Colossus Challenged: The Struggle for Caribbean Influence

edited by H. Michael Erisman
and John D. Martz

Westview Press / Boulder, Colorado

Westview Special Studies on Latin America and the Caribbean

Published in 1982 in the United States of America by
Westview Press, Inc.
5500 Central Avenue
Boulder, Colorado 80301
Frederick A. Praeger, President and Publisher

Library of Congress Catalog Card Number: 82-60034
ISBN 0-86531-362-8

Composition for this book was provided by the editors
Printed and bound in the United States of America

Contents

Tables

Preface

The Caribbean Basin is once again a hot item. Having languished for years on the periphery of the global stage, it has now moved into the limelight due to the political convulsions which have recently surged through it. The revolutionary dramas which have unfolded in Grenada and Nicaragua, the violence-scarred Manley/Seaga electoral confrontation in Jamaica, and especially the guerrilla wars raging in El Salvador and Guatemala--all have received extensive media coverage which has thrust the Caribbean into the public consciousness throughout the world. To international relations specialists, however, the significance of these developments lies not in the headlines and the notoriety which they generate, but rather in the fact that they are part of a larger process of structural alterations in the configuration of power and influence in the Basin.

Such changes are not unprecedented. Instead they represent yet another phase in a centuries-old battle for control which began in earnest with Colombus' arrival and has been highlighted by the ensuing European scramble for colonies (led by the Spanish and the British, but also including the French and the Dutch), Spain's displacement as the independence movement swept through most of Latin America in the early 1800s, and finally the United States' rise to dominance (with England, France, and the Netherlands maintaining a few small dependencies and neocolonial enclaves, primarily in the Lesser Antilles). Today another episode in this story is unfolding as U.S. hegemony is being contested directly by Cuba, Mexico, and Venezuela and indirectly, in many people's opinion, by the Soviet Union. This struggle, in which the challengers are trying to radically redefine political roles and relationships in the region, is examined in depth by Colossus Challenged.

In the United States over the past few years, a great deal of attention has been devoted to the Basin by the mass media, which has moved it from the travel sections to the front pages, and the academic community where area specialists who once labored largely unnoticed are now in heavy demand. But in all this outpouring of interest, no detailed comparative study of the foreign policies of the main actors competing for influence has appeared. This book, which grew out of a panel at the 1981 Caribbean Studies Association convention, seeks to fill that void. Five chapters focus on the Caribbean policies of the major contenders for power. Each includes the following: 1) background information regarding the policy's evolution; 2) an analysis of the main variables affecting the state's definition of its interests and the choice of its strategy to maximize its presence in the area, with particular attention being given to its capacity to exert ideological, economic, and/or military influence (i.e., what are its capabilities in these respects and how have they impacted its decision making?); and 3) an assessment of the current policy's effectiveness and of the country's prospects for exercising significant regional power in the foreseeable future. The other two chapters, aside from the Conclusion, investigate the perspectives on this rivalry of Eastern Caribbean and Central American governments.

Two features of the book deserve special mention. First, its definition of the Caribbean is rather broad. As explained in a Chapter 1 footnote, geopolitically the area can be visualized in terms of three concentric circles which from the smallest to the largest can be said to encompass respectively the Commonwealth Caribbean (i.e., the English-speaking islands), the Caribbean Archipelago (which includes all the islands as well as the mainland extensions of Guyana, Suriname, and French Guinea in South America and Belize in Central America), and finally the Caribbean Basin (consisting of the archipelago plus the South American littoral nations and Central America). The Basin conceptualization, which is becoming the most popular among foreign policy specialists, is used here, although some chapters naturally concentrate more heavily on certain parts of the region. Second, the book's topic is treated in a macroanalytical manner which strives to pinpoint and explain broad trends in Caribbean international relations and to project them into the future. The authors do not simply provide limited case studies of crisis diplomacy, but instead probe the larger phenomenon of systemic transformation and the wide-ranging, long-term power struggle inherent in that process. As such, their efforts should contribute to understanding not only contemporary Basin affairs, but also developments five to ten years from now.

As usual, there are a number of unsung heroes whose assistance was crucial in transforming this project from an idea in the editors' heads to a finished volume. In particular, we would like to thank Mercyhurst College and the Pennsylvania State University for their financial support; Lynne Rienner of Westview Press, whose promptness in deciding to publish is deeply appreciated and who was always readily available for editorial advice; JoAnn Alexander and Lee Belovarac, who typed the manuscript and moreover went through the occasionally traumatic experience of learning to use a computer as a word processor; Penn State graduate student Douglas Sears for subjecting himself to the tedium of preparing the index; Tom Kaliszak III and Dr. Detmar Straub of the Mercyhurst Computer Center, who invariably responded graciously to sometimes panic-stricken pleas for technical help; and Lisa Huffman, a Mercyhurst student assistant who did something of practically everything.

H.M.E.
J.D.M.

1
Colossus Challenged: U.S. Caribbean Policy in the 1980's

H. Michael Erisman

INTRODUCTION

During the hot Philadelphia summer of 1787 Benjamin Franklin supposedly whiled away time at the Constitutional Convention by wondering if the sun painted on the back of the presiding officer's chair was rising or setting. Today similar doubts exist about America's position in the Caribbean Basin. Throughout the 20th century the U.S. sun has burned brightly there, but now that is no longer the case. Washington's influence is not what it once was. Grenada and Nicaragua have joined Cuba in mounting a challenge to the Colossus of the North from the radical left with El Salvador and Guatemala threatening to follow suit. Venezuela and especially Mexico have displayed some independent regional leadership aspirations.[1] Thus the question arises as to whether the American sun is finally setting in the Caribbean or merely experiencing a momentary partial eclipse.

As a policy entity the Caribbean Basin encompasses the archipelago plus the littoral states of Venezuela, Colombia, Panama, and Mexico as well as all of Central America. Its total population is around 145 million and its overall GNP is approximately $120 billion.[2] Yet despite these rather impressive statistics, its status on Washington's international agenda has been rather low in recent decades. In fact, except for an occasional outburst of crisis-induced interventionism, the U.S. has generally ignored it.

This indifference disappeared as the 1980s dawned. The comfortable image of the Caribbean as a placid American lake was shattered and with it went Washington's complacency, to be replaced with a cacophony of storm warnings. Jack Anderson, for example, declared that

> ...our past treatment of Nicaragua, El Salvador, and Guatemala as banana republics is bearing bitter fruit.[3]

Time was much more funereal:

> Now the U.S. is faced with a chilling worst-case scenario formulated by its own policymakers. The scenario: a chain reaction of leftist revolutions that might turn the once subservient tropical basin into a rim of hostile Marxist states taking their cues from Castro's Cuba.[4]

And so American statesmen rediscovered the Caribbean. After the March 1979 revolution in Grenada, the State Department proclaimed it one of the globe's newest trouble spots.[5] Two years later Jeane Kirkpatrick, President Reagan's outspoken U.N. ambassador, called Central America the most important place in the world for the United States.[6]

Basically this concern is rooted in the fear that what is occurring is much more than simply another flurry of turbulence. The fact that Washington has not been able to control or contain the Basin's turmoil suggests that a process of structural change in the configuration of regional influence is taking place. In other words, what the U.S. once considered inconceivable--that its Caribbean hegemony could be seriously and irrevocably undermined--may indeed be happening. Certainly the signs are there in the drift of various nations toward America's old nemesis, Cuba, and Mexico's willingness to contest the United States' traditional pre-eminence.

This centrifugal phenomenon is hardly unique; it is but one aspect of a broader dynamic in the international system involving growing Third World nationalism and the emergence of new power centers such as OPEC.[7] Consequently to probe America's evolving Caribbean policy is to do more than just examine its relationship with one corner of the world. Rather it is to begin to define its place, particularly in reference to the developing countries where most of humanity lives, in today's changing global mosaic.

Keeping this larger perspective in mind, we now turn to describing U.S. responses to recent Caribbean developments, concentrating on the Reagan administration's initiatives. Later both intentions and capabilities analyses will be presented, the former dealing with the main variables shaping Washington's goals and the latter with internal and external factors affecting its capacity to achieve them. Finally, Reagan's policy will be critiqued in terms of both its internal consistency and its relevance to contemporary Caribbean realities and needs.

CARIBBEAN DEVELOPMENTS AND U.S. POLICY: AN OVERVIEW

The Basin's colorful history is dotted with periodic episodes of political violence whose varied cast of characters has included the early privateers who prowled the Spanish Main, colonial and neocolonial exploiters, military dictators, and modern-day guerrillas. Recently, however, the tempo has seemed to quicken with the United States being particularly troubled about outbursts of leftist radicalism in Grenada, Nicaragua, El Salvador, and Guatemala.

In early 1979 the first rumblings of the Caribbean's gathering storm emanated from Grenada, a tiny island of 110,000 people in the Lesser Antilles. From 1974, the year England granted independence, onward the country was ruled by Sir Eric Gairy, a corrupt eccentric enamored by the occult and UFOs. But on March 13, 1979 his regime came to an abrupt end in the English-speaking Caribbean's first successful armed coup. The uprising was led by Maurice Bishop, the young head of the New Jewel Movement. While few mourned Gairy's departure, Washington was worried about the Bishop government's left-wing proclivities, especially its rapidly expanding friendship with Cuba. When on April 16 Grenada formally established diplomatic relations with Havana,

> ...State Department spokesperson Tom Reston said that the United States "would be concerned about the establishment of any military or security arrangements between Grenada and Cuba." This concern had already been expressed to the Grenadian Government by U.S. Ambassador Frank Ortiz. Mr. Ortiz' communication said in part, "We would view with displeasure any tendency on the part of Grenada to develop closer ties with Cuba."[8]

Bishop ignored these warnings, accepting economic/military aid from Cuba as his revolution took on increasingly radical overtones.[9] Also, he frequently visited Havana and seldom missed an opportunity to praise Castro and the accomplishments of Cuban Marxism. The final straw was Grenada's vote against the U.N. General Assembly's resolution condemning Soviet intervention in Afghanistan.[10] Henceforth the U.S. considered the Bishop government firmly in the Russian orbit.

Following hard on the heels of the Grenadian revolt was Anastasio Somoza's downfall on July 17, 1979. Like the Shah in Iran, the Somoza dynasty had long enjoyed Washington's patronage and in return functioned as a bastion of pro-Americanism and anti-communism in Central America. Franklin D. Roosevelt's comment about Rafael Trujillo in the Dominican Republic could also serve as a cogent summary of the U.S. attitude toward Somoza--he may be an s.o.b., but he's our s.o.b. The problem was that too many Nicaraguans, disgusted by the new heights to which his corruption soared after the 1972 Managua earthquake and the repression he unleashed against those opposed to his dictatorship, reached the same conclusion about his basic character and rallied behind the Sandinista National Liberation Front to drive him from power.[11]

Although many feel that the Carter administration's human rights policy hastened Somoza's demise, Washington was hardly overjoyed at the prospect of a Sandinista victory and exerted considerable effort to prevent it. Subsequently it tried to use economic pressure to moderate the new government's behavior, but in vain. The Sandinistas consolidated their power, began to implement their revolutionary program, and enthusiastically embraced Cuba. By the end of 1979 Havana had poured in approximately 50 military advisors and 2,000 civilian workers, mostly doctors and teachers, to help to begin to rebuild the shattered country.[12] Besides being unhappy about this Cuban connection, U.S. fears that the Sandinistas were anxious to stir up trouble for neighboring pro-American regimes were fanned by such reports as:

> Free Nicaragua is preoccupied with the daily battles in El Salvador and Guatemala, guerrilla wars that could lead to Central American unity under a non-aligned banner in the 1980s. ...
>
> ...there are some outstanding priests [such as Nicaraguan Foreign Minister Miguel d'Escoto] who are playing an important role in fostering this unity that involves

> aiding--as is currently the case with El Salvador--liberation movements.[13]

Thus as the Reagan administration took office, attention shifted to El Salvador and Guatemala, two nations which were sinking into near-anarchy as leftist insurgents battled governments dominated by extreme right-wing military elements for control.

Instability has not, of course, been the case everywhere. Indeed in the eastern Caribbean quite the opposite has been true; essentially peaceful democratic elections have been held with moderates or conservatives generally triumphing over left-wing parties.[14] The most important race was held in Jamaica where in October 1980 conservative, Harvard-educated Edward Seaga won convincingly with 57.6 percent of the vote over incumbent Prime Minister Michael Manley, who had angered the U.S. with his nonaligned foreign policy and his close friendship with Fidel Castro. Nevertheless, spreading pro-Cuban radicalism along with the Mexican/Venezuelan challenge to American influence (to be discussed later) has been sufficiently upsetting to cause recent administrations to devote much more attention than before to Caribbean affairs.

Neglect was still the norm during the Nixon/Ford years. Nixon was preoccupied with southeast Asia, the Middle East, the opening to China, East-West detente, and finally the Watergate debacle while Ford concentrated on healing the traumas resulting from Watergate and the lost crusade in Vietnam. On those few occasions when the Caribbean did impinge on America's consciousness,

> The problems that arose were met and dealt with on an ad hoc basis. No Caribbean strategy was announced, because none was thought to be needed.[15]

Both administrations put symbolism before substance. Except for ongoing negotiations over a new Panama Canal treaty, they did little more than observe diplomatic rituals and issue bland statements promising a more cooperative relationship or, as Henry Kissinger liked to call it, a Good Partner Policy.[16] The only hint of any serious initiatives were stories alleging that in late 1975 Washington launched a destabilization campaign which included assassination plots to overthrow Manley after he rejected an ultimatum from Secretary of State Kissinger to

> ...cool his friendship with Cuban leader Fidel Castro and to stop interfering with U.S.-owned bauxite companies in Jamaica.[17]

The United States did cut off aid in 1975 after Jamaica nationalized an American firm, Revere Copper and Brass Inc., but no evidence to substantiate a charge of major intervention ever surfaced.

The Carter administration's relations began on a positive note. Its appointments to key policy positions, especially Andrew Young as U.N. ambassador and Terence Todman as Assistant Secretary of State for Inter-American Affairs, were generally well received. So also were its assurances that it would be more solicitous toward the Basin's sensibilities and special needs.[18] Andrew Young's ten-nation Caribbean tour in April 1977 represented an attempt to showcase this new sensitivity. During his highly successful trip Young

> ...made it clear that the Administration was concerned less with a government's ideological stance than with its commitment to help its own people...[19]

and repeatedly emphasized America's commitment to ideological pluralism with such statements as:

> Anything that's going to feed hungry people, anything that aids in rural development and anything that stabilizes population growth--the [U.S.] government can live with it, whatever it's called.[20]

Moreover, Carter actually delivered on two long-standing thorny issues--rapprochement with Havana and the Panama Canal. A breakthrough with Cuba occurred in April 1977 when, after the first government-to-government talks in sixteen years, the two countries concluded agreements on fishing rights and the delineation of a provisional maritime boundary in the Florida Straits. An even more significant step toward full normalization was taken in September 1977 with the opening of permanent interest sections in each other's capital staffed by diplomatic and consular officials. In addition to these formal bilateral arrangements, both nations moved unilaterally to demonstrate their good faith, Havana by releasing some Americans serving long prison sentences and Washington by relaxing its restrictions on travel to the island.[21]

Even greater progress was achieved on the Canal question. After thirteen years of often stormy negotiations, the United States and Panama signed two treaties in September 1977 providing for a gradual transfer of control to Panama. There was a strong opposition to the treaties in the United States, but Carter lobbied hard on their behalf and they were finally ratified by the Senate in April 1978.

But after this initial burst of good neighborism, Carter's momentum slowed as economic issues entered the picture. His performance in this sphere was not, at least from the Basin's viewpoint, very encouraging. Washington raised its sugar tariffs, sold tin from government reserves to drive down world prices, denied applications from Caribbean airlines for routes into the U.S., and tightened tax exemptions on business conventions abroad, all of which greatly hurt many of the region's economies and rekindled old animosities about Yankee arrogance. Abraham Lowenthal captured this sense of resentment with his comment that

> On matters of dollars and cents, the Carter administration has so far produced only small change.[22]

The thaw in U.S.-Cuban relations ended in early 1978 when Havana dispatched 11,000 combat troops to crush a Somalian invasion which threatened the survival of Lt. Colonel Mengistu Haile Mariam's new socialist government in Ethiopia. This contingent brought the total of Cuban military personnel in Africa to approximately 38,000, the largest concentration being 19,000 in Angola.[23] Infuriated by Castro's audacity in bolstering the power of radical elements in Africa and his growing influence in the Third World at large, Washington reverted to portraying Havana as untrustworthy, irresponsible, and a threat to international peace. By mid-1978 U.S.-Cuban detente had died under a barrage of angry American rhetoric.

> This administration has gone damn far to be friendly with Cuba, and we've gotten 12,000 Cubans in the Horn of Africa for it. We're all very disillusioned with Cuba.
>
> The Cubans are guns for hire, and they'll go anywhere. They have no compunctions.[24]

Carter's Caribbean problems multiplied in 1979. First the Grenadian coup caught him by surprise and then his attempts to control the deteriorating Nicaraguan situation failed. In its indecisive efforts to prevent a Sandinista victory while still trying to disassociate itself from the discredited Somoza, the United States managed to antagonize practically everyone. Right-wingers condemned it for abandoning a faithful anti-communist ally; anti-Somoza liberals, including the Mexican and Venezuelan governments, accused it of trying to perpetuate Somozaismo without Somoza; and the radical left resurrected the spectre of imperialistic Yankee interventionism.

The Nicaraguan fiasco marked a turning point for the Carter administration. Encouraged by Zbigniew Brzezinski, his contentious national security advisor, the President decided to get tough and to reassert U.S. primacy in the Basin. The issue he seized upon to do so was the discovery in late August 1979 of an alleged Soviet combat brigade in Cuba which he claimed represented a threat to the security of the hemisphere and the United States.[25] The new hard line which he announced during the troop crisis included

> ...a series of controversial moves clearly aiming to intimidate Cuba and other radical groups challenging the status quo in the region. Specifically the Administration:
>
> > ...Increased the U.S. military presence in the Caribbean with the new Caribbean Task Force Headquarters at Key West and the muscle-flexing exercises of 1,800 Marines at Guantanamo Bay.
> >
> > ...[Began] to consult with Latin American nations on the creation of some kind of "peacekeeping force" in Latin America. More specifically, [the U.S.] ... has been consulting with the Governments of Britain and Canada on the feasibility of forming a multinational Caribbean seaborne patrol force--a special Coast Guard-like force--to combat Cuban infiltration into Caribbean islands, which often have minimal security forces.
> >
> > Pursued its oft-stated intention to increase aid for the area in order

> to as President Carter said ..., "further insure the ability of troubled peoples to resist social turmoil and possible Communist domination."[26]

But in reality Carter's bark was much worse than his bite. Distracted by presidential electioneering and the hostage seizure in Iran, Caribbean policy drifted for the rest of his tenure. Admittedly there were some significant budgetary increases in economic and particularly security assistance programs, with the Dominican Republic, Barbados, and El Salvador receiving special attention,[27] but ultimately the indecisiveness which had often previously characterized his foreign policy behavior resurfaced. In El Salvador, for example, he first increased military aid in late 1979/early 1980, then cut it off in December 1980 following accusations that implicated government troops in the brutal murders of four American women, and finally resumed it shortly before leaving office in January 1981.[28]

Ronald Reagan entered the White House with a reputation as a Cold War warrior and quickly lived up to his billing. His general approach to foreign affairs has stressed bipolarity (i.e., world politics are dominated by the East-West confrontation), macrolinkage (i.e., all important international questions are connected to the bipolar power struggle and must be handled accordingly), and vigilant containment of Moscow. It is from this larger framework that his Caribbean policy has flowed.

Several central themes, advanced by such advisors as Jeane Kirkpatrick, Roger Fontaine of the American Enterprise Institute, former United States envoy to Nicaragua James Therberge, and Constantine Menges of the Hudson Institute, have dominated the Reagan administration's perspective of the Basin. These are: heavy criticism of Carter for supposedly downplaying Washington's traditional special relationship with Latin America by incorporating hemispheric issues into the overall global rubric of the North-South dialogue; the need to revitalize that special relationship; emphasis on the wisdom of supporting responsible rightists in order to prevent slippage to the left which would only benefit Cuba and the USSR; and the contention that a dramatic improvement in U.S.-Caribbean relations will result from America playing a more assertive role in the area because most of the countries there, including Mexico, actually want it to do so.[29] Translating these conerns into concrete initiatives has produced a basically three-pronged strategy.

The first prong has been aimed at solidifying cordial ties with key governments which the United States hopes can be persuaded to rally behind its policies. In the island Caribbean Jamaica has received top priority while on the mainland attention has been focused on Mexico. Clearly Reagan was elated with the outcome of Jamaica's October 1980 election, which he demonstrated by bestowing on Seaga the honor of being the first head of state whom he officially received at the White House. And even before he was inaugurated he was cultivating Mexico's friendship, making a special trip to Ciudad Juarez in early January 1981 to confer with its president, Jose Lopez Portillo. This courtship was consistent with a plan that he outlined during his campaign

> ...to move into a closer relationship with Mexico and Canada. Calling for a "North American accord," he said the three countries possessed the assets "to make it the strongest, most prosperous, and self-sufficient area on earth."[30]

It is safe to say that he sees the U.S. as this consortium's leader.

The second prong has been targeted on Cuba, employing classical carrot-and-stick tactics. On the one hand, the Reagan administration has made vague allusions to a magnanimous reconciliation if Havana behaves itself and moderates its Russian connection. But it also has threatened dire consequences should the Fidelistas involve themselves in the Caribbean's power struggles or attempt in any serious way to export their revolution. Caribbean Contact reported in December 1980 that

> Roger Fontaine, Reagan's most visible Latin American advisor, is on the record as saying that the President-elect will seek a major renegotiation of the relationship between Havana and Washington. He said that Reagan was willing to be generous on all outstanding matters between the two countries, so long as the Cubans were prepared to end their special relationship with the Soviet Union.

> In the absence of such an agreement, Reagan has suggested that a renewed blockade of Cuba would be a suitable form of retaliation... .[31]

Most comments by Reagan officials suggest that they lean much more toward the stick than the carrot.[32]

The third and most controversial aspect of Reagan's strategy has been his willingness, indeed some would say his eagerness, to become involved in El Salvador to demonstrate his determination to stop the spread of leftist influence. He has presented the situation there as a Cold War struggle, arguing that

> It is clear that over the past year the insurgency in El Salvador has been progressively transformed into another case of indirect armed aggression against a small Third World country by Communist powers acting through Cuba.[33]

Taking advantage of the honeymoon period traditionally accorded new presidents, he moved on several fronts in early 1981 to try to achieve a quick fix in El Salvador, stepping up the flow of weapons and ammunition to the Duarte regime, adding $25 million to the existing $10 million military aid package to help the government buy trucks, radar, and surveillance equipment, proceeding with plans to boost the $63.5 million U.S. economic assistance program by at least $100 million, and dispatching 50-55 military advisors to the country with indications that more would be sent if necessary. Also, to pressure the Sandinistas and the Cubans to stop acting as conduits for arms to the guerrillas, he suspended disbursement of the last $15 million of the $75 million that Carter had allocated for Nicaraguan reconstruction and threatened unspecified strong measures against Havana.[34] Throughout this escalation the administration was quite forthright regarding its basic philosophy.

> ...Secretary of State Alexander Haig said that America's mistake in Vietnam was its preoccupation with winning hearts and minds; in El Salvador, Haig said, the United States would concentrate instead on helping the government to win a military victory.[35]

Thus Reagan has, in Joseph Kraft's words, "rolled the dice in the Caribbean,"[36] markedly upping the ante in terms of overall U.S. security assistance programs (see Table 1.1) and laying a good deal of his prestige on the line.

REAGAN'S CARIBBEAN POLICY: AN ANALYSIS

It used to be fashionable to say that the United States stumbled blindly into Vietnam. This notion has, however, largely been laid to rest by the Pentagon Papers and other studies which have shown that American intervention resulted from a series of calculated choices. Likewise Ronald Reagan has not plunged into the Central American cauldron with his eyes closed. Nor is he a reluctant combatant who has been forced into the fray against his better judgement. Instead his administration has deliberately put Caribbean affairs at the top of its international agenda, giving them priority over other important issues such as SALT, the Mideast, and U.S.-PRC relations. Therefore we now want to discuss why it has done so, pinpointing some of the main considerations which have or could impinge on its decisions.

The Containment Doctrine has undoubtedly been the single most important variable motivating the Reaganites' actions abroad; it is in their opinion the very lifeblood of American foreign policy. Carter, they contend, blundered immensely by devaluing it to pursue detente and human rights, the result allegedly being a disastrous decline in U.S. influence which they are determined to reverse. Consequently they have been anxious for an opportunity to demonstrate that they mean business when they talk tough in order to establish the political/military credibility which they believe they must have to be able to deter any Soviet adventurism.

The Basin is an excellent low-risk place to do so because an anti-leftist campaign there is less likely to produce a serious confrontation with the USSR than might the case in, for example, the Middle East. This is attractive to Reagan not only from a tactical viewpoint but also because it minimizes his vulnerability to charges that he is irresponsibly shooting from the hip, thus putting him in a good position to neutralize his critics and to mobilize public support. Realizing that such favorable conditions for Cold War warrioring are rare, he has moved quickly to capitalize on them.

The second major factor shaping the administration's policy has been its conviction that the United States has vital national interests in the

TABLE 1.1

U.S. SECURITY ASSISTANCE PROGRAMS
(Millions of Dollars)

Foreign Military Sales

	1979	1980	1981 Estimated	1982 Request
Bahamas	-	-	-	1.0
E. Caribbean	-	-	5.0	7.5 (4.5)
Colombia	12.5	-	12.7	12.7
Domin. Rep.	0.5	3.2	3.0	7.0 (4.0)
El Salvador	-	5.7	10.0	25.0 (17.0)
Haiti	0.2	-	0.3	0.3
Honduras	2.0	3.53	5.0	10.0 (4.5)
Jamaica	-	-	1.59	1.0 (1.0)
Panama	1.0	-	-	5.0
TOTAL	16.2	12.43	37.59	69.5 (31.0)

( ) Direct FMS Credit on Concessional Terms

International Military Education/Training Program

Bahamas	-	-	.06	.06
Barbados	.006	.058	.084	.10
Colombia	.454	.255	.377	.85
Costa Rica	-	-	-	.06
Dominica	-	-	.008	.06
Domin. Rep.	.502	.25	.498	.60
El Salvador	-	.247	.498	1.00
Guyana	-	-	.025	.04
Haiti	.182	.127	.199	.415
Honduras	.250	.441	.495	.70
Jamaica	-	-	.025	.075
Mexico	.193	.128	.149	.245
Nicaragua	.007	-	.494	-
Panama	.399	.289	.489	.50
St. Lucia	-	-	.008	.06
St. Vincent	-	-	.008	.06
Suriname	-	.026	-	.075
Venezuela	-	-	-	.05
TOTAL	1.993	1.821	3.177	4.950

Emergency Grant Authority 1981 El Salvador = 25.0

Source: Data Provided By U.S. State Department

Caribbean whose protection demands that it maintain a dominant presence.[37] Exactly what are they? Unfortunately there is no neat, tidy answer. National interest is an extremely imprecise idea which can best be likened to a kaleidoscope; its coloration and configuration will vary as shifts occur in its economic, military/strategic, and ideological/political components. Thus its specific content is by no means fixed, but rather depends on the priorities of those who are mixing these three basic ingredients at a particular point in time and space.

There is an understandable temptation when discussing America's Caribbean interests to highlight investment and trade since the data show that it does have a large economic stake there (see Table 1.2).[38] Moreover, in the past Washington has frequently been willing to put its muscle behind the dollar, as illustrated by Major General Smedley Butler's famous statement that

> I helped make Mexico and especially Tampico safe for American oil interests in 1914. I helped make Haiti and Cuba a decent place for the National City Bank boys to collect revenue in. I helped purify Nicaragua for the international banking house of Brown Brothers in 1909-1912. I brought light to the Dominican Republic for American sugar interests in 1916. I helped make Honduras "right" for American fruit companies in 1903.[39]

One might add to Butler's hit list the frequent pre-World War Two military occupations (e.g., Nicaragua, 1912-1933; Haiti, 1915-1934), the 1954 overthrow of the Arbenz regime in Guatemala, and the hostile reaction to Castro's early economic nationalism. This track record has led many observers to conclude that U.S. behavior is motivated mainly by a desire to defend and expand its economic interests.

Yet despite the Reagan administration's pro-business orientation and indications that it would strongly support American corporations abroad,[40] military/strategic and ideological/political matters have thus far been more important to it. Apparently it feels that to maintain the Basin as a sphere of influence and thereby guarantee optimal conditions for securing U.S. economic interests, these two items must be dealt with first.

TABLE 1.2

U.S. DIRECT INVESTMENT
(Millions Of Dollars)

	1977	%	1978	%	1979	%
TOTAL	149,848	100	167,804	100	192,648	100
DEVELOPED STATES	108,225	72.2	120,471	71.8	137,927	71.7
DEVELOPING STATES	34,462	23.0	40,399	24.1	47,841	24.8
CARIB/C. AMER*	18,038		20,972		22,934	
% of Total		12.0		12.5		11.6
% of Developing		52.3		51.9		46.9

U.S. EXPORTS
(Millions Of Dollars)

	1977	%	1978	%	1979	%
TOTAL	121,212	100	143,663	100	181,802	100
DEVELOPED STATES	74,891	61.7	85,585	59.6	110,566	60.8
DEVELOPING STATES	43,307	35.7	52,895	36.8	62,982	34.6
W. HEMIS. MINUS CANADA	17,963		22,020		28,457	
% of Total		14.8		15.3		15.7
% of Developing		41.5		41.6		45.2
CARIB/C. AMER.*	12,703		15,835		20,253	
% of Total		10.5		11.0		11.1
% of Developing		29.3		29.9		32.2
% of W. Hemis. less Canada		70.7		71.9		71.2

TABLE 1.2 (cont.)

U.S. IMPORTS
(Millions Of Dollars)

	1977	%	1978	%	1979	%
TOTAL	147,671	100	171,978	100	206,327	100
DEVELOPED STATES	78,620	53.2	98,909	57.5	111,514	54.0
DEVELOPING STATES	67,703	45.8	71,230	41.4	92,345	44.8
W. HEMIS. MINUS CANADA	21,098		22,948		30,484	
% of Total		14.3		13.3		14.8
% of Developing		31.2		32.2		33.0
CARIB/C. AMER*	16,751		17,388		23,816	
% of Total		11.3		10.1		11.5
% of Developing		24.7		24.4		25.8
% of W. Hemis. less Canada		79.4		75.8		78.1

Source: U.S. Department of Commerce, Statistical Abstract Of The United States 1980 (Washington: U.S. Government Printing Office, 1980), pp. 865, 874-875.

*Does not include Puerto Rico. Josefina C. Tiryakian, "United States, Puerto Rico And The Caribbean: Rethinking Geopolitical Realities" (Paper presented at the 1980 conference of the Middle Atlantic Council on Latin American Studies in Newark, Delaware), p. 2 puts U.S. direct investments in Puerto Rico at $15 billion in 1978 and U.S. exports to Puerto Rico at $3.9 billion in 1978.

Given its near obsession with its global power posture and the international correlation of forces, no one should be surprised that more than anything else, military/strategic variables have molded the administration's perceptions of its paramount Caribbean interests. These issues have been given top priority not only in Basin affairs, but throughout the world.

On paper America's military presence in the area looks small. Its only notable bases are at Roosevelt Roads in Puerto Rico, Guantanamo Bay in Cuba, and the old Canal Zone in Panama. Nevertheless these installations (along with those in the southern United States) put Washington in a good position to control the region militarily should the need arise, which it almost surely would in a crisis since

> ...the Caribbean is a crucial military route. A major part of any U.S. military force destined for Western Europe or the Persian Gulf region would pass by ship or plane on or over the Caribbean or nearby southern states. This would include forces from the West Coast passing through the Panama Canal.[41]

They are therefore seen as significant assets to the Pentagon's long-range contingency planning which must be defended.[42]

This military dimension to Washington's policy must be viewed in conjunction with its broader strategic interests, the foremost being oil. Mexico and Venezuela ship large amounts to the United States. In addition, reserves are suspected in Guatemala and offshore Puerto Rico which could allow them to become substantial exporters. Access to this petroleum is vital and will be even more so as the Persian Gulf fields are depleted. In fact, a reorientation of sources may already be occurring.

> ...The CIA's recent report of the world's oil reserves ... points out that, in the near future, Latin America and other areas of the so-called Third World will be replacing the Middle East as world suppliers of hydrocarbons when deposits in the Middle East are exhausted.
>
> The accuracy of the report is made evident by the fact that the United States has been spending heavily on oil prospecting in

> more than 50 developing countries, many of them in Latin America, and chiefly in Central America and the Caribbean.[43]

Other strategic raw materials also come from the Basin, especially iron ore and bauxite (i.e., the U.S. imports approximately 50 percent of its bauxite from Jamaica). Finally, the Caribbean is the main artery for American trade with the rest of the world.

> The shortest connecting link between the Atlantic and Pacific oceans and between North and South America, the Caribbean sea is crisscrossed by 12 essential United States trade routes. The Caribbean is an important outlet for the Gulf of Mexico ports which handle some 37% of United States waterborne commerce. Through the Caribbean also transit Alaskan oil, Bolivian tin, Ecuadorian oil, Chilean and Peruvian copper, and innumerable commodities.[44]

Oil movement is particularly important; 52 percent of America's petroleum imports flow through the area with 30 percent of all its imported oil being processed there, the largest refineries operating in Curacao, Aruba, Trinidad, the U.S. Virgin Islands, and the Bahamas. Any situation which might endanger this resource flow (e.g., regional instability or a leftist takeover in a producer country) would, in the Reagan administration's opinion, constitute a serious threat to U.S. security.

Ideological/political concerns have likewise loomed large in Reagan's conception of U.S. vital interests due to the Containment Doctrine. As first proposed by George Kennan in 1947, containment was aimed primarily at preventing the further spread of Russian military power, especially into Western Europe and the eastern Mediterranean. But as it evolved and was globalized during the Cold War, it also came to mean stopping the spread of communist ideas and assuring that Marxists were kept from power everywhere.

Unlike some previous administrations which in the spirit of detente at least gave some lip service to the notion of tolerating ideological pluralism, Reagan has reverted to uncompromising containment in the Western Hemisphere--no leftist gains are to be permitted. Thus any challenge, especially one which employs violence, to the guardians of the Caribbean status quo has tended to be equated with a challenge to containment which justifies bringing American power to bear to restore stability and pro-Western ideological orthodoxy.

Politically the United States also has a large ego stake in the Caribbean. Exercising control there has always been an integral part of its image as a great power. It was in the Basin at the turn of the 20th century that it first sought to establish its credentials as an important international actor and ever since it has seemed convinced that its claim to great power status demands its continued hegemony. For instance, in 1980 Deputy Assistant Secretary of State James Cheek stated,

> If we cannot be a force for moderate and peaceful change in our own backyard, we cannot do it anywhere. And if we are irrelevant to revolutions, in this world we are doomed.[45]

In a similar vein, addressing himself specifically to the situation in El Salvador, columnist Joseph Kraft declared,

> El Salvador is a mini-state in the backyard of the U.S. If this country cannot sustain the junta by a limited application of muscle, then it should quit the Great Power business.[46]

The Reagan administration has pledged that under its tutelage America will not become, either in appearance or reality, a paper tiger or a helpless giant. To fulfill this promise, it has felt that it must take a strong stand against any challenges to its traditional preeminence in the Basin. Indeed reinforcing this great power reputation both at home and abroad may, from the Reaganites' bipolar viewpoint, be the most vital political interest they presently have in the area.

The third major consideration affecting the administration's Caribbean policy has been its conceptualization of the principal threats there to containment and to the various interests discussed above. Reducing the problem to its bare essentials, Washington has been worried about political instability in the region. What has been taking place has been a process of steady polarization resulting in confrontational politics and frequently violent power struggles between left and right. Reagan has decided that this situation is extremely dangerous and must be brought under control. But to do so effectively, it is first necessary to determine what has been causing it and here sharp disagreement has emerged between the economic crisis and external subversion theories.

The crisis school argues that economic conditions in the Caribbean have seriously deteriorated over the past several years due to oil price hikes, price drops on the world market for its commodity exports, burgeoning national debts to cover trade deficits, expanding foreign penetration and exploitation, and the transferral of U.S. stagflation through the mechanism of existing dependency relationships. Its advocates then go on to say that the poor majority which has borne the brunt of the burden has begun to demand drastic reforms which the rich oligarchy has refused to make, often responding instead with heavy-handed repression. All this, they conclude, has served only to increase class-based tensions and trigger spiraling violence whose first casualty has generally been the moderate elements in the body politic. Nicaragua, El Salvador, and Guatemala have repeatedly been mentioned as textbook cases for this analysis.

The external subversion school is much more conspiratorial. While recognizing that the Basin has been experiencing some unsettling economic problems, its adherents insist that the root cause of its political instability is Cuban/Russian agitation which is designed to overthrow moderate-conservative governments and replace them with radical left-wing regimes, thereby tipping the global power balance toward the communist bloc and contributing to an international environment inimical not only to America's general interests, but also to its very survival. This, predictably, has been the predominant view within the Reagan White House.

Cuba has been seen as posing a double-barreled threat. On the one hand, Havana has displayed a significant independent capacity to spread its influence in the Caribbean, occasionally doing so by extending moral/material support to leftist guerrillas and at other times relying on more conventional means such as economic aid programs and other demonstrations of its developmental successes.[47] While the former tactics tend to receive the most attention, the latter may in the long run be more effective because Castro's

> ...admitted achievements--notably the elimination of illiteracy--provide an

> alluring model for Cuba's neighbors. Says Abraham Lowenthal, a U.S. authority on Latin America, "These [Caribbean] countries are satellites in search of an orbit. They may become part of the Cuban orbit, but not for military reasons. If the Cubans succeed, it will be because Cuba is able to convey a greater sense of social and economic integration, a greater sense of nation-building and a greater ability to employ people."[48]

President Carter echoed these sentiments in April 1980:

> We tend to misunderstand the threat of Cuba. Certainly they contribute to violence and instability in the Caribbean region, but the real threat of Cuba is that they claim to offer a model to be emulated by people who are dissatisfied with their own lot or who are struggling to change things for the better.[49]

It has, however, been the second aspect of the Cuban challenge which Reagan has feared most--Havana's close ties, especially in the military realm, with the USSR. The administration has viewed this relationship in terms of the Surrogate Thesis, which holds that Cuba's foreign policy is in effect controlled by the Soviets and that the Fidelistas are little more than, as Senator Daniel Moynihan once labelled them, the "Gurkhas of the Russian Empire." Applying this concept to the Basin, the Cubans simply become a stalking horse, stirring up leftist political violence on Moscow's behalf and serving as a conduit for Kremlin-dispatched arms. What do the Russians hope to gain? Asssuming a worse-case scenario, their goals could include: establishing a strong military presence in the eastern Caribbean (e.g., Grenada) in order to interdict strategic U.S. trade/logistical routes; encircling the Caribbean oil reserves off the Mexican coast and perhaps ultimately bringing Mexico itself under their influence; and diverting America's attention from other vital areas such as the Persian Gulf by brewing trouble in its backyard.[50]

The administration has been so mesmerized by the Cuban/Russian question that it has not devoted any serious attention to other developments in the area, such as intensifying economic/political nationalism, which may not be conducive to its pursuit of its national interests. These matters have not been completely ignored, but instead have tended to be subsumed within the larger rubric of Cold War confrontationism and containment.

Finally, implementation considerations have affected the administration's calculations. A cardinal rule of politics is to avoid reaching beyond your grasp; otherwise your fingers may be badly burned. As such, a nation's capacity to carry out its plans inevitably becomes a crucial variable in its foreign policy-making process.

In a purely quantitative sense, Washington's ability to project power and influence into the Basin seems overwhelming; its financial and human resources are more than adequate to sustain a high level of economic assistance programs, military training/advising missions, and even combat operations. But to possess such material assets does not necessarily translate into a free hand to use them. Rather, the White House operates within a context of potential domestic and external constraints on its behavior which cannot be ignored when assessing its overall implementation capabilities.

Domestically the Reagan administration has been most concerned about solid backing for a hardline Caribbean policy. It has faced two main problems, the first being the Vietnam syndrome. Although America's fiasco in southeast Asia is only a dim memory for many, its trauma has nevertheless remained deeply embedded in the country's political psyche, reemerging to generate opposition to serious involvement in hot spots such as Angola, Iran, and most recently El Salvador. Vietnam's restraining influence will probably remain strong until Washington has had an unambiguously successful engagement somewhere. But since that has not yet occurred, its specter still hangs over the Reagan team. The second problem has been apathy. Many Americans simply do not see the Basin as something important enough to get excited about or to make any sacrifices for (especially given the tenuous economic situation in the United States), a fact reflected in the plaintive observation of a Guatemalan Foreign Ministry official that

> Reagan won't be able to take as hard an anti-communist line down here as he would like. The bottom line will be that it costs

> too much and that the American people don't give a damn about a bunch of sweaty little countries down here.[51]

Such indifference, which prior to the Indochina War would probably have benefitted the President by allowing him to take advantage of the public's trust to develop policy momentum in a particular direction, could now put the administration in the difficult position of not being able to rally sufficient mass support to neutralize opposition fueled by the Vietnam syndrome.

Thus far these domestic factors do not seem to have greatly affected Reagan's policies.[52] Apparently the administration has concluded that the emotional upsurge of patriotism (some might call it jingoism) surrounding Iran's release of its American hostages has created a climate favorable to a tougher, more assertive U.S. stance, especially in low-risk areas like the Caribbean. Also, it may believe that its quick-fix approach, epitomized by Haig's emphasis on a military victory in El Salvador, will allow it to present its critics with a fiat accompli.

The external dimension, however, has been more troublesome, involving pressures for moderation from three main quarters. First, some of Washington's Western allies have been decidedly cool toward an American crusade in the Basin. In a few cases this sentiment has reflected basic policy differences. For example, West Germany's ruling Social Democrats and England's Laborites have become active in the Socialist International (SI), an organization of progressive left-wing parties (including among its sixteen Caribbean members and informal associates Manley's People's National Party, Nicaragua's Sandinistas, and Grenada's New Jewel Movement) which in recent years has been devoting increased attention to spreading its political ideals in Latin America.[53] Consequently they have been extremely unhappy about Reagan's pro-right policy, correctly viewing it as detrimental to their leadership interests in the SI. Most NATO dissidents, however, have reacted negatively because they fear that the U.S. will become so entangled in the Basin that it will neglect its responsibilities in areas like the Middle East which they consider much more vital.

Also, many smaller Caribbean governments have joined the opposition chorus, some because they have increasingly begun to identify with the Third World's antipathy to any muscle-flexing by the developed states and others because they resent what they believe to be Washington's disinterest in them except when its hegemony is threatened or it needs them as pawns in its international machinations. As one disgruntled leader said,

> It's the same old story ... when the Americans get scared of Communism, they offer us money.[54]

Whatever its roots, this anti-Yankeeism was graphically illustrated in June 1979 when many Caribbean members joined the successful effort to defeat a Carter proposal to dispatch an OAS peacekeeping force to Nicaragua which was obviously designed to prevent the Sandinistas from assuming power.

Third and most important has been Reagan's anxiety about the Basin's two oil powers--Venezuela and Mexico. Should these states decide to do so, they could put great pressure on Washington and severely limit its Caribbean options. And both have displayed aspirations for regional influence which are incompatible with continued American domination.

In the mid-1970s President Carlos Andres Perez embarked on an ambitious attempt to make Venezuela a Third World as well as a Caribbean leader. Buoyed by the flood of money produced by OPEC price hikes, he launched impressive foreign aid programs; in 1975, for example, they consumed 12 percent of the country's Gross Domestic Product (compared to approximately 1 percent in most industrialized nations). He also was a co-architect along with Mexico's Luis Echeverria of the Latin American Economic System (SELA), which was to foster integrated development and serve as a vehicle for hemispheric states to achieve a united front to push demands for a new international economic order. The U.S., incidently, was specifically barred from SELA membership while Cuba was admitted.[55]

Carlos Perez was succeeded by Luis Herrera Campins in 1979. The new administration, while less flamboyant, less enamored with a major Third World role, and less inclined to assume leftist positions than its predecessor, has nevertheless maintained an interest in exerting influence in the Basin. Whether it has sufficient resources and political skill to compete successfully with the United States over the long run remains to be seen. So far, however, it has been more worried about Cuba than Washington. In early 1980 relations between Caracas and Havana began to deteriorate badly as the two governments traded bitter recriminations over a variety of issues.[56] Cuba, for instance, charged that the Herrera Campins regime

> ...is cooperating with the United States in its genocidal murder of the sister Salvadoran people.[57]

Naturally Reagan has been delighted by this turn of events, seeing it as having secured his Venezuelan flank by creating conditions conducive to a sympathetic response from Caracas to his thrusts against Havana.

With Venezuela adopting a lower Caribbean profile, Mexico has moved to the forefront of non-Marxist regional challengers to the United States. Mexico has made it clear that it opposes Reagan's anti-leftism and has even demonstrated a willingness, beginning during Luis Echeverria's presidency (1970-1976) and continuing under Jose Lopez Portillo's administration (1976 onward), to align itself closely with anti-Yankee elements in the Basin (e.g., Castro and the Sandinistas).[58]

Echeverria was determined to take Mexico out from under America's shadow and into the political front ranks of the developing nations. This scenario included mobilizing Caribbean countries behind Third World issues and leading them into the mainstream of nonaligned politics. His most dramatic move in this direction was his Charter of Economic Rights and Duties of States calling for a new international economic order which was overwhelmingly adopted by the U.N. General Assembly in late 1974 despite opposition from the United States and most other Western industrialized nations.

Although Echeverria's global ambitions were never realized, he did set some crucial precedents for his successor. Perhaps most important was his break with the Estrada Doctrine, which calls for swift, automatic recognition of <u>all</u> new Latin governments and was integral to Mexico's tradition of a noninterventionist foreign policy. Specifically, in 1973 he refused to recognize the Chilean military junta which had overthrown Salvador Allende. Thus he set the stage for Lopez Portillo's successful attempt to help oust Somoza.

Many expected Lopez Portillo, who was depicted as being much more conservative than Echeverria, to abandon his predecessor's left-wing proclivities and to return to a more restrained international stance. Initially this seemed to be happening. Certainly his style was less theatrical and he did not seem very interested in playing a significant Third World role. But following the announcement of Mexico's petropower status, he pointedly embraced Havana and then unveiled a much more assertive, radical Caribbean policy as the Nicaraguan power struggle unfolded.

Lopez Portillo fully supported the Sandinistas. Ignoring the Estrada Doctrine and noninterventionism, he severed Mexico's ties with the Somoza regime in May 1979 and immediately thereafter sent high-ranking delegations to five other important Basin states--Venezuela, Colombia, Panama, Jamaica, and the Dominican Republic--to try to persuade them to do likewise. He was also instrumental in defeating Washington's plan to send an OAS peacekeeping force into Nicaragua. The extent of Mexico's aid to the insurgents was strikingly symbolized by the fact that after Somoza fled, the country's new leaders were flown into Managua on Lopez Portillo's presidential plane.

These actions had significance which went far beyond Nicaragua.

> Mexico's break with Somoza was taken by knowledgeable observers as a signal to other military-dominated governments of Central America that Mexico intended to play a larger role in the area.[59]

Lopez Portillo's policy has been a direct threat to the Reagan administration's affinity for exercising Caribbean influence through right-wing regimes, military or otherwise. And given Mexico's new oil clout, it is not a threat which has been taken lightly.

> Since Mexico has become a major oil producer, Lopez Portillo has been making a quiet bid for influence in turbulent Central America and the Caribbean. "Mexico's in there with the old troupers," says a State Department official. "Let's hope they know their lines."[60]

Reagan has worked hard at courting Mexico in order to coax it back to a noninterventionist stance and although he has not yet achieved any spectacular results, Joseph Kraft has suggested that

> In moving toward harmony with Mexico, Reagan has some notable assets. As a friend of big oil, he is prepared--as Jimmy Carter was not--to have the U.S. pay top dollar for Mexican oil and gas. As a friend of the growers, and with slim ties to labor, Reagan can open the U.S. job market to Mexican workers. As a free marketeer, he opposes restriction on Mexican exports.
>
> In return for an accommodating American stand on the issues of immigration, energy and trade, Mr. Reagan can fairly ask Sr. Lopez-Portillo for a discreet lowering of Mexican support for radical forces now surging in Central America.[61]

Should such persuasion fail, the administration will have to hope that those observers who contend that Mexico's basic conservative impulse will soon reassert itself, especially as the leftist tide in Central America begins lapping at its borders, are correct. Indeed Edward J. Williams suggests that this may already be occurring, noting that there have been reliable reports of

> ...Mexican military cooperation with their Guatemalan counterparts to squelch Guatemalan guerrilla activity along the binational border. As the threat of turbulence moves north from Nicaragua to Guatemala, ... Mexico's sympathy for revolutionary activity decreases and its support of a tyrannical role increases.[62]

Reagan would, of course, like to capitalize on such sentiment to enlist the Mexicans as a (silent?) partner in restoring calm in the Caribbean.

These overtures to Mexico are symptomatic of a thread in Reagan's policy which has often been overlooked--his preference for a multilateral approach to stabilizing the Basin. To a great extent the administration itself has been responsible for this oversight by spotlighting El Salvador where its determination to send an unequivocal message to Moscow has caused it to plunge ahead unilaterally. In general, however, it has been attracted to joint ventures. In the eastern Caribbean, for example, the U.S. has been relying on the English and the French to use their influence to help hold the line. Both have responded positively, with England's Foreign Minister announcing that

> ...Britain's Tory Government stood ready to assist "friendly" Caribbean Governments with arms sales and military training to combat internal subversion.[63]

Thus, just as Carter attempted to organize a collaborative effort to quiet the Sandinista storm in Nicaragua, so also is Reagan likely to explore similar options before acting alone.

REAGAN'S CARIBBEAN POLICY: A CRITIQUE

One way to critique Reagan's Caribbean policy would be to challenge his assertion that the United States has legitimate vital interests which justify and even necessitate involvement in the region. If such interests are few or nonexistent, then U.S. intervention can at best be characterized as misguided and at worst an exercise in raw exploitive imperialism. And strong cases can be made that:

A) America's stake in the Basin's essential economic status quo is not crucial. The nation would not fall apart or even be seriously injured if some significant alterations in its present economic relationships resulted from political change there;

B) Washington's military/strategic interests, while perhaps vital in some respects like oil routes, do not require it to maintain a military presence via in-country bases or advising/training missions. They can be protected by naval/air units operating from the U.S. mainland;

C) Ideological containment, whether in the Caribbean or elsewhere, is not a valid concern. As sovereign entities, all states have the right to utilize whatever political philosophy they wish to structure their societies and any

> outside interference is illegitimate according to accepted norms of international custom and law.

The problem raised by each of these points ultimately boils down to how to define "legitimate" and "vital," a controversy which has been raging in one form or another for years and still remains unresolved.

The approach to be used here, however, recognizes that the Basin's proximity to the United States means that Washington will almost inevitably <u>think</u> that it has interests there. Whether or not one deems them legitimate and vital, they nevertheless exist because the U.S. believes they do and behaves accordingly. Therefore, rather than continuing the debate, it is more productive to move on and evaluate Reagan's policy in more specific terms of: A) the accuracy of its perceptions regarding threats to U.S. interests; B) its viability as a means to achieve its stated goals; and C) its relevance to evolving Caribbean (and perhaps by inference Third World) realities and needs.

Much of the rationale for Reagan's initiatives rests on the contention that there is a major Cuban/Soviet threat to the Basin's security and to America's vital interests there; it is a central theme in practically every administration statement. But this is not a very convincing argument when subjected to close scrutiny.

Regardless of all the shrill rhetoric about Russian bears prowling the Caribbean, Moscow has not displayed any great enthusiasm or aptitude for expanding its presence beyond Cuba. In 1977, for example, it passed up an opportunity to provide desperately needed economic support to Jamaica after Manley rejected the conditions which the International Monetary Fund had attached to its aid offer and broke off negotiations. The Kremlin's response to Kingston's request for help was not that of a government anxious to win friends.

> The Russians, already enjoying the geopolitical privilege of subsidizing one Caribbean island [Cuba] at the rate of $1 billion a year, offered the Jamaicans less money, on more stringent terms, than the IMF.[64]

Also, the Sandinista regime can hardly be said to have been drawn into the USSR's orbit. Managua has received some Russian assistance and has established trade relations with the Soviet bloc, but at the same time it refused to back Moscow on Afghanistan and has tried to maintain cordial ties with Western nations. In short, it has been nonaligned. Basically, then, rather than being on the offensive as portrayed by Reagan, the Kremlin has not made any direct military/economic investments of any consequence to increase its Caribbean influence.

Given this lack of overt expansionism, the existence of a Soviet threat then becomes dependent on the Cuban Surrogate Thesis, which in essence argues that the Castro regime's need for constant injections of massive Russian aid in order to survive has transformed it into a puppet which Moscow regularly uses for indirect penetration of Third World countries. This idea first gained wide popularity in official American circles when Cuban combat troops became heavily involved in the Angolan and Ethiopian conflicts. But most Cuban specialists saw it as a grossly simplistic, inaccurate explanation of Havana's African activities[65] and such skepticism has continued, if not grown, with regard to its Caribbean policy, as the following comments by Anthony Payne and Raymond Duncan illustrate.

> Whatever may be the case in respect of Cuba's African adventures, in the context of the Caribbean Cuba has to be seen as an autonomous actor in its own right rather than as a pliable agent of the Soviet Union.[66]

> Developing an active Caribbean policy allows Havana to gain flexibility vis-a-vis the Soviet Union and, in fact, to augment its power. Havana's Caribbean diplomacy demonstrates an independence in foreign policy perhaps not found in its African adventures... .[67]

Those voicing these opinions span the political spectrum; they include both friends and well-established critics of the Cuban Revolution. Nevertheless they basically agree that while the USSR has encouraged and materially supported Havana's exploits abroad, thereby allowing it to take on more ambitious tasks and carry them out more effectively than might otherwise have been the case, the Surrogate Thesis is invalid. Actually, rather than being subservient to Moscow, Cuba has been pursuing a complicated foreign policy combining independent action and close but selective collaboration with the Russians designed to serve its own interests and to enhance its own stature.[68]

Without the Surrogate Thesis, the whole idea of a Soviet/Cuban threat simply is not persuasive. Naturally both countries will, if given an opportunity, try to improve their positions internationally. Such behavior is normal for states; the U.S. routinely does it all over the world. Havana in particular has been active in the Basin as its focus has shifted from Africa back to the Western Hemisphere and it has, along with Moscow, enjoyed some success there. But not unqualified success, for as Raymond Duncan cautions,

> ...the argument that the Caribbean's leftist governments have become increasingly pro-Soviet or pro-Cuban seems weak. The evidence suggests more strongly that most governments in the region--leftist or not--intend to maximize their development opportunities and their flexibility, favoring whatever financial channels are available and consistent with their development objectives.
>
> ... it would be quite erroneous to take the position that Cuban and Soviet policies in the Caribbean have had no effect on leftist trends in the region. But Caribbean leftism marches essentially to its own drumbeat. No amount of stress on the "Cuban" or "Soviet" threat changes this fact.[69]

The foregoing critique leads to but one conclusion--the external subversion scenario which Reagan has used as grounds for his militaristic approach to dealing with Caribbean instability is basically incorrect. This fundamental miscalculation is the source of practically all subsequent flaws in his policy.

With external subversion discredited, economic crisis emerges as the most plausible explanation for the Basin's political upheavals. Typical are Anthony Lewis' comments about El Salvador:

> El Salvador is under attack by "terrorists," General Haig and the president say; Cuba and

> the Soviet Union are trying to infiltrate terrorism into the Americas. But anyone who cares to ... knows that the revolutionary movement did not originate abroad but began as an indigenous response to a century of right-wing exploitation enforced by state terrorism.[70]

Frequently such analyses point to the United States rather than Moscow or Havana as the outside troublemaker, accusing it of contributing heavily to the Basin's difficulties by having sustained repressive oligarchic governments in office for years. Obviously reducing these regimes to American clients has helped Washington control the region. But guaranteeing their survival has also removed much of the incentive for them to institute any serious reforms in order to generate domestic support, an option which has never attracted them because they have always feared that mass politization and mobilization might backfire by getting out of hand and endangering the status quo from which they benefit so immensely. Consequently no broadbased modernization has occurred, the Caribbean has sunk deeper into dependency on the U.S., and the internal gap between the haves and the have-nots has widened. As matters have reached crisis proportions, demands for change have almost invariably taken on an anti-Yankee tone, reflecting the conviction that American intervention is integral to the area's problems.

The Reagan administration's "get tough" reaction has not really resolved anything. Instead it has prolonged and will probably even intensify tensions by helping local elites perpetuate what is to many people a totally unacceptable social order. At best,

> ... arms can bring only short-term order to the region. ... Only by improving frail economies and miserable living conditions can peace be achieved.[71]

Washington therefore has been making a cardinal error--it has been pursuing a policy which actually aggravates the situation which it is supposed to ameliorate. From such contradictions fiascos are born.

Even if the Reaganites would shift to a developmental strategy to alleviate the Basin's economic crisis, it is doubtful that they would be able to make much progress because their commitment to ideological containment makes their parameters of acceptable reform too narrow. Their basic instinct is to insist that Caribbean modernization must essentially follow the American capitalist model; any deviation is seen as a threat to containment and hence to the United States' power to protect its vital interests. This approach is, however, very unlikely to work.

> If the history of modern Latin America teaches no other lesson, it should by now be clear that the combination of formal democracy ... and late-industrializing capitalist economies has not and probably cannot significantly reduce the appalling inequities in economic and social conditions... .
>
> In U.S. policy circles, this key fact of hemispheric life is not understood.[72]

Indeed the status quo of dependent capitalism which has been widely rejected in the Basin is the result of previous efforts at Americanization. Thus another contradiction emerges--the administration's developmental perspective is rooted in an ideological framework which almost certainly would function to preclude the structural changes necessary to modernize the region. Consequently the economic crisis would remain and with it the potential for instability which the President so fears as a breeding ground for leftist challenges to the U.S. Once this became apparent, he almost surely would revert to more forceful tactics to assure (American) law and order.

In the final analysis, then, Reagan's policy, whatever its stated motivations and goals, whatever its misperceptions or deviousness, boils down to another unimaginative exercise in hegemonic clientelism. As such it is simply old wine in old bottles, a reaffirmation of the Pax Americana, sphere of influence mentality which has long characterized Washington's attitude toward the region. Given this perspective, it really does not matter what the specific threats or causes thereof to U.S. dominance are because <u>all</u> must be confronted and overcome, militarily if necessary. The fact that the external subversion thesis is untenable or that American intervention may generate more economically-induced instability is immaterial to the administration. Imperial powers, which is what the United States has been and seeks to remain in the Basin, seldom worry about such technicalities.

Even if Reagan scores some victories against the Caribbean left, which America's massive economic/military resources and its experience at political manipulation may very well allow him to do, it is doubtful that the effort will be worthwhile in the long run. Instead he will probably discover that what he has done is irrelevant and/or counterproductive.

For example, his idea that anti-leftist initiatives in the Basin are required to demonstrate his continuing commitment to the Containment Doctrine makes little sense. The Soviets do not need such a message to tell them what they already know--that the U.S. has never abandoned containment. That being the case, there is no reason to think that his restatement of the obvious will seriously worry them. They were not intimidated when they were weaker than the United States and they surely will not be now that they have achieved rough military parity. Indeed American intransigence may have exactly the opposite effect.

> ...consider the argument that Haig is using El Salvador to signal the Russians--to warn them that they had better behave in Afghanistan and Poland. Is that really the message that Moscow is likely to get? Not bloody likely.
>
> The message of the Haig policy is that a superpower will not tolerate political upsets in its own backyard. If that is true for us in El Salvador, why should it be any different for the Soviet Union in Poland or Afghanistan?[73]

The containment rationale for a hard line is also related to the belief that superpower politics is a zero-sum game; any loss by one party translates into a direct or indirect gain for the other. However,

> There are two basic flaws in this interpretation ... . First, there is no reason for the a priori assumption that the superpower game is of the zero-sum variety. Logically they could both gain or lose at the same time: it is a question of fact, not of theory. And second, a serious examination of the record clearly points to the conclusion that during the past two

decades both superpowers have in fact been losing power and influence.[74]

Containment, bipolarity, macrolinkage--all suggest that there is a compelling Cold War logic behind U.S. Caribbean policy. But when examined critically, the argument lacks substance. To believe otherwise and behave accordingly is absurd.

Equally questionable is Reagan's notion that helping to establish and consolidate center-right coalition governments in the Basin represents an effective way to impede the spread of anti-Yankeeism. According to the administration, such regimes will pursue moderate reformist policies which will generate widespread public support and keep the influence of the radical left, the main instigator of anti-Americanism, to a minimum. The problem is that in many instances there is no viable political center to incorporate into this scheme; it either never existed, has been decimated by attacks from the left and/or the right, or has gravitated toward the political extremes. U.S. involvement then puts it in a position where in reality it is throwing its weight behind traditional elites who are not interested in reform or pluralist politics and who will capitalize on Washington's support to defend their exploitive perogatives by repressing their opponents, thereby further polarizing their countries and undermining their legitimacy by exposing themselves to charges that they are being maintained in power by outsiders. Such a situation is ideal for the flowering of left-wing, anti-Yankee nationalism, which means that the administration's own actions, not foreign agitators or local radicals, provide the main impetus for the development of the anti-American sentiment which it perceives as a serious threat to U.S. interests.

Finally, Reagan's interventionist policy is incompatible with his desire for extremely cordial, cooperative relations with Mexico and Venezuela. Neither country, particularly Mexico, is likely to stand idly by while the United States tries to perpetuate its dominance under the guise of combatting leftist subversives. Instead they want Washington to accept the fact that a new era is dawning involving fundamental structural change in the configuration of regional power, change which demotes the Colossus of the North from director/producer to just another actor on the Caribbean stage. The administration's refusal to do so puts it on a potential collision course with them. And in any confrontation, oil is their trump card. Should they play it, it not only would be disastrous to U.S. economic/strategic interests, but also might unleash shock waves that could further destabilize the entire area.

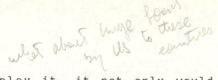

CONCLUSION

The most charitable thing that one can say about Reagan's Caribbean policy is that it has not yet achieved its full catastrophic potential. Overall it has been responsive to neither concrete American interests (including many accorded high priority by the administration itself) nor contemporary Caribbean realities and needs. Even a few successes (e.g., in El Salvador or Guatemala) will not compensate for the self-defeating contradictions in it; they will merely provide a reprieve while Washington ventures farther down its dead end road.

A viable policy demands that Reagan first come to grips with the new facts of international and hemispheric life. And perhaps the most difficult of these for him and many other Americans to recognize is that a colossus challenged is a colossus no more. Only after this psychological Rubicon has been crossed and the United States accepts, both pragmatically and normatively, the limitations of its power will it be able to play a truly constructive role in the Caribbean.

NOTES

1. Anthony Payne, "Giants and Pygmies In The Caribbean," *World Today* (August 1980), p. 289 groups the leading actors on the Caribbean scene as follows:

> "...hemispheric powers, by which is meant the United States and Canada; old colonial powers like Britain and France; Communist powers, including the Soviet Union, China and Cuba; and Latin American powers, notably Venezuela and Mexico."

Add to this list Japan and European Social Democratic and Christian Democratic parties and it is obvious that the Caribbean political stage is becoming rather crowded.

2. William G. Demas, "Foreword" in Richard Millet and W. Marvin Will (Eds.), *The Restless Caribbean: Changing Patterns of International*

Relations (New York: Praeger Publishers, 1979), pp. vii-x explains that geopolitically the Caribbean can be seen in terms of three concentric rings. These are, from the inside outward: A) the English-speaking or Commonwealth Caribbean; B) the Caribbean archipelago, which includes all the islands plus the mainland extensions of Guyana, Suriname, and French Guinea in South America and Belize in Central America; and C) the Caribbean Basin, consisting of the countries of the archipelago plus the littoral states of Central and South America. Here we are using the Basin conceptualization, which is gradually replacing the insular view as the most popular among area specialists.

3. Jack Anderson, "Storm Warnings At Our Doorstep," Parade Magazine (September 21, 1980), p. 35.

4. "Land of The Smoking Gun," Time (August 18, 1980), p. 35.

5. Reported in Payne, op. cit., p. 289.

6. Reported in "Storm Over El Salvador," Newsweek (March 16, 1981), p. 34.

7. Too often Caribbean studies tend to become mesmerized by the region's supposed special relationship with the United States and thus neglect its linkages with the rest of the world, especially the Afro-Asian developing nations. Consequently the erroneous impression is created that the Basin has somehow acquired subsystemic immunity; that, in other words, events and transformations in the larger global environment do not significantly affect it. Among the more recent analyses which avoid this mistake and instead emphasize the Caribbean's sensitivity to the international system are Luis E. Agrait, "Whither The Non-Independent States of the Caribbean?" (Paper presented at the 1979 conference of the Southeastern Council on Latin American Studies in Tampa, Florida); Josefina C. Tiryakian, "United States, Puerto Rico, and The Caribbean: Rethinking Geopolitical Realities" (Paper presented at the 1980 conference of the Middle Atlantic Council on Latin American Studies in Newark, Delaware);, and Jacqueline Braveboy-Wagner, "Changes In The English-Speaking Caribbean: An International Systems Perspective With Implications For The United States" (Paper presented at the 1980 conference of the Latin American Studies Association in Bloomington, Indiana).

8. "Grenada--Consolidating The Revolution," Caribissues, Vol. 3, No. 6 (April 1979), p. 7. This issue contains nine pages of very useful news summaries about the New Jewel revolution in Grenada. Similar news summaries covering the Bishop government's first two weeks in power can be found in "Revolution In Grenada," Caribissues, Vol. 3, No. 5 (March 1979), pp. 1-7.

9. H. Michael Erisman, "Cuban Internationalism: Impact of Nonaligned Leadership And Afghanistan" (Paper presented at the 1980 Latin American Studies Association conference in Bloomington, Indiana), pp. 21 and 26 provides data indicating that by late 1979 Cuba had 50 military and 350 civilian aid personnel working in Grenada. Its major project was to build a new $50 million international airport for which it supplied 50 percent of the funds and practically all of the construction expertise.

10. The January 14, 1980 vote was 104 to 18 in favor of the resolution (with 30 abstentions or absences). Cuba and Grenada were the only hemispheric nations opposing it: Nicaragua abstained and Dominica was absent. For voting details, see "The Roll Call In The General Assembly," New York Times (January 15, 1980), p. A8.

11. Among the best of the many studies analyzing Somoza's ouster are William LeoGrande, "Revolution In Nicaragua: Another Cuba?," Foreign Affairs, 58:28-50 (Fall 1979) and Waltraud Queiser Morales, "Nicaragua 1979: Why, How, and What's Ahead?" (Paper presented at the 1979 Annual Third World Conference in Omaha, Nebraska).

12. Erisman, op. cit., pp. 21 and 26.

Details about the Cuban presence in Nicaragua are murky. U.S. Department of State, Bureau of Public Affairs, Current Policy #167 (April 17, 1980), "Cuban-Soviet Impact on The Western Hemisphere," p. 2 stated that in late 1979 the Cuban mission in Nicaragua numbered at least 2,000 and included about 200 military/security advisors, a minimum of 1,200 teachers, and several hundred developmental assistance personnel.

"Reagan's Goal: Cutting Castro Down to Size," U.S. News and World Report (April 6, 1981), p. 20 puts the 1981 total of Cuban military/civilian personnel in Nicaragua at approximately 5,000.

13. "Nicaragua, The Church, And The USA," Caribbean Contact (September 1980), p. 12.

14. These moderate-conservative victories included those of Milton Cato in St. Vincent (December 1979), Kennedy Simmonds in St. Kitts-Nevis (February 1980), Vere Bird in Antigua (April 1980), Eugenia Charles in Dominica (July 1980), and Tom Adams in Barbados (June 1981).

15. Roger Fontaine, Cleto DiGiovanni, Jr., and Alexander Kruger, "Castro's Specter," Washington Quarterly (Autumn 1980), p. 4.

16. Representative samples can be found in U.S. Department of State Publication 8770, Inter-American Series 107, The Inter-American Relationship (June 1974) and U.S. Department of State Publication 8848, Inter-American Series 110, Major Statements on Latin America By Secretary of State Henry Kissinger (March 1976).

17. Facts on File, Vol. 37, No. 1932 (November 19, 1977), p. 884.

18. Two good summaries of the Carter administration's initial policies can be found in U.S. Department of State, Bureau of Public Affairs, "The United States and Latin America: President Carter before the Permanent Council of the Organization of American States" (April 14, 1977) and U.S. Department of State, Bureau of Public Affairs, "U.S. Relations In The Caribbean: Assistant Secretary for Inter-American Affairs, Terence A. Todman, before the Subcommittee on Inter-American Affairs of the House International Relations Committee" (June 28, 1977).

19. Facts on File, Vol. 37, No. 1920 (August 27, 1977), p. 646.

20. Ibid., p. 647.

21. For an analysis of the rise and later demise of U.S.-Cuban rapprochement, see H. Michael Erisman, "La Normalizacion De Relaciones Entre Cuba Y Estados Unidos: El Caso De Cuba En Africa," Arieto, Vol. 5, No. 17 (November 1978), pp. 20-25.

22. Abraham F. Lowenthal, "Latin America: A Not-So-Special Relationship," Foreign Policy, 32:107-126 (Fall 1978), p. 119.

23. Much has been written about the Cuban military presence in Africa. Probably the most thorough treatments are William Durch, "The Cuban Military In Africa And The Middle East: From Algeria To Angola," Studies in Comparative Communism, 11: 34-74 (Spring/Summer 1978); Nelson Valdes, "The Evolution Of Cuban Foreign Policy In Africa" (Paper presented at the 1979 convention of the International Studies Association in Toronto, Canada); and William LeoGrande, "Cuban-Soviet Relations And Cuban Policy In Africa," Cuban Studies (January 1980), pp. 1-45.

24. Both quotes are reported in "Cubans In Africa: Moscow Tests Carter," Newsweek (March 13, 1978), pp. 36-37. The first quote is attributed to an anonymous high-ranking U.S. official and the second to an anonymous White House official.

25. Carter's explanation of the crisis and a general outline of his administration's response can be found in U.S. Department of State, Bureau of Public Affairs, Current Policy No. 92, "President Carter: Soviet Troops in Cuba," which is the text of his television address to the nation on October 1, 1979.

Moscow insisted that the 2,000-3,000 men which Carter labelled a combat unit were actually a training brigade which the U.S knew had been in Cuba for years. Castro accused Washington of manufacturing a crisis to discredit Cuba immediately prior to the September 1979 nonaligned summit in Havana and to wreck the conference. In any case, the troop issue itself faded rather quickly with the Carter administration backing down from its previous statements that the presence of those forces was totally unacceptable. However, the U.S. continued its military/economic initiatives in the Caribbean which the incident had spawned.

26. Elizabeth Farnsworth, "Keeping The Caribbean Safe From Castro," The Nation (December 15, 1979), p. 617.

Further details on the Carter administration's efforts to increase America's visibility and influence in the Basin can be found in U.S. Department of State, Bureau of Public Affairs, Current Policy No. 177, "U.S. Relations With The Caribbean and Central America" (December 1979).

27. For specifics regarding Carter's economic/military aid policies at this time, see U.S.

Department of State, Bureau of Public Affairs, Current Policy No. 166, "Foreign Assistance Proposals: Latin America And The Caribbean" (April 16, 1980).

Washington's concern about developments in the Lesser Antilles resulting from the Grenadian revolution explains Barbados' unprecedented prominence. Indeed Karen de Young, "The Caribbean: A Gathering Storm," Washington Post (September 30, 1980), p. A16 noted that

> "There have been reports that the United States hopes to turn the island of Barbados, perhaps the closest U.S. ally in that region, into a sort of 'Iran of the Caribbean.' Barbados maintains the only army-like defense force in the area and many within the Pentagon and the Carter administration would like to see it as the center of a regional defense force.
>
> But Barbados so far has balked."

Yussif Haniff, "Barbados Warming Up For Elections," Caribbean Contact (August 1980), p. 6 reported that Barbados had agreed to send troops to the American Virgin Islands to be trained by the U.S. National Guard and to allow the U.S. Virgin Islands National Guard to spend some time in the country, but nothing remotely similar to U.S.-Iranian military cooperation seems to have been established.

28. Carter's El Salvador policy is discussed in Cleto diGiovanni, Jr. and Alexander Kruger, "Central America," Washington Quarterly, 3:175-186 (Summer 1980), pp. 179-183; William LeoGrande and Carla Ann Robbins, "Oligarchs and Officers: The Crisis In El Salvador," Foreign Affairs (Summer 1980), pp. 1084-1103; Richard Millet, "Central American Paralysis," Foreign Policy (Summer 1980), pp. 99-117; and James Petras, "The Junta's War Against The People," The Nation (December 20, 1980), pp. 657+.

29. Probably the best presentation of these themes can be found in Jeane Kirkpatrick, "U.S. Security And Latin America," Commentary, 71(1):29-40 (January 1981).

30. Facts on File, Vol. 39, No. 2036 (November 16, 1979), p. 866.

31. "Reagan, Latin America, And The Caribbean," Caribbean Contact (December 1980), p. 3.

32. Reagan's basic antipathy toward Castro's Cuba is reflected in the New York Times reconstruction of what is called his basic campaign speech, reported in Facts on File, Vol. 40, No. 2048 (February 8, 1980), p. 91, which said with regard to Cuba,

> "Why should we respect the experiment of an American-hating dictator who betrayed the Cuban people and converted that country into a penal colony for the Soviet Union?"

See also "Reagan's Goal...," op. cit., pp. 20-22.

33. U.S. Department of State, Bureau of Public Affairs, Special Report No. 80, "Communist Interference in El Salvador" (February 23, 1981), p. 1.

34. Apparently arms shipments through Nicaragua dropped markedly in February/March 1981. It is unclear, however, whether this decline was due primarily to U.S. economic pressure or to Nicaraguan disillusionment with the El Salvadoran insurgents. Clearly there was some disillusionment. In "El Salvador: The U.S. Gets Tougher," Newsweek (March 9, 1981), p. 38 a high-ranking Sandinista official is quoted as complaining with regard to the guerrillas' abortive January 1981 final offensive that

> "They told us they were going to show what great public support they had. They either lied to us or they are completely ignorant of their own weakness."

35. "Storm Over El Salvador," Newsweek (March 16, 1981), p. 35.

36. Editorial column by Joseph Kraft, "Caribbean Gamble Seen" (February 26, 1981).

37. The development of this tradition is examined by James Petras, H. Michael Erisman, and Charles Mills, "The Monroe Doctrine and U.S. Hegemony In Latin America" in James Petras (Ed.), Latin America: From Dependence to Revolution (New York: John Wiley and Sons, 1973), pp. 231-268.

38. "Powder Keg On Our Doorstep," U.S. News and World Report (May 19, 1980), p. 21 puts U.S. direct investment in the Caribbean Basin at $13.7 billion, which is apparently a 1979 figure. Also, data provided the author by the U.S. State Department

contains the following updated export/import information: U.S. exports to the Caribbean, 1980 = $27.7 billion; U.S. imports from the Caribbean, 1980 = $24.1 billion.

39. Quoted in John Gerassi, The Great Fear In Latin America, revised ed. (New York: Collier Books, 1965), p. 231.

40. For example, Kirkpatrick, op. cit., p. 31 strongly implies that sanctions should be used to aid American businesses in the hemisphere and that U.S. power should be employed to protect American corporations from expropriation.

41. Jeffrey Antevil, "The Caribbean: America's Vital Underbelly," Today (May 30, 1980), p. 1.

42. Regarding naval macroplanning, Tiryakian, op. cit., p. 4 says that

> "The increasing threat to the sealanes and to the free flow of Western trade posed by the spectacular growth of Soviet maritime and naval power has prompted naval strategists to pose the need for extending the reach of NATO beyond the Tropic of Cancer and to integrate the defense of the North and South Atlantic. In such an eventuality, Roosevelt Roads naval station would be the logical connecting link."

43. "The Danger Behind The Vile Campaign Against Cuba," Granma Weekly Review (April 20, 1980), p. 6.

44. Tiryakian, op. cit., pp. 6-7.

45. Quoted in "Land Of The Smoking Gun," op. cit., p. 35.

46. Kraft, op. cit..

47. For a comprehensive discussion of these activities, see Erisman, "Cuban Internationalism...," op. cit..

48. "Troubled Waters," Time (October 22, 1979), p. 49.

49. U.S. Department of State, Bureau of Public Affairs, Current Policy #174 (April 1980), "President Carter: Caribbean/ Central America," p. 2.

50. These Russian foreign policy goals in the Caribbean are mentioned in Anderson, op. cit., p. 18; Richard Buel, "Grenada: Cold War In A Hot Country," National Review (November 14, 1980), pp. 1392+; and Daniel James, "Mexico: America's Newest Problem?," Washington Quarterly (Summer 1980), pp. 89 and 105.

51. Quoted in "El Salvador's Short Fuse," Newsweek (January 18, 1981), p. 49.

52. During a one-week working session at the U.S. State Department in early April 1981, it was apparent to the author that high officials there felt that they had somewhat of a public relations problem regarding El Salvador. They seemed particularly unhappy with criticism coming from the U.S. academic and Catholic communities. Their concern, however, was clearly with managing these nuisances rather than altering policy.

53. For further information, see James Petras, "Social Democracy In Latin America," NACLA Report on The Americas, 14(1):36-39 (January-February 1980).

54. Quoted in Tad Szulc, "Radical Winds In The Caribbean," New York Times Magazine (May 25, 1980), p. 70.

55. Two good investigations of Andres Perez' foreign policy are Robert Bond (Ed.), Contemporary Venezuela And Its Role In International Affairs (New York: New York University Press, 1977) and Winfield J. Burggraaff, "Oil And Caribbean Influence: The Role Of Venezuela" in Millet and Will, op. cit., pp. 193-203.

56. This brief summary is based on John D. Martz, "Ideology And Oil: Venezuela In The Caribbean" (Paper presented at the 1981 conference of the Caribbean Studies Association in St. Thomas, U.S. Virgin Islands).

57. "Threatening U.S. Military Maneuvers In Vicinity of Cuba," Granma Weekly Review (April 20, 1980), p. 1.

58. Three good overviews of recent Mexican foreign policy are George W. Grayson, "Mexican Foreign Policy," Current History, 72:97-101+ (March 1977); John F. McShane, "Mexican Foreign Policy: A Return To Restrained Nationalism" (Paper presented at the 1979 convention of the Southern Political Science Association in Gatlinburg, Tennessee); and James, op. cit..

59. Quoted in Facts on File, Vol. 39, No. 2012 (June 1, 1979), p. 409.

60. "Mexico: A New Leadership Role," Newsweek (September 15, 1980), p. 62.

61. Joseph Kraft, "A Mexican Tradeoff?", Erie (Pa.) Daily Times (January 6, 1981).

62. Edward J. Williams, "Between North and South: Mexico, The United States And Central America" (Unpublished manuscript), p. 3.

63. "Britain's Strange Anti-Opposition Arms Offer To Caribbean Governments," Caribbean Contact (September 1980), p. 6.

Additional information about British and French activities can be found in Szulc, op. cit., p. 58 and Payne, op. cit., pp. 291-292.

64. T.D. Allman, "Killing Jamaica With Kindness," Harper's, 258:30-36 (May 1979), p. 33.

65. For a representatitve sample, see Valdes, op. cit., LeoGrande, "Cuban-Soviet Relations...," op cit.; Jorge Dominguez, "Cuban Foreign Policy," Foreign Affairs, 57:83-108 (Fall 1978); Edward Gonzalez, "Complexities Of Cuban Foreign Policy," Problems of Communism, 26:1-15 (November/December 1977); and Durch, op. cit.. Durch's negative conclusions about the Surrogate Thesis are particularly interesting since his article resulted from a study financed by the Pentagon.

66. Payne, op. cit., p. 293.

67. W. Raymond Duncan, "Soviet and Cuban Interests In The Caribbean" in Millet and Will, op. cit., p. 144.

68. This line of analysis is developed more fully in H. Michael Erisman, "Cuban Foreign Policy And The Sino-Soviet Split" (Paper presented at the 1980 International Studies Association convention in Los Angeles, California) and Erisman, "Cuban Internationalism...," op. cit..

69. W. Raymond Duncan, "Caribbean Leftism," Problems of Communism, 27:33-57 (May/June 1978), pp. 44 and 56.

70. Anthony Lewis, "Haig's Best Laid Plans," Erie (Pa.) Times-News (March 8, 1981).

71. These comments are attributed to reflective Panamanians and strategists elsewhere in Central America in "The Ferment In Central America," Newsweek (March 16, 1981), p. 46.

72. Richard R. Fagen, "The Carter Administration And Latin America: Business As Usual?," Foreign Affairs, 57(3):652-669 (1978), pp. 666-667.

73. Lewis, op. cit..

74. "U.S. Foreign Policy In The 1980s," Monthly Review, 31:1-12 (April 1980), p. 2.

2
Soviet Policy and the Crisis in the Caribbean

Jiri Valenta

INTRODUCTION

With the victory of the Sandinistas in Nicaragua in July 1979 and the ongoing civil war in El Salvador, Soviet strategy and tactics in Central America are being analyzed with new seriousness. According to some observers, the revolution in Nicaragua is transforming that country into a "second Cuba." Meanwhile, the Reagan administration has presented an array of evidence of cautious yet active support (armaments and military instruction) to left-leaning guerrillas in El Salvador. This aid is relayed by the Cubans by way of Nicaragua.

These recent developments not only are significant within the context of the Caribbean basin, but they also shed new light on the more crucial issue of Soviet strategy in the Third World in general.[1] The Soviet-backed, Cuban-orchestrated support to allies in Central America follows a decade of limited military and security assistance to other Third World countries--to Mozambique, Guinea, and Zambia in Africa, to Syria and South Yemen in the Middle East--and comes on the heels of two Soviet-Cuban military interventions on behalf of revolutionary and government forces: in Angola in 1975-1976 and in Ethiopia in 1977-1978. Along with Soviet support for the 1978 intervention in Kampuchea (Cambodia) conducted by the North Vietnamese (the Cubans of the Orient

---

Reprinted, with some revisions, by permission of the author and the publisher, from Orbis: A Journal of World Affairs (Fall 1981). This article adapted from a chapter in Richard E. Fineberg (Ed.), Central America: The International Dimensions of the Crisis (New York: Holmes and Meier, 1982).

as the Chinese call them) and the Soviets' own military intervention in Afghanistan in 1979, these activities are perceived by many U.S. policymakers as fitting into an overall Soviet plan.

Secretary of State Alexander Haig views developments in Central America as part of "a very clearly delineated Soviet-Cuban strategy," the clear objective of which is "to create Marxist-Leninist regimes in Central America--Nicaragua, El Salvador, Guatemala, and Honduras."[2] In Haig's view, the Soviet-sponsored interventions in Central America are "an extension of the 'Brezhnev doctrine' [once applied only to Eastern Europe] outside the area of Soviet hegemony." This school of thought was echoed by President Reagan himself, who explained that "the terrorists aren't just aiming at El Salvador," but "at the whole of Central and possibly later South America [and], I'm sure, eventually North America."[3] The Reagan administration has apparently decided to counter what it sees as Soviet implementation of the Brezhnev Doctrine by acting on the principle of the Monroe Doctrine, whereby the U.S. government announced its intention to oppose outside interference in the Americas. Thus the crises in Central America in general and El Salvador in particular have become crucial tests of this administration's determination to challenge Soviet designs in the Western Hemisphere and perhaps in other areas of the Third World.

The present analysis will be limited to Soviet perceptions of and strategies toward Central America and the Caribbean and will emphasize the specific tactics employed in Nicaragua and El Salvador. First, however, something should be said about the complex beginnings of the ongoing conflict in the region and the reasons for the revolutionary transformation occurring there. The present crises in Central America cannot be attributed solely to outside interference. What is happening in El Salvador and to varying degrees in other Central American countries is rapid decay of long-entrenched and autocratic power.[4] This process has been witnessed already in other Third World countries, such as Ethiopia. The decay of outmoded political, economic, and social orders is the result of a number of factors internal to the countries themselves. The societies of Central America are polarized by antagonism between a very small upper class and a very poor majority; in most of these countries, the middle class remains weak and underdeveloped. Socioeconomic polarization and past and existing oppressive regimes have contributed significantly to the rise of internal and interregional conflicts.

Moreover, several decades of U.S. hegemony and shortsighted policies, ranging from intervention to benign neglect, have also contributed to the development of nationalist reaction in the region. The prevailing feeling of many nationalists and radicals south of the Rio Grande regarding the United States resembles the traditional attitude of the Poles and Hungarians toward the Soviets. This view was well articulated by prerevolutionary Mexican President Porfirio Diaz, who once lamented, "Poor Mexico: so far from God, so near the United States." More recently, the tensions have been exacerbated by Cuba, the USSR, and some other communist and Third World states that have sought to exploit radical currents and capitalize on the tides of revolution.

In this examination of Soviet strategies and tactics in Central America, the following questions will guide the discussion: How and why did the Soviets become involved in Central America? What are their ties both with the more traditional communist parties and with the guerrilla groups of the region? How does Central America fit into Soviet global strategy? To what degree does Cuba exercise its own strategy in the region? Are Cuba, the USSR, and their allies competing with the United States for influence in Nicaragua and El Salvador as they have done for several years in Africa, particularly in Angola and Ethiopia? If so, are they prepared to risk further deterioration of U.S.-Soviet relations to accomplish this? Are the Soviets motivated merely by the desire to cause problems for the United States or by more complex aims? Do Soviet commitments in Angola, Ethiopia, and South Yemen and its preoccupation with the war in Afghanistan, the crisis in Poland, and the Iran-Iraqi war limit its ability to become heavily involved in Nicaragua and El Salvador?

A HISTORICAL PERSPECTIVE

Unlike Cuba, which is an integral part of the Caribbean basin, the Soviet Union has no long-standing cultural, political, or commercial ties with the countries of Central America. It began to develop such ties only as recently as the 1960s. In contrast to those with Europe and Asia, its interactions with Central and South America have recently been modest. This is chiefly because of the area's geographic remoteness and therefore marginal importance to the USSR and the traditional hegemony there of the United States.

The element of geographic remoteness, it should be noted, has been an asset to the Soviet Union in its efforts from the 1960s onward to become involved in the region. Like the United States in Eastern Europe, the USSR does not have a strong imperial record in Central and South America. Like the American image in Eastern Europe, its image in some Central American countries has been a conspicuously favorable one. As "enemies of American imperialism," early Bolsheviks were viewed as natural allies by revolutionary and patriotic circles in Mexico. Despite U.S. intervention in favor of revolutionary forces in 1916, two years later the military boss of a Mexican region said, "I don't know what socialism is but I am a Bolshevik, like all patriotic Mexicans--the Yankees do not like the Bolsheviks. They are our enemies; therefore the Bolsheviks must be our friends and we must be their friends. We are all Bolsheviks."[5]

Although revolutionary elements were sympathetic to the Bolshevik revolution and the Soviet regime, the Soviets were ostracized for several decades by the ruling elites of Central America and handicapped by the absence of diplomatic relations. Soviet relations with the countries of the Caribbean basin, with the exception of Mexico, were limited up to the 1960s to relations with their respective communist parties. In fact, until the Cuban revolution, Mexico, Uruguay, and Argentina were the only Latin American countries with which the USSR had diplomatic relations. Thus, first-hand Soviet knowledge of the Caribbean basin was effectively limited to Mexico.

Before World War II, Mexico was the principal center for the dissemination of Comintern publications to Spanish-speaking countries in the region. With the help of Mexican Communist party officials, the Comintern was able to supervise the founding of the Communist party of Guatemala and assist with the founding of other communist parties. The communist parties of Central America were illegal, their memberships ranging from several dozen to a few hundred. In Cuba, with Soviet encouragement, the party even entered into a coalition with the government of Fulgencio Batista during the Popular Front era of the 1930s and again briefly in the 1940s. On the other hand, with the notable exception of the Communist party of Costa Rica, the Central American parties have traditionally operated in a conspiratorial or semilegal fashion. Even in Costa Rica the Communist party is weak and has participated in only a limited manner in the politics of the nation.

Comintern officials had traditionally discounted the prospects for communism in Central and South America, displaying, like Marx and Engels, a certain Eurocentric disdain for Latin peoples and viewing the countries within a colonial framework in which the United States was firmly in command. Until the victorious Cuban revolution, the Communist Party of the Soviet Union (CPSU) had had only sporadic contacts with its Latin American counterparts through individual party and Comintern officials. Soviet financial subsidies to these parties have been small, though regular.[6]

Local communist parties have been involved in several unsuccessful insurrections in Central America's past. In 1932 there was an uprising in El Salvador that was crushed by government forces. In Guatemala in 1953-1954, the nationalistic regime of President Jacobo Arbenz attempted a swing toward radicalism with the backing of the Communist party of Guatemala, a small but influential party that was in control of the labor movement. Available evidence suggests that the Soviets provided Arbenz's regime with financial and political support and even shipped 2,000 tons of Czech-manufactured weapons to Arbenz and his supporters. This support was marginal, however, and there is little evidence pointing to direct Soviet involvement. The meager level of support was determined in part by the Soviets' then-limited capabilities and in part by the fact that the United States treated Guatemala as a major issue, thus warding off further Soviet involvement. With covert support from the U.S. CIA, anti-Arbenz forces launched an invasion from Honduras and soon overthrew the regime.[7]

The turning point in Soviet relations with Central America came in 1959-1960 after the Cuban revolution. When U.S.-Cuban differences became unbridgeable and the United States withdrew from Cuba, the Soviets, after a period of hesitation, tried to fill the political and economic vacuum thus created. After the Bay of Pigs invasion attempt, Nikita Krushchev and his colleagues painstakingly went about building a major alliance with Cuba. Despite ups and downs and disagreements about strategies in the Third World and in Latin America, the alliance begun at this time has remained solid.

Initially--at least until the Cuban missile crisis in 1962--the Soviets were exuberant about the success of the Cuban revolution. The revolution spurred Soviet research into Latin American affairs and in 1961 the Soviet leadership established a new Institute for the Study of Latin America. For a brief time during this period of euphoria, Moscow seemed to believe that the Cuban style of revolution could be exported, with Soviet backing, to Central America. Thus in 1959 and 1960, respectively, the communist parties of Nicaragua and El Salvador tried to overthrow their countries' regimes. The Cuban missile crisis, however, which the Chinese describe as the "Caribbean Munich," soon reminded the Soviets of the limits of their power in the area.

Not surprisingly, Krushchev's decision to remove the missiles had some repercussions for USSR-Cuban relationships. In the aftermath of the Soviet capitulation, marching militia in Havana chanted "Nikita mariquita, lo que se da no se quita (Nikita, you little braggart--what one gives, one doesn't take away)."[8] Fidel Castro was naturally worried at this time about the degree of Soviet commitment to protecting Cuba against the United States. Like many others, he did not realize what would become clear only in the 1970s: though humiliated, Krushchev achieved at least one of his objectives during the missile crisis--while agreeing to remove the missiles, he was able to extract an American pledge not to topple the revolutionary Cuban regime. In retrospect, considering the success of joint Soviet-Cuban operations in the Third World in the 1970s, it appears that Krushchev and not John Kennedy may have been the winner in the 1962 confrontation.

The resolution of the Cuban missile crisis had a sobering effect on Soviet perceptions of the potential for revolution in the Caribbean basin. So did U.S. intervention in the Dominican Republic in 1965, when the motto "Never a second Cuba" became the imperative for U.S. policy in Latin America. The failure of Cuban-backed guerrilla revolutionaries in the 1960s in Guatemala, Nicaragua, and in South America (Bolivia, Peru, and Venezuela) further ingrained this Soviet attitude, which Castro did not (at least not immediately) share.

In the 1960s the Soviets and the Cubans had profound disagreements about which strategies to pursue in Latin America. As a result of doctrinal differences, Soviet-Cuban relations in 1966-1967 were strained almost to the breaking point. It was not only their pessimistic assessment regarding "revolutionary potential" in the Caribbean basin nor their realistic appraisal of the U.S. response to Soviet-Cuban-supported guerrilla revolution that restrained the Soviets; there were other internal and external factors as well. Because of their preoccupation with the power struggle after Krushchev's dismissal in 1964, the course of the Vietnam War, and the deepening of the Sino-Soviet dispute, the Soviets in the late 1960s were unwilling and unable to sponsor Castro's call to create "two or three" and even "four or five more Vietnams" for the United States in Latin America. Castro, who was in favor of a "genuine revolutionary road," criticized the USSR for dealing with capitalist governments in Latin America. He even clashed over the issue with pro-Soviet leaders in some Central American parties, such as those of Guatemala and Venezuela, where young, pro-Castroist elements resisted Soviet advice to proceed gradually and with caution.

After the death of Ernesto "Che" Guevara in 1967, however, when most of the guerrillas were wiped out, the Cubans soon came to realize the need for overcoming their differences with Moscow and coordinating their policies with those of the Soviets. As Castro saw it, there were no immediate revolutionary opportunities in Latin America in the 1970s. Thus he grudgingly approved the Soviet policy of employing diplomatic, commerical, and cultural channels (in addition to revolutionary tactics where feasible) in order to expand relations with "progressive forces" in Latin America. Until very recently, the Soviets and Cubans have been less successful in dispelling traditional anti-communist hostilities from the Caribbean basin than from the South American continent. Besides those in Mexico and Jamaica, prior to the revolution in Nicaragua the USSR had only one other ambassador to the Caribbean region, stationed in Costa Rica. In some other countries of the area, however, the Soviets were able to accredit nonresident ambassadors (Panama and Honduras) and to negotiate trade representation (El Salvador).[9] They were also able to promote better economic cooperation with a friendly Mexico by helping to bring about a new cooperation treaty between Mexico and COMECON in 1975.

Soviet diplomatic initiatives in Latin America in the 1970s yielded some political payoffs, among other things helping to invalidate the political and economic blockade of Cuba. Subsequently Cuba was able to normalize relations with many Latin American countries. It exchanged consuls with Costa Rica, established diplomatic relations with Panama, and extended its influence to the Caribbean countries of Jamaica, Guyana, Barbados, and Trinidad-Tobago.

It is misleading to suggest that because of these trends the Soviets had given up the notion of supporting revolutionary movements in the region. Although their posture was realistic, it was not one of acquiescence. The USSR did not renounce the efficacy of revolution as a means for overthrowing unfriendly, anti-communist governments. In the mid 1970s, when conditions were not ripe for revolution in Latin America, the Soviets were busy supporting their allies elsewhere, particularly in Africa. This situation changed dramatically with the successful revolution in Nicaragua in 1979 and the upswing in guerrilla warfare in El Salvador in 1980.

A STRATEGIC PERSPECTIVE

The USSR and Central America

The behavior of the Soviets in the Third World is not, of course, motivated solely by historical ties and opportunism. They have developed a coherent strategic vision with an integrated, though flexible, plan of action aimed at achieving specific long-term objectives. What are these objectives and how does Central America figure in them? In Soviet strategy there are four distinct components that can be verified from their own sources: ideology, politics, security, and economics.

Ideology. With respect to ideology, the Soviet objective is to create Marxist-Leninist regimes in the Third World (although in the long run this does not always work to the benefit of the USSR, as was the case with China's conversion to communism). While it is misleading to assume that the Soviets support revolutionary political movements in the Third World chiefly because of ideological affinity, it cannot be discounted. They believe that some radical Third World nations will someday embark on a path of truly socialist development, as Cuba did in the 1970s. Meanwhile, because of Moscow's bad experience in the 1960s and 1970s--when revolutionary or radical regimes were overthrown and when more moderate regimes substantially reduced Soviet presence and influence in the countries in question--they feel impelled to exercise caution in making commitments to socialist and would-be socialist regimes in developing countries.

Indeed, with the probable exception of Cuba, in the early 1980s the Soviets hardly view the radical regimes of the Third World as truly Marxist-Leninist. Thus Soviet officials in the Central Committee responsible for dealing with Third World revolutionary regimes refer to them as being "progressive," "anti-imperialist," or "revolutionary-democratic" and at most (when referring to Angola and Ethiopia) as having a "socialist orientation" and pursuing "noncapitalist" (but not "socialist") development. Soviet experts on Latin America such as M. F. Kudachkin, who is responsible for the Latin American section of the Central Committee of the CPSU, appreciate the diversity and uneveness of economic and political development in Latin America. They recognize that the region holds a special place in the Third World because of its success in throwing off the Spanish colonial yoke in the nineteenth century and because, unlike Africa and most of Asia, capitalism has reached a high state of development in parts of Latin America--particularly in Argentina, Chile, and to a certain degree in Mexico.[10] These countries also possess a significant working class and, in Mexico and Chile (before the anti-Allende coup), large communist parties. In the Soviet view, the situation in the Caribbean basin is different, not only because of a lower level of capitalist development, but also, as stressed, because of a weak communist movement and a more pervasive U.S. hegemony. The Marxist inclination of new regimes in such countries as Nicaragua and Grenada, however, cannot but be appreciated and applauded by the Soviets. Because of it, the Soviets are better able to justify to their domestic constituencies the aid extended to these countries. By the same token, as demonstrated by Jerry Hough, a debate is evolving among Soviet experts over the prospects for revolution in Latin America.[11]

Politics. The USSR also has political objectives in the Third World. These appear to center on the fermentation and furtherance of "progressive" anti-American and anti-Chinese regimes. By exploiting growing anti-American currents, the Soviets hope to win influence at U.S. expense without directly projecting military power. Moreover, they hope to counter the activity of their other major rival,

China, in such areas of the Third World as Asia, East Africa, and the Middle East; China's influence in Latin America is minimal. Although some Marxist groups in the region have sided with Maoism, most communist parties have taken a pro-Soviet position in the Sino-Soviet conflict, identifying Maoism with Trotskyism and adventurism.

Because the Soviets view Central America as the "strategic rear" of the United States,[12] they have until recently exercised caution in forming policy toward the region. From the Cuban revolution onward, however, they have challenged the Monroe Doctrine. As early as 1960, Krushchev declared that "the Monroe Doctrine has outlived its times." U.S. acceptance of the Cuban revolution was proof that it had died "a natural death."[13] In spite of this new attitude, Soviet strategy in Central America during the past two decades has been refined and subtle. It provides for a revolutionary transformation that can use violent methods while following a "peaceful road" (that is, a prolonged political process during which anti-American "progressive forces" build national coalitions to challenge U.S. hegemony). As pointed out in the Havana Declaration adopted at the 1975 regional conference of Latin American and Caribbean communist parties:

> The utilization of all legal possibilities is an indispensable obligation of the anti-imperialist forces....Revolutionaries are not the first to resort to violence. But it is the right and duty of all revolutionary forces to be ready to answer counter-revolutionary violence with revolutionary violence.[14]

The formulation of Moscow's strategy in the 1960s was affected significantly by the Soviet-Cuban dialogue and even by Soviet-Cuban disputes. In this period, the Cubans decided to promote revolution when the Organization of American States levied sanctions against them. They favored and at first even insisted on Soviet-Cuban support of revolutionary guerrilla movements in Latin American countries, with the exception of such friendly states as Mexico. By adhering to Che's and Regis Debray's concept of guerrilla-peasantry insurgency (see Debray's *Revolution in the Revolution?*), Castro's strategy in Central America in the 1960s contradicted and even challenged the Soviet doctrine of allowing for diversified roads to socialism. Yet, as Herbert Dinerstein notes, in the late 1960s the Soviets and Cubans arrived at a kind of compromise strategy by making mutual concessions. Thus the Soviets approved support for guerrilla activities in some Latin American countries with extremely pro-American and anti-communist regimes while the Cubans gave their blessing to the pursuit of diplomacy with other, friendlier nations.[15] Overall, the Cubans basically accepted the Soviets' more gradual and realistic "anti-imperialist" strategy.

Thus in the 1970s diplomatic channels were pursued in Panama (where the late Omar Torrijos's dictatorial yet "progressive" regime was avidly courted by the Cubans and the Soviets), in Costa Rica to a certain degree, and rather more intensely in Mexico--both the latter being (in the Soviet view) liberal-democratic regimes. In the Caribbean proper, the Cubans courted the "progressive" Jamaican regime of Michael Manley. Available evidence suggests that the Soviets and Cubans have dissuaded the local communist parties and other leftist groups from trying to overthrow these regimes, encouraging them rather to expand their influence and work toward the greater goal of building "anti-imperialist" coalitions.

The Soviet strategy in Central American countries having pro-American, anti-communist regimes--that is, Nicaragua, El Salvador, Guatemala, and Honduras--has been to encourage revolutionary struggle, although not necessarily by fostering terrorism. In the late 1970s more emphasis was placed on revolutionary struggle than on peaceful coexistence. Yet even at that time the party's role was designated as one of gradual coalition-building among all revolutionary forces and of leadership of their struggle (insofar as possible). In the Soviet view, the "correlation of forces" in the 1970s was shifting worldwide because of the U.S. defeat in Vietnam. In Central America, this shift manifested itself in a growing wave of radical anti-U.S. sentiment. This and the Soviets' greater military and economic capabilities paved the way for a more mature, assertive globalism in the Third World. Moreover, the 1973 ouster of Allende in Chile seems to have increased their doubts about the feasibility of a "peaceful path" toward socialism in Latin America.[16]

<u>Security</u>. Another important component of the Soviet strategic vision regarding Central America and the Caribbean is concern over security. Moscow's security objectives in the region fit into its overall "anti-imperialist" strategy in the Third World. This

scenario includes gradually securing access to and maintaining naval and air facilities in the Caribbean basin to improve the projection of its influence while undermining that of the West--particularly of the United States. The basin--a geopolitical concept--constitutes a key transit zone for oil and vital raw materials from Guatemala, Venezuela, and the Caribbean islands to the United States as well as for all seagoing vessels approaching the Panama Canal. In an extreme case, such as wartime, a substantial Soviet military presence in the basin would endanger logistics support for the U.S. allies in Europe and the delivery of oil and other strategic materials to the United States. During such times, Cuba, though highly vulnerable, might nevertheless serve as a forward base for submarines and aircraft carriers. In general the Soviets recognize the strategic importance of Latin America as an area of special security concern for the United States (much as Eastern Europe is for them). They see it as a sort of hinterland on whose stability freedom of U.S. action in other parts of the globe depends.[17] Thus far, the Soviet military presence is limited by a lack of facilities necessary for permanent deployment. At present, the Soviets do not have sufficient strength in the region to disrupt the flow of oil to the United States. Moreover, they would probably attempt such action only in case of an all-out war.

Despite these limitations, the Soviets were able to establish a military presence in Cuba after 1961, one that has grown considerably in the past two decades. In return for financial and advanced technical assistance, they are today permitted to use modern docking facilities, potential submarine facilities in Cienfuegos, air facilities for reconnaissance aircraft, satellite stations, and sophisticated intelligence facilities for monitoring U.S. satellite and microwave conversations as well as NATO advanced weapons testing in the Atlantic. Since 1978, Soviet pilots have been flying MiG-27s on patrol missions in Cuba while Cuban pilots serve in Africa. Meanwhile, Soviet TU-95s conduct regular missions to monitor U.S. naval activities in the Atlantic. Thus Cuba is a center for close Soviet-Cuban coordination in gathering intelligence information in the basin itself.

Although proceeding with caution, the Soviets would undoubtedly like to see their military presence in the Caribbean basin expanded. Witness the increasing number of Soviet submarine visits to Cuba since 1969, an indication of Soviet plans to make permanent use of the facilities at Cienfuegos, which were partly shelved in 1970 because of vociferous U.S. protests. They are trying to establish other strategic footholds in the area. In revolutionary Grenada, for instance, Soviet equipment and financial assistance from the USSR and Libya have enabled the Cubans to start building a new international airport capable of handling all types of jet aircraft, including the Soviet Backfire bomber. As the Cubans work to build a revolutionary army, the Soviets assist in developing and promoting a fishing industry. After Sergei Gorshkov, commander-in-chief of the Soviet navy fleet, visited the island in 1980, there were unconfirmed reports about Moscow's intention to build naval facilities there are well.[18] It may be seeking similar facilities in Nicaragua.

Up to the present, in view of the Soviets' awareness of the basin's paramount importance to the United States, their naval activities in the area, including regular visits by warships, seem to have been designed to establish the legitimacy of Moscow's naval presence. There have been twenty such visits by warships to the Caribbean in the past twelve years. During the most recent visit, in April 1981, the force included a cruiser equipped to carry small nuclear weapons. Besides warships, the Soviets deploy intelligence, fishing, and merchant vessels. They have also sponsored joint marine cruises with Cuba for the purpose of conducting fishery and oceanographic research as well as for gathering and establishing future channels of information. Soviet naval deployment is designed to help encourage the long-term political and economic transformation of the area along the lines of what Gorshkov refers to as "progressive changes" offshore. In this respect, the security, political, and economic aspects of Soviet strategy in the region are mutually complementary, for naval visits to the Caribbean are facilitated by the establishment of diplomatic and economic relations. As the Soviets see it, "progressive changes" offshore make the environment more amenable to their interests in the region.

Economics. Economic calculations also play a role in Soviet strategies in Central America. Soviet trade and investment in the region, although growing, are limited chiefly to Costa Rica, where Moscow is apparently running a large deficit (like everyone else in Latin America). Since they generally have to pay for imports in hard currency, the Soviets would not be expected to view Central America as a priority interest in strictly economic terms. Soon, however, one may look for them to establish regular trade relations with the new regime in Nicaragua.

The discovery of natural resources--particularly in Guatemala, Mexico, and the Caribbean proper--have doubtless spurred increasing interest in the basin. Thus the Soviets are working with the Mexicans on long-term cooperation in oil matters and may be interested in similar cooperation with other oil producers in the region. (Mexico has also agreed to supply crude oil to Cuba, to assist with Cuba's oil exploration efforts, and to help expand Cuban oil-refining facilities.) Eastern bloc trade and economic aid to such "progressive regimes" as the one in Nicaragua encourage the Soviets' overall "anti-imperialist" strategy in the area. The Soviets may calculate that in the long run Central America will offer a more lucrative opportunity for COMECON trade than do many of the much-courted African and Asian countries. A full COMECON member since 1972, Cuba can play a key role in this effort. The Soviets view Cuba as a useful instrument in restructuring the economic base of the Caribbean basin by reducing the preponderance of U.S.-based multinational corporations. Thus they applauded Cuba's important role in founding the Caribbean Free Trade Association (CARIFTA) and the Latin American Economic System (SELA), cosponsored by Mexico and Venezuela. With Cuban help, COMECON was able in 1975 to work out a special agreement with Mexico that may soon be followed by a similar arrangement with Nicaragua.

Relations With Cuba and Soviet Caribbean Policy

Two extreme views are current regarding the Soviet-Cuban alliance in the Third World. The first portrays Cuba as a surrogate of the USSR, merely carrying out Soviet orders. The second pictures Cuba as an almost totally unconstrained, autonomous actor, having its own independent strategic vision. As I have argued elsewhere, Cuba is neither of these.[19] The view that Cuban policy is necessarily subservient to that of the USSR is unsophisticated and obscures the existence of mutual constraint and leverage in the alliance. While the USSR plays the dominant role and exercises great influence over Cuban foreign policy, Havana in turn provides certain inputs into Soviet decisionmaking regarding the Third World. The degree of Cuba's autonomy in the Third World seems to vary with the area of involvement. In Africa, it appears to exercise little autonomy; in the Caribbean basin, its autonomy seems to be significant.

Even Soviet African policy, however, has been dependent to some extent on the willingness of Castro and his colleagues to provide ground forces for joint enterprises. In Angola and Ethiopia, unlike Afghanistan, the Soviets were cautious about committing their own troops in direct military fashion. The use of Soviet combat units might have elicited a firmer response from the United States, with resulting detrimental consequences for the USSR. Furthermore, the similarity of the physical environment of Africa, particularly in Angola, to that of Cuba and the presence of a substantial number of blacks and mulattos in the Cuban forces, who share a racial and cultural affinity with the black Africans, make the Cubans much more suitable for the task than the Soviets. Soviet strategic decisions regarding the Third World thus reflect, at least marginally, Havana's desire to support revolutionary operations there and its willingness to supply the necessary manpower. Castro, who is currently president of the Nonaligned Movement, has exercised some influence on the USSR both directly (by consulting with Soviet leaders) and indirectly (by serving as a broker between Moscow and Third World leaders, many of whom admire his courage, self-confidence, and personal charm). As in Africa, Castro can serve as a useful mediator between the USSR and Central American leaders because he is viewed by many radicals and revolutionaries in the region as a new type of leader, one signally worthy of being emulated and followed--if not as a second Bolivar, then as a modern continental liberator.[20]

Although Castro's foreign policy cannot be viewed as totally subservient to that of the USSR, it would be far-fetched to think of Cuba as an independent or even a semi-independent actor. The basic subordination of Cuban foreign policy to that of the Soviet Union seemed to be acknowledged at the First Cuban Party Congress of December 1975.[21] Cuba's emergence as a major player in the Third World in the 1970s and early 1980s has been possible mainly because of Moscow's growing military and economic power and its willingness to exploit changes in the international system. More specifically, Cuban ascendancy in the Third World--particularly in Africa and the Middle East-- in the 1970s and more recently in the Caribbean basin has been possible because of the Kremlin's military-strategic cover and Cuba's expectation that its support and protection will be forthcoming in the event of an attack on the island. Moreover, the Soviets subsidize the Cuban economy with an estimated $7 million a day. Without this help, Cuba's faltering economy could never have absorbed the cost of the military intervention in Africa. Certainly in Africa the major portion of these expenses has been picked up by the Soviets or by the recipient countries, who in turn have received the money from the USSR.

Another important factor suggesting Moscow's preponderance in the Soviet-Cuban alliance is its growing military and economic presence in Cuba during the 1970s. At present there are some 2,700 Soviet soldiers in Cuba as well as several thousand intelligence personnel, technicians, and other specialists. In addition to protecting sophisticated communications facilities, the Soviets train the Cuban armed forces.

Cuba's dependence on the USSR in carrying out military operations in Africa was first demonstrated during the Angolan crisis of 1975-1976. The view that the Soviet role was confined chiefly to the supply of weaponry is mistaken. It is true that because of initial uncertainties regarding the U.S. response, the Soviets were cautious about committing themselves in a direct military fashion in Angola. Nevertheless, in early November 1975 they took over the Cuban air- and sealift, transforming the Angolan campaign into a massive operation during which both the Soviet air force and navy were operationally active. A small yet effective naval task force provided physical and psychological support to the Cuban combat troops, protected the Cuban staging areas against local threats, served as a strategic cover for established sea and air communications, and worked as a deterrent against possible U.S. naval deployment.

The alliance between the Soviets and the Cubans was even tighter in the case of the intervention in Ethiopia in 1977. While the Cubans initially functioned independently in Angola, four Soviet generals in Ethiopia ran the entire operation from start to finish. Cuba functioned as a very subordinate actor, if not a proxy, during the conflict between Somalia and Ethiopia in the Ogaden.

Also, Cuba is highly vulnerable to politicoeconomic coercion, which the Soviet leaders used to their advantage in the late 1960s when they slowed down the supply of oil and arms in order to encourage Castro to appreciate the subtleties of their "anti-imperialist" strategy. They are likely to use this leverage again should the need arise.

Cuba and the Kremlin basically agree regarding the coordination and implementation of strategy in the promotion of Soviet global interests and policies. Cuban strategic priorities, of course, are not necessarily identical to those of Moscow. As a result, subtle and not so subtle differences tend to distinguish Soviet from Cuban policies. This is more the case in the Caribbean basin than in Africa. Although the basin is of marginal geopolitical concern to the USSR, it is of paramount importance to Cuba. The USSR is a superpower with global interests, responsibilities, and capabilities; Cuba, notwithstanding its abundant rhetoric, is basically a regional power, culturally and historically a part of the Latin American community.

In spite of past disagreements and existing differences, the Soviets and Cubans in the 1970s discovered that their strategies in the Third World, a subject of disagreement in the 1960s, were inexorably linked. Moscow has made enormous ideological, political, security, and economic investments in Cuba. To turn its back on Castro's regime now would seriously undermine Soviet strategies in Africa and in Central America. Likewise, Soviet strategic, economic, and political support is essential to Cuba. Cuba is too dependent on the USSR to try to alter the relationship and it is still too committed to revolutionary change to do so.

SOVIET TACTICS

The Nicaraguan Revolution

For the jubilant Soviets and Cubans, the triumph of the Sandinistas in Nicaragua in 1979 signaled an important juncture in the revolutionary transformation of the Caribbean basin, equal in importance only to the victory of the Fidelistas twenty years earlier. In both cases, the United States was perceived as suffering a humiliating political defeat. In the view of such Soviet officials as V. Zagladin, deputy head of the international department of the Central Committee, the Nicaraguan revolution was one of the "starlets" of the "anti-imperialist" movement in Latin America. Zagladin has tried, at least implicitly, to link the "victory of Nicaragua" with Soviet-Cuban-supported "anti-imperialist" strategy and has expressed the hope that Nicaragua will "have its continuators."[22] As during the Allende period (1971-1973), revolutionary change in Latin America has become a favorite topic in Moscow.

Was the triumph in Nicaragua indeed the result of coordinated Soviet-Cuban strategies and tactics in Central America or of a complex interplay of internal and regional as well as external forces? Like Cuba in 1959, the revolution in Nicaragua was conditioned by various internal forces: the unpopularity of the Somoza regime among all classes, underdevelopment, unequal distribution of wealth, enormous poverty, and other deep social and economic cleavages. Nicaragua has long been dominated by dictators such as Anastasio "Tacho" Somoza (1936-1956) and his son Anastasio "Tachito" Somoza (1967-1979). Also, the great powers have traditionally played a role in national policymaking.[23] The fact that Nicaragua contains a promising site for an interocean canal and lies in close proximity to the existing Panama Canal has caused its foreign policy to be of some concern to the United States. Thus U.S. strategic interests were largely the motivating force behind the American interventions in 1912 and 1927, when, except for a brief interlude from 1926-1927 until 1933, Nicaragua was virtually a U.S. protectorate.

U.S. interventionism in Nicaragua gave rise to a "Yankeephobia" characterized by resentment of and even violent resistance to the United States. The human symbol of this resistance in 1927-1933 was Augusto Cesar Sandino, who, like Castro in the 1950s, was a staunch radical nationalist and opposed both the corrupt dictatorship in his country and what he saw as U.S. interference. Although the Soviet press exalted him in the early 1980s as an "anti-imperialist" hero, in the 1930s the Soviets and the Comintern had criticized Sandino and his "rebel bands." They had condemned the U.S. intervention of 1927, but they had failed to display much admiration for the orginal Sandinistas. While Sandino had cooperated with the communists in the 1920s, he then denounced their activities in 1936. After the withdrawal of U.S. troops from Nicaragua, Sandino actually made peace with the government. The Comintern meanwhile accused him of "capitulation...over to the side of the counterrevolutionary government.[24]

Communism in Nicaragua, as elsewhere in Central America, has traditionally been a weak movement. In the past two decades, three Marxist parties have existed in Nicaragua--all of them illegal and clandestine or semiclandestine: a very small Maoist group; the anti-Soviet Communist party of Nicaragua; and the pro-Soviet Socialist party of Nicaragua (PSN), a semiclandestine organization founded in 1937 and never boasting more than 250 members. Some members of the PSN had links with the Sandinistas in the 1960s and 1970s, but the PSN was not the main force behind the revolution. The Sandinista National Liberation Front (FSLN) was founded in 1961 by radical, left-leaning nationalists led by the late Carlos Fonseca Amador, who, though not a communist, had visited the USSR in 1957. The Sandinistas, inspired and supported from the very beginning by Castro, tried to overthrow the Somoza regime but were soon crushed by the National Guard. In time, the FSLN evolved into a conglomerate of Marxist and non-Marxist elements united under an anti-Somoza banner, yet still separate from the PSN. Although Amador later died while fighting Somoza, the Sandinistas continued their struggle in the 1970s with only limited support from the USSR and Cuba. (Havana actually sent material aid to the Somoza regime following the earthquake in 1972.) Despite the fact that the revolutionary struggle in Nicaragua coincided with Soviet-Cuban "anti-imperialist" strategy, geographic remoteness and general pessimism about the prospects for revolution in Latin America following the anti-Allende coup of 1973 caused the Kremlin to be rather pessimistic about the prospects of the Sandinista struggle. Another probable reason for Moscow's low-keyed support up to 1979 was Soviet and Cuban military involvement in Angola, Ethiopia, and elsewhere in the Third World as well as events in Afghanistan--all of which occupied the greater part of the Kremlin's attention from 1975 to 1979. Soviet support of the FSLN continued to be modest even as late as 1978, when a unified FSLN directorate brought together in one coalition all the guerrilla factions, whose struggle had begun to assume a genuinely revolutionary character. Even during this high point, the role of the PSN was limited mainly to propaganda support, clandestine radio broadcasts, and some financial aid.

Although by 1978 the Soviets probably knew of Somoza's critical situation, they may have thought that President Carter, despite his human rights rhetoric, would not let Somoza fall. Nevertheless, in the 1970s the Cubans, with Soviet blessings and perhaps even financial help, were training the FSLN in Cuba and providing them with arms (primarily rifles) and money.[25] However, the FSLN was securing weapons from elsewhere as well. Evidence at this time is insufficient to suggest that the Soviets and Cubans coordinated arms transfers for the Sandinistas as they were to do for the guerrillas in El Salvador in 1980; still, we do know that some weapons flowed from Cuba to the FSLN by way of Costa Rica and Panama. We also know that the FSLN used weapons from Venezuela, Panama, the Middle East, and, as the Sandinistas maintain, from Mafia sources in the United States and Europe. Although many guerrillas were trained in Cuba, there is no evidence that Cubans were involved in command and control functions for the Sandinistas before early 1979. The Cuban factor was important but it was not crucial.

The Sandinistas also received active political, economic, and moral support from various groups in Venezuela, Panama, and Mexico and found sanctuaries and a place to train on the territory of democratic Costa Rica. The Costa Rican capital of San Jose was the site of the FSLN government in exile. Leftists from other Central American countries, such as the Victoriano Lorenzo Brigade from Panama and various groups from Costa Rica, fought alongside FSLN forces in Nicaragua.[26]

The Cubans and particularly Moscow exercised considerable caution prior to the Sandinista victory of 1979. Indeed the Soviets published few analyses of the Nicaraguan struggle and only in 1978 did they and the Cubans begin to reassess the chances for a successful revolution. In early 1979 Havana finally set up intelligence headquarters in Costa Rica to monitor the anti-Somoza struggle and sent military personnel to advise the Sandinistas. Within months of the Sandinistas' assumption of power on July 19, 1979, Castro sent specialists in significant numbers to help with the reconstruction of Nicaragua: 1,200 teachers, 250 doctors and health personnel, technicians, some security and propaganda experts, and forces of construction workers to build a road uniting Nicaragua's east and west coasts. At the same time, Castro reportedly cautioned the Sandinistas not to push their socialist program too far or too fast. The Cubans perceived the victory of the Sandinistas as an opportunity for them to pursue their own strategic objectives in Nicaragua as well as elsewhere in the region. Unlike the 1960s, the risks of Cuban involvement seemed to be low both because of apparent U.S. inability to intervene and because the United States basically opposed Somoza and recognized the Sandinistas.

In contrast to the Cubans, the Soviets were typically guarded in their willingness to make commitments to the new Sandinista regime, just as they had been in 1959 with Cuba. The only Soviet initiative at this time was the provision of emergency donations in the weeks following the overthrow of Somoza. These were much smaller, however, than U.S., Mexican, and Venezuelan donations. Only after a gradual reassessment of their options did the Soviets decide to become more assertive in Nicaragua. This "new chapter," as they called it, opened in March 1980 during the first high-level visit of Sandinistas to the USSR since the overthrow of Somoza.[27] Subsequently the Soviets concluded various economic, technical, and trade agreements, mainly in the areas of fishing and marine affairs, water power resources, mining and geological surveys, communications, and air traffic. The FSLN and the CPSU also agreed on future party-to-party contracts, apparently along the same lines pursued by the Soviets with other revolutionary organizations whom they consider to be reliable, long-term partners such as the regimes in Angola and Ethiopia. By the spring of 1981 the Soviets, Cubans, and East Europeans (particularly the East Germans and Bulgarians) had concluded several other related agreements with Nicaragua for economic aid (including the donation of 20,000 tons of wheat), scientific and cultural cooperation, and technical assistance in telecommunications, agriculture, and transportation. There were also signs of future military cooperation, as evidenced by the Soviet loan of a few helicopters to the FSLN and by East Germany's credit sale to the FSLN of 800 military trucks. As the crisis in neighboring El Salvador began to mount in late 1980, there were also unconfirmed reports of the influx of additional Cuban military officials into Nicaragua (officials who were supposedly running training camps) and of the transfer of tanks and helicopters, possibly for use in El Salvador. Western reports that Moscow was building naval facilities in Nicaragua were denied by the Soviet ambassador to Nicaragua, G. Schlyapnikov. The Nicaraguan government, however, has confirmed that a Soviet floating workshop, designed for repairing ships, will be operating off the Pacific coast of Nicaragua.[28]

El Salvador

How do Soviet perceptions of the crisis in Nicaragua (before the overthrow of Somoza) compare with their perceptions of the ongoing crisis in El Salvador? The victory of the Sandinistas in Nicaragua prompted them to anticipate a chain reaction of leftist upheavals and revolutions throughout Central America. Thus, in an important speech on October 20, 1980, B. Ponomarev, candidate Politburo member and secretary of the Central Committee of the CPSU, added the countries of Central America to the list of states in Africa and Asia that could be expected to undergo revolutionary changes of "a socialist orientation." Ponomarev described the revolution in Nicaragua as a "major success" and compared it with the revolutions in Angola and Ethiopia.[29] Professor Viktor Volskii, president of the Soviet Association of Friendship with Latin American Countries, assessed the Nicaraguan revolution as a "triumph for the people of Latin America and the Caribbean" and a "model for all peoples fighting for liberation."[30]

After Nicaragua, the Central American country singled out by Soviet writers as being most pregnant with revolutionary opportunities was, of course, El Salvador, which Moscow sees as occupying "an important strategic position in the region."[31] Like Nicaragua, El Salvador has a strong heritage of instability caused by a rigid class structure, unequal distribution of wealth, and 30 per cent unemployment. In El Salvador--the smallest yet most densely populated country in Latin America (400 people per square mile)--the socioeconomic life has been dominated by an oligarchy of wealthy familiies while military strongmen have controlled the country's politics.

In El Salvador, as in Nicaragua, the communist movement has been very weak. The pro-Soviet Communist party in El Salvador (PCES), founded in 1930, was actively involved in a massive peasant insurrection in 1932 which was crushed by the military and resulted in 30,000 deaths. Since that time, the PCES has been an illegal, clandestine organization. As late as 1979, it had only 225 members. In the 1960s and 1970s, however, the PCES, like the PSN, had to compete with more radical and relatively larger groups such as the Maoist-leaning People's Revolutionary Army (ERP) and the Trotskyite Popular Liberation Force (FPL). The latter organizations, and not the miniscule PCES, were responsible for the organized terrorism and guerrilla activities of the 1970s. In fact, well-known General

Secretary of the PCES Schafik Jorge Handal published a severe critique of these groups in the Soviet journal Latinskaia amerika in early 1979, before the fall of Somoza. He accused them of violence and nihilism.[32]

Unlike those in Nicaragua, the various guerrilla factions in El Salvador have not yet united, in spite of rhetoric to the contrary. In El Salvador there is no Sandinista legacy. In contrast to the meager support given the Nicaraguan party, Soviet public support of the PCES has been strong, particularly of its leader Handal, who seems to be following Moscow's tactical advice. With the Sandinista victory in Nicaragua and the increase in political violence in El Salvador, the PCES and the Kremlin have become more optimistic about the revolutionary potential of the region, especially in El Salvador. These changing perceptions are certainly shared by the Cubans. Although in their public reports the Cubans continue to be somewhat more cautious than the Soviets, they nevertheless have begun to increase their direct support to the various competing guerrilla factions. In addition, they have played an important role in minimizing factional differences and in trying to unite the various groups.[33]

The Soviets, for their part, have proceeded with deliberation. Although they promised initially, during a meeting organized by Castro in Havana in December 1979, to supply weapons to the guerrillas, only in the spring and summer of 1980 did they switch completely to the new support tactics, agreeing to provide military training for a few dozen Salvadoran youths. This change in tactics was reflected by the pro-Soviet PCES endorsement of violent revolution at its Seventh National Congress in May 1980. As noted above, up to that time the PCES opposed armed struggle and terrorism as revolutionary means in El Salvador. In the fall of 1979, though jubilant over the victory in Nicaragua, Handal was cautious about commenting on prospects for revolution in El Salvador. In April 1980, however, he became much more optimistic and, according to Soviet sources, expressed "confidence" in the "defeat of internal reaction, despite the fact that the latter is backed by imperialist forces."[34]

The example of Nicaragua, however important, was not the only motive for the changing perceptions and tactics of the PCES and Moscow in the spring of 1980. Both the Soviets and the Cubans probably feared that if the PCES did not use violence to implement its "anti-imperialist" strategy, it would soon be overtaken by its more radical rivals who were quickly gaining popular strength. The PCES, they reasoned, should not be suddenly surprised by successes of the noncommunist guerrillas and deprived thereby of credit for the victory, as happened in Nicaragua to the PSN which was outshone by the Sandinistas. Thus Soviet tactics since the spring of 1980 have been directed at transforming the numerically small PCES into a leading force in the guerrilla struggle in El Salvador.

Moscow's assessment of U.S. ability to maintain hegemony in the region also seems to have changed. Despite the example of the Cuban revolution, the Soviets continued to believe throughout the 1960s and 1970s that the United States had the ability and will to challenge outright revolution in Central America. In Nicaragua, however, the U.S. administration made one mistake after another. It failed to break completely with Somoza and it tried too late to modify the outcome of a Sandinista victory. A Soviet analyst, quoting an anonymous official in Washington, wrote in July 1980 that the Carter administration was "too late and too indecisive" with its intervention in the Nicaraguan crisis, that it therefore could not prevent the complete victory of the Sandinistas, and that "a different course of action" must be taken by the United States in El Salvador.[35] According to the analyst, the situation in El Salvador, which was arousing the "anxiety" of American strategists, was even more "tense" than in Nicaragua before the fall of Somoza.

The main reason for fomenting turmoil in El Salvador is probably to pin down the United States in its "strategic rear." Developments in El Salvador may also be linked to perceived changes in Soviet-American relations in the wake of the Iranian and Afghan crises in late 1979. In the Soviet view, as I have argued elsewhere, the U.S. administration was veering toward a dangerous new cold war by encouraging a semialliance with China, threatening Iran, and sabotaging SALT II negotiations.[36] Most grievous was U.S., Chinese, and Egyptian "allied" support of the Afghan rebels with Soviet-made weapons. (Whether or not this was true in 1979 is still a matter of speculation; the Kremlin professes to have believed that it was and sometimes the perceptions of policymakers are more important than the facts.) The Soviet invasion of Afghanistan, a matter of necessity as Moscow saw it, was met with retaliatory policies by the zigzagging Carter administration aimed at further punishing the USSR. After Nicaragua, the Soviets may have thought that El

Salvador provided an easily exploitable opportunity in the same geographic proximity to the United States as Afghanistan is to the USSR. The idea of making El Salvador an "American Afghanistan" in retaliation for perceived U.S.-Chinese-Egyptian support for the Afghan rebels and using the issue as a bargaining chip in future negotiations may have played a part in their decision to back the Cuban orchestration of support for the guerrilla struggle.

One can only speculate, of course, on the motives for Moscow's decision. Nevertheless, the facts of the story are well known. Unlike the case in Nicaragua, the Cuban orchestration of the supply of armaments from Kremlin-allied countries has been significant. It appears that the Soviet-backed involvement of Cuba has significantly strengthened the guerrillas in El Salvador. Handal's search for arms in the East, which seems to be well documented by the U.S. administration, began around the time of the Seventh Congress of the PCES, during which a passive line was exchanged for one of organized violence intended to topple the government. After the congress, the Cubans took charge of clandestine operations in El Salvador and Castro actively assumed the role of broker in attempting to unify the various revolutionary groups. In June and July, with the assistance of officials responsible for Third World affairs in the Soviet Secretariat (such as K. Brutens and his deputy Kudachkin), Handal visited the USSR and certain East European countries and obtained American-made weapons (M-14 and M-16 rifles, M-79 grenades) from Vietnam and Ethiopia, countries with large stocks. Thus the USSR could, by proceeding with caution, deny its involvement if accused. East European allies (minus Poland and Rumania) promised to provide communications equipment, uniforms, and medical supplies while Moscow helped to arrange for the transport of the weapons to Cuba in the fall of 1980. From Cuba, the weapons were conveyed to Nicaragua and from there directly by ship or air, or by land through Honduras, to El Salvador. Following the U.S. presidential elections, Cuban experts, with cautious yet active Soviet backing, played a key role in the arms transfer and the preparation of the "final" guerrilla offensive. A U.S. State Department report concludes: "The political direction, organization, and arming of the insurgency is coordinated and heavily influenced by Cuba--with active support of the Soviet Union, East Germany, Vietnam, and other Communist states."[37]

CONCLUSIONS

The joint strategy for dealing with Third World countries worked out by the USSR and Cuba in the late 1960s and 1970s is not necessarily designed to create Marxist-Leninist regimes in these countries but rather to achieve a variety of "anti-imperialist" ideological, political, security, and economic objectives. Soviet and Cuban strategic visions have not always been identical, particularly in the 1960s when there were serious disagreements regarding doctrine and tactics. As recent Soviet-Cuban policies in Africa and Central America attest, however, most of these differences have now been overcome. Although Cuba is not subservient to the USSR, for a variety of reasons its foreign policies are basically dependent upon Moscow's support (Africa) or linked to its foreign policy (Central America). The Soviets and Cubans seem to have linked strategic visions regarding Central America. Although the Soviets are newcomers there, with Cuban help they have been able to exploit the socioeconomic malaise and anti-U.S. sentiment characteristic of the region. In doing so, they have employed a variety of tactics: peaceful and legal, violent, or often combinations of both.

Undoubtedly, deep socioeconomic cleavages are the main cause of the ongoing crisis in Central America, particularly in the countries located in the northern tier: Nicaragua, El Salvador, Guatemala, and to a certain degree Honduras. The more southern countries of Costa Rica and Panama do not have such pronounced social problems, but they face severe economic difficulties (particularly Costa Rica) and are by no means immune to revolutionary change. The civil war in El Salvador could escalate into a regional war, perhaps even leading to the involvement of Mexico and Venezuela, with Guatemala and Honduras assisting the regime and Nicaragua and Cuba assisting the guerrillas.

Internal forces were the main impetus for local insurgency and revolution in Nicaragua in 1979; the Soviets and Cubans were deeply involved in Africa prior to 1978-1979, when the insurgency peaked, and their involvement in Nicaragua was marginal. Afterward, however, the Nicaraguan revolution became an inspiration to other revolutionaries in the region and a catalyst in changing the perceptions and tactics of the USSR, which seems to have believed that the Nicaraguan "example" could be repeated soon in "strategically located" El Salvador. The dramatic change in Moscow's tactics in the spring of 1980, after the Nicaraguan revolution, is proof of its flexibility in the implementation of its "anti-imperialist" strategy.

Although the socioeconomic problems in Nicaragua and El Salvador are similar, there are profound differences between the political situations in the two countries. Nicaragua's revolution was more genuine in that it expressed the will of a majority of the people in overthrowing the hated dictatorship of Somoza while El Salvador's revolution is less so, having significant Cuban support with cautious backing from the Soviets. Both Cuba and the USSR supported, if not encouraged beforehand, a dramatic change in the tactics of El Salvador's Communist party in May 1980 and facilitated an impressive arms transfer in the fall of the same year. In late 1980 the guerrillas in El Salvador announced the creation of a united liberation front--the Farabundo Marti People's Liberation Front--whose general command includes Handal. Although the so-called final offensive in early 1981 failed, El Salvador may still develop into a "second Nicaragua." Up to now, however, the guerrilla offensive has failed to spark a popular insurrection of the Nicaraguan kind; the majority of the people do not appear to support the leftist guerrillas. One can "spur" revolutionary struggles,[38] but one cannot sustain them without genuine popular support.

The vigorous Soviet and Cuban support of Salvadoran leftists and the new closer relationship with Nicaragua since last year are the result of more than a preconceived strategy. They also illustrate the Kremlin's tactical skill in exploiting opportunities. In the case of Nicaragua, such an opportunity was furnished by the hesitancy of the U.S. Congress in providing aid to that country and U.S. failure to assume a more active role.

The Soviets' position in El Salvador may go beyond the desire to exploit revolutionary opportunities. It may be that by taking a tough stand concerning that country, Moscow is trying to pin Washington down and eventually place itself in a position to bargain on other issues, such as Afghanistan and Poland. The internal situations in both of these border countries are causing the Soviet Union serious problems, which it has attributed to outside provocation and assistance. It may be, as suggested by some Central American observers, that the Kremlin's tactics in El Salvador are being used to divert Western attention from its domestic failures and the problems faced in Poland and Afghanistan in order to prepare a hardening of its policies in these countries, perhaps including some kind of intervention in Poland. In exchange for U.S. acquiescence to such hard-line policies, Moscow would change its tactics in El Salvador. The Soviet leadership appears to link the crises in Poland and Central America. Indeed, while delivering an important speech on the Polish crisis on April 7, 1981, Brezhnev unexpectedly concluded his remarks by stressing the Soviets' role as the protector of Cuba's security.[39]

As of the fall of 1981, any firm conclusions about the outcome of the struggle in El Salvador are, of course, premature. Indeed, a number of internal and external constraints could mitigate assertive Cuban and Soviet implementation of "anti-imperialist" strategy in the Caribbean basin. The Cuban economic situation has reached its lowest level since the revolution, despite massive Soviet economic support. Cuban economic difficulties, however, failed to elicit any major antiwar movement, or, for that matter, any visible opposition to or even political debate about its involvements in Africa. Despite the difficulties arising from its alliance with the USSR, Cuba in 1980-1981 has succeeded in maintaining its overseas commitments and even in expanding them, as seen in Nicaragua and El Salvador.

Furthermore, local conditions in the Caribbean basin may not always favor revolutionary upheaval and its exploitation by the Soviets. A crucial setback for them was the October 1980 defeat of the left-leaning regime of Manley in Jamaica by the more pro-Western Edward Seaga. In recent years, Soviet economic backing had allowed the Cubans to expand their influence in Jamaica. Like Nicaragua and Grenada, Jamaica was offered financial credits by Havana (perhaps with Moscow's help) and the assistance of several hundred Cuban civilian teachers, technicians, and construction workers as well as some security officials to train the Jamaican security forces. Additional setbacks in the region include the electoral defeats of other parties with close Cuban ties on the small Caribbean islands of St. Vincent, Dominica, and Antigua.

Also, given the Kremlin's preoccupation with the Polish crisis, the continuing resistance of Muslim rebels in Afghanistan, and the ongoing war between Iran and Iraq, its concerns in the next year may be directed toward Eastern Europe and the strategic "arc of instability" to the south of its borders in Asia (that is, Afghanistan and Iran). Continuous preoccupation with Poland and Afghanistan could impose hard choices on the Soviet leadership with regard to its strategy in the Third World, including Cuba. What effect will all this have on Soviet-Cuban commitments in other parts of the Third World, particularly in Angola and Ethiopia, but also in Central America? How long can Soviet-backed Cuban deployment in Angola and Ethiopia be maintained and how effectively? These questions, for which there are no pat answers, are probably being posed now by foreign policy experts in the USSR who may feel that Caribbean and Central American anti-U.S. nationalism simply cannot be exploited as vigorously as Havana's leaders believe, at least not in the foreseeable future.

The most important factor affecting Moscow's strategy in Central America is the future course of U.S. policy. And as the U.S.-Soviet struggle for Caribbean influence unfolds, one thing is almost certain: the Soviets themselves are not going to undertake a direct military intervention in Central America. They still do not have the capability to do so effectively, in spite of what they see as a "weakening of U.S. hegemony" in the region.

U.S. Interests and Options in the Caribbean Basin

For the United States the Caribbean is not just a refuge from the inconvenience of the American winter. Washington has vital security, political, and economic interests in the area. The U.S. military installations at Roosevelt Roads in Puerto Rico, the Panama Canal zone, and Guantanamo Bay in Cuba as well as the existence of key shipping lines from Venezuela and the Caribbean island oil refineries, the networks of U.S. listening posts monitoring ships and submarine activities, and potential supply routes to U.S. allies in Western Europe and the Middle East which would need to be activitated in case of war make the basin a strategic hinterland for the defense of America's southern flank.

Because of the presence of natural harbors which, as shown in Cuba, could be used for visits and repairs of naval vessels, the United States wants to deny possibly hostile powers like the USSR the use of the Caribbean basin. Moscow's growing naval and air presence in Cuba (as well as growing Cuban naval power) and its spreading influence in other countries such as Nicaragua, Grenada, and El Salvador would be felt in wartime. These factors could make a major difference by tying down American forces needed in other theaters. The Pentagon's freedom of action depends on stability in its Caribbean "southern flank". Also, tolerance of unfriendly regimes there could be detrimental to Washington's political credibility in other important regions such as the Persian Gulf.

Finally, the basin is important to the United States because of its potential as a supplier of oil and other raw materials which are indispensable to American industry and because of the investments made there by U.S. business. Protecting these interests requires preventing abrupt dislocation and hostile radicalization of the region's economies, which in its cumulative and ultimate implications would put U.S. interests in jeopardy.

Given such concerns and its capability for challenging the USSR, American policy in the basin is an important factor affecting Soviet strategy and tactics there. In the wake of Vietnam, Moscow's initiatives were scarcely constrained by the United States because of the unwillingness of the American public and Congress to support a forceful response. This point was well illustrated during the Soviet-Cuban interventions in Angola and Ethiopia. Furthermore, President Jimmy Carter's empty rhetoric in 1979 about the "unacceptable" Soviet combat brigade, which suddenly became "acceptable," hardly served as a meaningful deterrent to the Kremlin's activities in the Caribbean.

It seems, however, that Soviet perceptions about U.S. willingness to defend its vital Caribbean interests are now changing, as demonstrated by Moscow's uncertainty regarding the policy of President Reagan, who already in 1980 suggested a naval blockade of Cuba in response to the invasion of Afghanistan. In 1981 Reagan and his advisors repeatedly warned that they would take all necessary measures to stop the arms transfer to El Salvador, not excluding military action against Nicaragua or even Cuba.

Considering its interests in the basin, the United States should move decisively to curb further Soviet activities there, particularly the expansion of its naval presence and its military support for future clients. Nicaragua may be the best place to begin. The Reagan administration wisely did not rule out the use of a blockade or other military action against Nicaragua or even "going to the source" (e.g., Cuba), as Secretary of State Alexander Haig put it, to prevent further Cuban involvement in El Salvador. Although the use of force should be considered the last option and most certainly is, the threat was taken seriously by Havana, which subsequently decided to organize a territorial militia defense system, call up its military reserves, and declare a state of emergency. If the drift toward establishing a Soviet-Cuban military presence in Nicaragua and/or significant Soviet-Cuban military aid to El Salvador continues, Washington may be forced to take drastic measures which could be very costly and would hinder American capabilities in other areas (Europe, the Middle East and the Pacific) as well as entail great international risks. Technical problems must also be considered. For example, although perhaps less dangerous than outright military intervention, it is much harder to impose an effective naval blockade on a continental nation like Nicaragua than on an island such as Cuba. Furthermore, a blockade at the present time would be much more difficult than in 1962 because of a smaller U.S. Navy.

Needless to say, there are other less hazardous military measures Washington might opt to take wherein its navy would play a significant role. It could expand its naval presence in the basin, acting on but surpassing Carter's 1979 plan to establish a Caribbean Contingency Joint Task Force (CCJTF) in Key West and Reagan's December 1, 1981 decision to upgrade the CCJTF as a new military command for the Caribbean. These steps could include building more facilities to monitor ship and air movement at Key West and perhaps elsewhere in the basin, the assignment of permanent forces to the CCJTF, and scheduling regular patrols of an air carrier task force in the region. The United States should heed Admirals Mahan and Gorshkov's writings on how to use sea power during peacetime to further political objectives. After all, it has routinely carried out successful operations in the Mediterranean and Pacific for quite some time. The United States could also initiate with her Latin American allies a multilateral deployment. In any case, given the advanced Soviet arms transfers to Cuba and lately to Nicaragua, the U.S. has little choice but to sell advanced weapons to friendly nations in the Caribbean basin.

What is needed most, however, is a comprehensive American strategy with coherent objectives encompassing a variety of different instruments, not only military but also political, psychological (Nicaragua as well as Cuba is vulnerable to criticism via broadcasts regarding treatment of its dissidents), cultural (wide-range scholarly exchange programs), and above all economic. It is of enormous importance that while resisting Soviet activities, Washington not lose track of the complex nature of the conflict. The present crisis in the Caribbean cannot be attributed solely to Cuban and Soviet interference. What is occurring in El Salvador and to varying degrees in other countries in the Caribbean basin is, as noted previously, the rapid decay of outmoded political, economic, and social orders. Socio-economic polarization and the specific political culture have contributed significantly to the rise of internal and interregional conflict in the area.

As the Jamaican elections of 1980 suggest, a patient wait-and-see approach, together with support for democratic forces, can bring fruitful results. The same technique may not, of course, work elsewhere. Nicaragua seems to bear this out. Nevertheless it is important that each country in the basin be treated as a special case and that the wide-ranging cultural, social and political diversity in the area be appreciated. If necessary, military aid should be upgraded to countries such as El Salvador, but it should be coupled with comprehensive economic, financial and technical assistance. The roots of the region's problems are socio-economic and, as this author argued in early 1981, call for a kind of "new Marshall Plan" in support of the beleaguered and often weak local democratic forces. This effort should be coordinated with Mexico, Venezuela, Colombia and Costa Rica. The United States should take the initiative in protecting its interests by a variety of means that include but also go beyond the emergency first-aid measures needed to arrest Soviet "anti-imperialist" strategy in Central America.

NOTES

1. See my earlier work on the Soviet-Cuban alliance in the Third World: "The Soviet-Cuban Intervention in Angola, 1975," Studies in Comparative Communism (Spring-Summer 1978), pp. 3-33; "Soviet Decision-Making on the Intervention in Angola" in David Albright (Ed.), Communism in Africa (Bloomington, Ind.: Indiana University Press, 1980); "The Communist States and the Conflict in the Horn of

Africa" in J. Valenta and D. Albright (Eds.), Communist Countries and Africa (Bloomington, Ind.: Indiana University Press, forthcoming); "Comment: The Soviet-Cuban Alliance in Africa and Future Prospects in the Third World," Cuban Studies/Estudios Cubanos (July 1980), pp. 36-43; and "The Soviet-Cuban Intervention in Angola," U.S. Naval Proceedings (April 1980), pp. 51-57. For an expanded version of the last article, see Steven Rosefield (Ed.), World Communism at the Crossroads: Military Ascendancy, Political Economy and Human Welfare (Boston: Martinus Nijhoff, 1980).

2. Time (March 16, 1981), pp. 24-25.

3. Ibid., p. 10.

4. For a more detailed discussion, see R. Feinberg's forthcoming volume, Central America: The International Dimensions of the Crisis (New York: Holmes & Meier, 1982).

5. M. N. Roy, Memoirs (London: Allen & Unwin, 1964), p. 154.

6. For studies dealing with early Soviet relations with Latin American communist parties, see Rollie E. Poppino, International Communism in Latin America: A History of the Movement, 1917-1963 (Glencoe, Ill.: The Free Press, 1964); Robert J. Alexander, Communism in Latin America (New Brunswick, N.J.: Rutgers University Press, 1957); Karl M. Schmidt, Communism in Mexico: A Study in Political Frustration (Austin, Tex.: University of Texas Press, 1965); Ronald M. Schneider, Communism in Guatemala, 1944-1954 (New York: Praeger, 1959); and Robert J. Alexander, "The Communist Parties of Latin America," Problems of Communism (July-August 1970), pp. 37-46.

7. Cole Blasier, The Hovering Giant: U.S. Responses to Revolutionary Change in Latin America (Pittsburgh, Pa.: Pittsburgh University Press, 1976).

8. K. S. Karol, Guerrillas in Power: The Course of the Cuban Revolution (New York: Hill & Wang, 1970), p. 272.

9. Blasier, Soviet Relations with Latin America in the 1970s (Washington: The National Council for Soviet and East European Research, 1980).

10. M. F. Kudachkin, Velikii Oktiabr' i kommunisticheskie partii Latinskoi Ameriki [The Great October and Communist Parties of Latin America] (Moscow: Progress Publishers, 1978). The "anti-imperialist" strategy has also been argued for in many articles published in Latinskaia Amerika in the 1960s and the 1970s. There were, of course, some significant disagreements in formulating this strategy. These are well analyzed in a forthcoming book by Jerry F. Hough, to whom I am indebted for his comments.

11. For a very perceptive analysis, see Jerry F. Hough, "The Evolving Soviet Debate in Latin America," Latin American Research Review (vol. 10, no. 1), pp. 124-143.

12. S. Mishin, "Latin America: Two Trends of Development," International Affairs (Moscow)(July 1976), p. 450; Leon Goure and Morris Rothenberg, Soviet Penetration of Latin America (Miami, Fla.: Miami Center for Advanced International Studies, 1973).

13. Tass (Moscow)(July 12, 1960).

14. Declaration of the Conference of Communist Parties of Latin America and the Caribbean (Havana 1975), p. 42.

15. For an excellent analysis, see Herbert S. Dinerstein, Soviet Policy in Latin America (Santa Monica, Calif.: Rand, May 1966), pp. 28-30.

16. Kudachkin, "The Experience of the Struggle of the Communist Party of Chile for Unity Among Leftist Forces and for Revolutionary Transformation," Voprosy istorii KPSS, no. 5 (May 1976), pp. 72-76.

17. L. I. Kamynin, International Affairs, no. 3 (1967), pp. 27-33.

18. Radio Paris (January 21, 1981) in Foreign Broadcast Information Service (FBIS), Daily Report (Latin America), (January 21, 1981).

19. See my "Comment: The Soviet-Cuban Alliance in Africa," op. cit.

20. Edward Gonzales, Cuba Under Castro: The Limits of Charisma (Boston: Houghton Mifflin, 1974), p. 220.

21. Jorge I. Dominguez, Cuba: Order and Revolution (Cambridge, Mass.: Harvard University Press, Belknap, 1978), p. 149.

22. Vadim Zagladin, "On the Threshold of the Eighties," New Times (January 1, 1980), pp. 5-7.

23. Charles W. Anderson, "Nicaragua: The Somoza Dynasty" in Martin C. Needler (Ed.), Political Systems of Latin America (New York: Litton Educational Publishing, 1978), pp. 108-131.

24. Compare "USSR-Nicaragua: Building Cooperation," New Times (March 1980), pp. 13-14 with "Struggles of the Communist Parties of South and Caribbean America," The Communist International, vol. 12, no. 10 (May 20, 1935), pp. 564-576. See also Alexander, op. cit., pp. 347-378.

25. See statement of W. H. Duncan, a vice-president with the American Chamber of Commerce of Latin America in Nicaragua, in U.S. House, Committee on Foreign Affairs, Central America at the Crossroads, Hearing Before the Subcommittee on American Affairs (September 11-12, 1979), p. 47.

26. James N. Goodsell, "Nicaragua" in R. F. Starr (Ed.), Yearbook on International Communist Affairs, 1979 (Stanford, Calif.: Hoover Institution Press, 1980), pp. 369-371.

27. See "USSR-Nicaragua: Building Cooperation," op. cit.

28. Baltimore Sun (February 26, 1981); La Prensa (Managua)(July 30, 1980); The News Gazette (San Salvador) (February 1-7, 1981); Prela (Havana)(April 26, 1981) in FBIS, Daily Report (Latin America) (April 29, 1981); Managua Radio (March 27, 1981) in FBIS, Daily Report (Latin America) (March 30, 1981).

29. Ponomarev's report can be found in Kommunist, no. 6, (November 1980), pp. 30-44.

30. Moscow Radio (July 17, 1980).

31. V. Korionov, "El Salvador: The Struggle Sharpens," Pravda (December 30, 1980); and Ruslan Tuchnin, "Reign of Terror," New Times (April 1980), pp. 9-11.

32. Thomas P. Anderson, "El Salvador" in Starr (1979), op. cit., pp. 347-348. See also Anderson's analysis in Starr (Ed.), Yearbook on International Communist Affairs, 1980, pp. 354-355.

33. "Communist Interference in El Salvador," Special Report, no. 80 (Washington: U.S. Department of State, Bureau of Public Affairs, February 23, 1981).

34. Interview with Handal, Tass (Moscow)(October 22, 1980); V. Dolgov, "Mounting Struggle," New Times (April 1980), p. 11. In November of the same year, the leading theoretical journal of the CPSU published a lengthy article by Handal in praise of the guerrilla struggle. See "Na puti k svobode" [On the Road to Liberty], Kommunist, no. 17 (November 1980), pp. 94-103.

35. Ye. V. Mityayeva, "The United States Interference in El Salvador," SShA: ekonomika, politika, ideologiia, no. 7 (July 1980), pp. 60-64.

36. See J. Valenta, "From Prague to Kabul," International Security (Fall 1980), pp. 114-141.

37. "Communist Interference in El Salvador," op. cit. Although several critics have rightly pointed out inconsistencies in this report, none has proved that it is a forgery or that the USSR and other communist countries did not actively support Cuban assistance to the guerrillas of El Salvador. For a critique of the report, see T. Segel, Washington Star (May 18, 1981); and James Petras, The Nation (March 28, 1981).

38. One is reminded of the eloquent words of Jose Marti, Cuba's national hero: "The Russians are the ship of reform. But these impatient and generous men, darkened as they are by anger, are not the ones who are going to lay the foundation for the new world! They are the spur, and they come in time as the voice of man's conscience. But the steel that makes a good spur will not do for the builder's hammer." (1883)

39. See Brezhnev's speech delivered at the Sixteenth Party Congress of the Czechoslovak Communist Party, Prague, in Pravda (April 8, 1981).

3 Cuba in the Caribbean and Central America: Limits to Influence

W. Raymond Duncan

INTRODUCTION

Cuban foreign policy since the Revolution of 1959 completed a full cycle by the outset of the 1980s. It began by advocating armed struggle as the path to change in the early 1960s, especially in Latin America, then shifted toward peaceful government-to-government relations in the early 1970s. By 1975-76, however, emphasis on military power reappeared, first in Africa with the Angolan affair and eventually in Nicaragua and El Salvador as the decade closed.[1] The military thrust in turn produced major local, regional, and international repercussions, just as it had in previous years, owing largely to friction between Washington and Havana on the one hand and, on the other, between Washington and Moscow.[2]

One might conclude from Cuba's military activities, with its approximately 50,000 military and economic advisers supporting revolutionary movements in the Third World from Angola to El Salvador by 1980, that it had been transformed into an irresistible armed power in the western hemisphere, destined to shape the future of that region.[3] Yet ironically, this Cuban shift toward support of armed struggle in the Caribbean and Central America which has so strained the international system has come at a time when Havana's fortunes in the region appear to be on the decline. This conclusion suggests a reorienting of American foreign policy to address less a perceived Cuban-Soviet security threat and more the conditions that invite outside intervention in the first place.

Cuban Intervention and International Strains

The strain on the international system created by public attention to Cuba's military roles in the Caribbean and Central America is indeed serious. It is not so much that Cuba's stepped-up support for clandestine arms shipments to left-wing guerrillas, first in Nicaragua and later in El Salvador, violates international law, for such transgressions are frequent in world politics. Nor is it that Havana's work in arming and training a Grenadian army of 2,000 out of a population of 120,000 or its sending in military and security advisers to Nicaragua after the Sandinista victory in 1979 does not violate international law since the Cubans were invited to do so by recognized governments.[4] Actually the nature of the problem lies more in the realm of power politics than international law.

Havana's military escalation of the late 1970s and early 1980s comes at a time of major global and regional tension. Renewed United States ideological confrontation with the Soviet Union, coupled with a massive increase in military spending, have transformed the early 1980s into perhaps the most volatile period in superpower relations since the onset of the Cold War in 1947-1949 -- completing still another cycle in world affairs.[5] Thus, given its close economic, military, and political ties to the U.S.S.R., Cuba's intervention in Central America and its other activities in the Caribbean escalate adversarial hostility not only between Washington and Havana, but also between Washington and Moscow. Moreover, the Caribbean and Central American states, which are in great need of economic development, lack consensus on how to change internally to achieve it and their neighbors cannot agree precisely on how to help them modernize. Cuban military intervention makes consensus-building all the more difficult within the affected countries and hinders the formation of a cohesive U.S. longrun strategy of development for the area. These trends worsen the internal conditions of the very countries Cuba seeks to help.

The scope of Cuba's renewed armed intervention in the 1980s, then, is magnified by the current nature of the international setting. Washington's reactions to Havana widens the scale of military competition with Moscow, which in turn affects major world order issues. It raises, for example, not only the spectre of nuclear confrontation, but also stimulates major non-nuclear spin-offs as United States and Soviet military spending grows. Not least of these negative effects are potential drains on scarce natural resources, rising world energy and raw materials costs, and potentially another round of global inflation generated by increased demand for oil.[6] These negative interdependent tremors heighten the sensitivities and vulnerabilities of all states within the world system, including the Soviet Union and Cuba.

Regional reaction to Cuba's increasingly military-oriented approach to Caribbean and Central American politics, meanwhile, heightens interregional conflict as well as affecting the methods of developmental problem solving in the area. Certainly it does not improve state-to-state relations between Nicaragua on the one hand and El Salvador, Guatemala, and Honduras on the other. And does it not encourage diversion of scarce resources to military spending within the region, especially Central America, when those resources are so desperately needed for non-military developmental projects? At the same time, Havana's actions condition the diplomacy of oil-rich Mexico and Venezuela, whose external postures increasingly shape the nature and style of developmental alternatives in the area -- including those within Havana itself.

Decline in Cuba's Fortunes

The second major trend -- a decline in Cuba's fortunes in the Caribbean and Central America as the 1980s began -- is not so discernible at first. It is obscured because the military shift is the latest example of Cuba's greatly expanded presence in the region, a process dating back to the early 1970s. Here it should be noted that compared to its virtual isolation in the 1960s, Havana's diplomatic contacts reached out to eleven countries by 1980, including its highly publicized ties with Grenada, Guyana, and Jamaica in the Caribbean and Costa Rica, Nicaragua, and Panama in Central America.[7] Within this historic perspective, Cuba's newer military ties to leftist movements in Nicaragua and El Salvador are part of a consistent record of policy alignment with evolving external opportunities where the choice of policy depends upon the situation. In addition to the pattern of Cuba's widening activities in the region, Soviet and East European links have also spread during the past decade, which adds to the portrait of irresistible influence emanating from Fidel Castro's regime.[8] And when a United States Secretary of State announced the existence of a Soviet-Cuban "hit list" for control of Central America in 1981, a scenario within which Nicaragua had been already "lost", it is all too easy to perceive substantial Cuban power on the loose in and around Caribbean waters.[9]

Yet behind this record are undeniable declines in Cuba's apparent smooth-sailing performance of the 1970s. As a number of observers now stress, the Soviet-Cuban tide began to ebb in 1980. Guyana developed rifts with Cuba and became disillusioned with Cuban political interference and poor economic assistance.[10] Cuban and Venezuelan relations turned sour over an airline incident and parties friendly to Cuba lost elections in Antigua, St. Vincent, Dominica, St. Christopher, and St. Kitts-Nevis.[11] Cuba's showcase operation in Jamaica lost headway with the election of Mr. Edward Seaga in 1980, who vowed to rid the island of Cuban influence.[12] Mexico, long a supporter of Cuba's revolutionary model, nevertheless supplied El Salvador's ruling junta with oil and food despite its media attention to the leftwing guerrilla cause which received Cuban military supplies.[13] No less significant is Cuba's waning image as a revolutionary model to be emulated elsewhere, due largely to its continued dependence on Moscow, the flight of the refugees from the island, its unspectacular economic performance, its past economic and political mistakes, and its rigid society.[14]

Behind these events are even more significant trends which suggest that Cuba's capacity for attaining lasting influence in the Caribbean and Central America may be more elusive than imagined.

To provide a balanced perspective on this proposition, we can probe four key dimensions of Cuba's foreign policy. They are: (1) the motivating factors in Cuban diplomacy; (2) the evolution of Havana's recent influence seeking; (3) Havana's evolving opportunities and capabilities to shape favorable outcomes within the context of Caribbean and Central American economic and political realities; and (4) the emerging constraints on Cuban foreign relations.

MOTIVATING FACTORS IN CUBAN FOREIGN POLICY

Like other states in the international political arena, Cuba pursues its national interests through the application of power. By national interests is meant the quest for territorial security, economic development, and the affirmation of Cuba's own identity and roles within the global political community, largely through support of other leftist revolutionary struggles. Within this agenda must be included a strong commitment to internationalist solidarity (less for reasons of national security than of ideological affinity) which sets Cuba apart from the traditional pursuit of national interest through power politics.[15] By power is meant the capacity to influence political and economic outcomes externally which are supportive of Cuban national interests. The precise nature of Cuba's translation of its national interests into specific policy outcomes abroad and the types of techniques adopted to implement external policy, however, are conditioned by other _sui generis_ forces operative on the Cuban foreign policy psyche. This observation is made in light of Fidel Castro's pronouncements over the years, the statements made by other leaders in the Cuban foreign policy elite, and by the evolving patterns of foreign policy since the early days of the Revolution.

Among those special forces that condition the evolution of Cuban external goals and policy techniques must be included its nationalist revolutionary past, the adoption of a Marxist-Leninist ideology in the early 1960s, and the continued dependence on the Soviet Union for economic and military aid. Without going into these factors in detail, for they have been well analyzed elsewhere, brief observations about them can be made.[16] The first motivating force, Cuba's national revolutionary image, dates back at least to the early independence struggles against Spain from 1868-1878 and 1895-1898 when Cuban national leaders -- such as Jose Marti, Antonio Maceo, Maximo Gomez, Ignacio Agramonte, and Carlos Manuel de Cespedes -- emerged. Pride in these past struggles and the rebirth of the nationalist revolutionary tradition exploded with Fidel Castro's overthrow of Fulgencio Batista in 1959.[17] Since then nationalism has been and continues to be a constant theme in Cuban domestic and foreign affairs -- a _leitmotif_ systematically pursued in the arts, literature, cinema, sports, and indeed practically every walk of life. Fidel Castro's era, then, has been largely an era of nation-building as he linked his movement to the earlier historic events of 1868 and thereafter. To appreciate the thrust of Cuba's external support of other revolutionary movements and the drive to put Cuba on the map -- in Africa, in the Nonaligned Movement, in the United Nations, in opposition to the United States which for so long held back Cuban national pride after 1898 -- one must come to grips with the nationalist force.

Nor can the role of Marxism-Leninism be discounted, for it has been grafted onto Cuban nationalism. It provides a set of perceptions about reality in world affairs which is compatible with Cuban nationalism; defining in part the nature of the international political game, the natural adversaries faced by Cuba, and the friends it should support through internationalist solidarity. Given its prism of a bipolar world divided into the capitalist/imperialist camp and the communist/socialist camp -- a world in constant tension and struggle with inevitable victory posited for the latter -- Cuba, like the U.S.S.R., is led into a model of world politics emphasizing through ideology the role of power to encourage friends and trends favorable to the communist/socialist group. As leader of the capitalist/imperialist group, the United States becomes Havana's natural enemy, thus reinforcing the nonideological facts and perceptions of Cuba's historic national image where the United States dominated it for so long during and after the Spanish-American- Cuban war. The Marxist-Leninist ideological perception, then, is a second constant force molding Cuban foreign policy since the early days of Fidel Castro's victory over Batista.

Castro's adoption of Marxism-Leninism and his swing into the Soviet camp, it must be stressed, produced tangible benefits for both the U.S.S.R. and Cuba over the past two decades. In Moscow's case, Cuba's performance as an ideological and political ally provided the Soviet Union with its first significant leverage in the Caribbean and Latin America -- a geographic arena of increasing strategic importance to the U.S.S.R.[18] At the same time, Cuba became a means to promote Soviet interests in the Third World, which Cuban involvement in Africa and the Middle East from 1975 onwards so vividly illustrates. For these reasons, Moscow has continued its heavy economic and military support to the island despite Cuba's low economic performance and growing indebtedness to the U.S.S.R.[19] For Havana, the benefits derived from adopting Marxism-Leninism and joining with the Kremlin are clear: the acquisition of a partner without whose help in the economic and military domain Cuba could not have survived these past two decades. Even more, the Soviet association greatly enhanced Cuba's economic and military capacity to play the role of a major regional actor in Africa and the Western Hemisphere as well as to become a prestigious leader within the broader Third World.

Cuba's dependence on the Soviet Union for economic and military aid, as suggested above, must be isolated as a third force behind Havana's foreign policy in the Caribbean and Central America. The problem is to identify precisely what kind of relationship evolved over the years and here the scholarly analyses offer a variety of interpretations.[20] One version of the relationship holds that Cuba is strictly a surrogate of the U.S.S.R., undertaking whatever assignments requested by the Kremlin as repayment for all the material and political support received by Havana since the early 1960s.[21] A second view is more centered on Cuba, emphasizing that Havana attempts to maximize its goals of security, economic development, and establishment of its identity in the world within the constraints imposed by Moscow's aid and by the limits created by the dynamics of international politics in specific Third World regions where the United States must be included among the actors. Insofar as both Cuban and Soviet interests are promoted through their ideological and political alliance, what emerges is a two-way relationship of <u>convergence</u> of Soviet and Cuban interests.[22] The concept of convergence highlights the importance of Cuba's own independent dimension of foreign policy, but one not discounting the role played by Soviet support.

EVOLUTION OF HAVANA'S RECENT INFLUENCE SEEKING

With these underlying forces in Cuba's external posture now made clear, we can probe Havana's recent policy in the Caribbean and Central America. Much of the island's diplomacy in the past decade reflects the projection of its presence and capabilities in quest of national interests essentially along peaceful state-to-state relations. The range of its policy techniques includes expanded diplomatic contacts which helped to end its hemispheric isolation of the 1960s. And as Cuba's capabilities in the areas of health services, education, agriculture, and other developmental-oriented activities increased, the government began to send medical teams, teachers, agricultural technical assistants, and construction workers to selected countries when invited to do so -- as it did in the cases of Grenada, Guyana, Jamaica, Panama, and more recently Nicaragua.

By January 1980 1,200 Cuban teachers had arrived in Nicaragua to match its over 300 medics, 200 construction workers, and other advisers in that country who worked on agricultural and fisheries projects.[23] In 1980 Cuban construction workers also began to arrive in Grenada to build a new airport, for which Cuba supplied the materials, while other Cubans participated in educational, agricultural, medical, and political indoctrination activities.[24] In Jamaica, meanwhile, Cuba had become very active during the Michael Manley era (1972-1980) by helping that country to improve its water supply, to build houses and schools, to modernize its agricultural and fishing techniques, and to provide medical services.[25] All this, however, met enormous opposition from Edward Seaga and his followers, who won the 1980 national election and then asked the Cuban ambassador to leave. The broad profile of Cuban economic and technical, compared to its military, personnel in the Caribbean and Central America is presented in Table 3.1. Observe the remarkable build-up in 1979 and into 1980.

In addition to sending its teams out into Caribbean and Central American countries, as it also did in Africa and parts of the Middle East, Cuba began to train foreign students inside its own territory. Since 1975 Cuba has trained approximately 1,000 Jamaicans in a variety of areas, including sports, while other Caribbean and Central American students came from Grenada, Guyana, Nicaragua, and elsewhere. In late 1979, for example, about 600 students were from Nicaragua while altogether Havana was hosting approximately 6,000 foreign students by September 1980.[26] These more peaceful policy instruments were part of the island's overall spectacular growth of involvement in the Third World as a whole, which by 1981 included its 50,000 economic and military advisers supporting revolutionary movements.[27]

During the 1970s, Cuba also participated in regional and global intergovernmental organizations. It became an active member of the Latin American Economic System (SELA), which did not include the United States, and the joint Caribbean Shipping Company (NAMUCAR) as well as the United Nations Committee on Decolonization where it supported the Puerto Rican independence movement. Not the least important is Fidel Castro's chairmanship of the

TABLE 3.1

CUBAN ECONOMIC AND TECHNICAL PERSONNEL COMPARED TO MILITARY PERSONNEL IN THE CARIBBEAN AND CENTRAL AMERICA: 1978-1980

	1978		1979		1980	
Country	E&T	MIL	E&T	MIL	E&T	MIL
Grenada			350	50	1000	100
Guyana		10	65			
Jamaica	100		450		600	
Nicaragua			1600	50	1700	200
TOTAL	110		2565		3600	

Sources: Communist Aid Activities in Non-Communist Less Developed Countries, by year; Central Intelligence Agency, National Foreign Assessment Center; Tad Szulc, "Confronting The Cuban Nemesis," The New York Times Magazine (April 5, 1981), pp. 36ff.; Impact of Cuban-Soviet Ties in the Western Hemisphere, Spring 1980, Hearings before the House Committee on Foreign Affairs (Washington: U.S. Government Printing Office, 1980).

Nonaligned Movement, a three-year position which he assumed at its Sixth Summit Meeting in Havana in September 1979.[28] During the 1970s, however, it should be noted that the Cuban government continued its contacts with leftwing guerrillas in Nicaragua, Guatemala, Honduras, and El Salvador and from 1975 onwards it greatly expanded its military involvement in Africa.[29]

The Shift Toward Military Aid in the Caribbean and Central America

This pattern of essentially peaceful diplomacy in the Caribbean and Central America shifted toward a renewed emphasis on military aid in the late 1970s. Table 3.1 captures this transition in part. The shift found expression through a number of activities. Having provided low-level assistance to the Sandinistas in Nicaragua for over two decades previous to their victory over Somoza, the Cuban government began in early 1979 to increase its training, funds, arms and advice.[30] The July 1979 Sandinista victory in turn stimulated leftist guerrillas to renewed activity and vigor in El Salvador, which led Cuba to step up its training and the flow of its arms to them.[31]

It is the Sandinista victory, then, which seems to have pressed Havana toward increased military influence seeking in the Caribbean and Central America -- coupled of course to its previous experience and training in Africa since the mid-1970s. By 1980 Cuba had emerged as a major weapons supplier to the Salvadoran guerrilla factions -- in association with Soviet efforts -- as well as the overall "driving organizational force," in the words of one analyst, behind the broad insurgency movement in Central America.[32] The role of Cuba in Central American armed struggle is documented by the U.S. Department of State's February 1981 "White Paper" entitled <u>Communist Interference in El Salvador</u>. It cites evidence of Cuban military involvement in El Salvador, a point with which other Latin American governments subsequently were to agree.[33] The White Paper identifies Cuba's efforts in helping to organize the Salvadoran guerrilla factions, its assistance and advice to guerrillas in planning their military operations, and its role in supplying insurgents with tons of the most modern arms and equipment while trying to disguise this activity by providing mostly weapons of Western manufacture.[34]

The key question to raise is why would Havana embark upon the path of military involvement, given its previous failure and in light of predictable United States opposition? The answers to this question lie within the realm of evolving opportunities and Cuban capabilities.

EVOLVING OPPORTUNITIES AND CAPABILITIES

Cuba's expanded economic, political, and eventual military involvement in the Caribbean and Central America results from two basic conditions. First, Havana's capacity to become involved has increased over the years, notably in the military dimension but also in the fields of education and medicine. Secondly, the opportunities to extend its presence clearly expanded throughout the 1970s as some left-wing governments emerged in the Caribbean and Central America and as revolutionary leftist groups sought governmental power through force in other countries. Behind these generally radical trends in the region were forces well documented elsewhere, such as the deteriorating economic and social conditions, the quest for more independence of action _vis a vis_ the United States, and the deepening identity of regional leaders with those developmental aspirations expressed elsewhere in the Third World and clearly articulated through the New International Economic Order (NIEO).[35] As these conditions stimulated the wave of leftism in its many forms, the Cuban government demonstrated a sense of pragmatic opportunism to ride the tides of change.

Beyond the identifiable forces leading to Cuba's growing shadow over the region must be added two additional factors that contributed to Havana's posture, especially the turn toward militarism in 1979. The first of these is rising Soviet interest in the region, which supported Cuba's own policies, at precisely the same time that Moscow demonstrated a distinct orientation toward increased military aid and direct military intervention in developing countries, as in Africa and in Afghanistan. As Cuba turned toward the armed struggle thesis, then, it did so in line with a shifting Soviet posture of the same type, unlike the late 1960s when Havana's armed struggle interests conflicted so remarkably with those of Moscow.[36] The second factor is the Cuban military experience in Africa since 1975, which must have generated the inertia toward expanded military operations elsewhere when opportunities arose, coupled with a distinctly enhanced military capability as a result of the African experiences and its associated Soviet military aid. Each of these propositions can be examined briefly.

Rising Soviet interest in the Caribbean and Central America became quite clear during the 1970s, a trend matched by the continued very strong Soviet interest in the Third World dating back to its inception in 1954-55.[37] The motivation for Soviet interest stems from its view of the Third World as a new center of power and influence. It is perceived as an arena in which communism can be encouraged, where markets for Soviet economic goods and military weapons can be found, and as a region of strategic interest to expand the Soviet presence and security while reducing the Western presence.[38] The Caribbean and Central America understandably play significant roles within this overview, given their strategic locations near the United States and especially since the early 1970s as leftist movements swept through many of the area's countries. The resulting Soviet interest naturally supported and undoubtedly encouraged the Cuban thrust.

The Soviet Union also began to demonstrate a growing tendency to use military intervention as a key technique of power from the mid-1970s onward, a trend that clearly affected the Cubans since they were so deeply involved in it. By the late 1970s, not only had Moscow occupied Afghanistan, but it also supported 6,825 military technicians in Africa (these included East European military technicians), 5,780 in the Middle East, and 4,150 in South Asia. And Moscow escalated its arms sales in 1974-79 to more than $34 billion, thereby capturing one-fourth of the world arms market and ranking it second behind the United States as an arms supplier.[39] Cuban troops, meanwhile, rose to 33,060 military technicians in Africa and 1,000 in the Middle East during the last half of the 1970s.[40] One inescapable conclusion relative to the Soviet use of military intervention in Africa and elsewhere from the mid-1970s onward is its increased convergence with the older Cuban belief in armed struggle dating back to Castro's days in the Sierra Maestra.

Cuba's experiences in Africa with the Soviet Union and the enhanced power capabilities which they provided probably generated renewed acceptability for armed struggle among its policy makers. During their years in Africa, the Cubans acquired advanced weaponry by supporting Soviet objectives and they also gained new military experience. As one Cuban observer notes, "In the last several years the Cuban Armed Forces have graduated from what was a defensive force to one which, with Soviet assistance, can deploy a large number of troops to distant conflicts on short notice."[41] This escalation of military capability undoubtedly increased Havana's prestige among leftist groups in the Caribbean and Central America, stimulating the ties with Jamaica, Nicaragua, Grenada, and El Salvador. Indeed, again in the words of a Cuban observer, "It is doubtful that the Sandinistas could have achieved victory without Cuban support."[42]

A final observation on Cuban capabilities must be directed to the government's political skills. The Cubans, by all indications, have emerged as astute political tacticians in advising leftist revolutionaries in the Caribbean and Central America -- drawing upon experiences from their own movement, but also from new experiences abroad. While this phenomenon is reflected in Cuban efforts at political indoctrination in Grenada, it is more visible in the case of El Salvador. Before receiving large-scale Cuban aid, Salvadoran guerrilla leaders met in Havana in May 1980 to form three political organizations designed to unify their previously fragmented forces in order to augment their political strength. The meeting led to the formation of the Unified Revolutionary Directorate (DRU) as their central executive arm for political and military planning, the Farabundo Marti People's Liberation Front (FMLN) as the coordinating agent of the guerrilla groups, and the Revolutionary Democratic Front (FDR) to disseminate propaganda abroad.[43] Given the enormous political fragmentation in many of the Central American countries, Cuba's role in mediating such agreements should not go unnoticed in any analysis of its capabilities to extend its influence in the region.

EMERGING CONSTRAINTS ON CUBAN FOREIGN POLICY

Four major types of constraints operate against the long-run Cuban efforts at influence seeking in the Caribbean and Central America. These are: (1) problems created by Cuba's links to the Soviet Union;

(2) weaknesses in Cuba's own capabilities as measured against the developmental needs of the region's countries; (3) limitations to Cuban influence that arise from internal political characteristics in the Caribbean and Central America; (4) the waning image of Cuba as a viable alternative model of development in the area; and (5) obstacles generated by regional systematic changes. Each of these dimensions merit attention.

Cuban-Soviet Ties

While Cuban interests are clearly promoted through association with the U.S.S.R., those bilateral relations are not free of stresses and strains that work against both short and long-term Cuban objectives in the western hemisphere. The list of these strains is long, for it deeply involves the impact of Cuba's close economic, political, and military links with its Soviet patron, suggesting that those forces which work against the U.S.S.R. in the Third World cannot but affect the fortunes of Cuba as well. A synthesized set of these difficulties includes:

-- Recent growing disenchantment with the Soviet Union in Africa (e.g., Angola and Mozambique) which suggests a pattern of Third World response that can be reproduced in Cuban ties in the Caribbean and Central America, as is already visible in Jamaica's break from Cuba in late 1980.

-- A legacy of Soviet failures elsewhere in the Third World that also can be replicated in Cuban-Third World relations.

-- Cuba's pressing of Soviet interests in the Nonaligned Movement against the wishes of many of its members, especially since the Soviet military invasion of Afghanistan in late 1979, which makes Havana appear as a surrogate to the U.S.S.R.

-- Growing Third World discontent with Moscow for not carrying its weight in meeting the modernization needs of the lesser developed countries, a pressure not likely to soon disappear in light of the efforts which are supported by many Caribbean/Central American countries to establish a New International Economic Order (N.I.E.O.).

-- Long-run forces operating against Moscow's capacity to continue to support Cuba in an emerging era of resource scarcity in a globally interdependent economic system.

-- Negative overall economic and political effects of Soviet encouragement of Cuban militarism in terms of the Cuban economy and its image in the Caribbean and Central America.

Angola and Mozambique are two fascinating cases of the limits to influence produced by Soviet economic and military aid, a pattern from which Cuba is not immune. Consider first the extent of aid in these countries. By 1979 the Soviets had 1,000 military officers in Angola, with East Europeans providing ground forces equipment, while the Cubans were supplying 19,000 (mainly combat) troops.[44] In addition, by 1979 U.S.S.R. and Eastern European economic technicians amounted to 2,760 in Angola.[45] But despite these large forces on the scene,[46] Angola and Mozambique have recently become disenchanted with Moscow. Both countries increasingly are determined not to become a Soviet satellite, are not overly attracted to the socialist planned economy, and show a distinct proclivity to go their own way on international issues.[47] The presence of Soviet and Cuban economic and military personnel, then, does not guarantee automatic influence. In fact, it may encourage quite the opposite trend. Certainly this pattern is demonstrated by Jamaica's adverse reaction to the substantial number of Cubans in that country following the defeat of Michael Manley's pro-Cuban government in 1980.[48]

As to Cuba's leadership in the Nonaligned Movement and how seriously it may have been damaged by the Soviet invasion and continued occupation of Afghanistan, two points can be made. First, the immediate wave of indignation created serious problems for Havana, which had just assumed the chairmanship of the movement in 1979. Strong anti-Soviet reactions found Cuba isolated from the majority of Third World countries, including most Caribbean and Central American states, who censured the U.S.S.R.'s behavior and the Afghan affair soon cost Havana the seat on the United Nations Security Council for which it had fought so hard.[49] And had there been lingering infatuation within the Third World over Havana's argument that the U.S.S.R. was their "natural ally," that romance was laid to rest in Afghanistan.[50] Indeed Cuba's position on the Afghanistan matter lent increased credence to the Havana-as-a-Soviet-surrogate thesis,[51] which could not improve its leadership position in a movement populated in part by Caribbean and Central American states.

Secondly, there remains the question of the long-term effects of Afghanistan on Havana's leadership role in the Nonaligned Movement. One notes, for example, the disagreement among Cuban observers on this matter.[52] There is, to be certain, Cuba's stepped up efforts at economic and other developmental assistance in trying to moderate the damage created by the Afghanistan invasion. This activity is especially pronounced in the Caribbean and Central America where Cuba can exploit the fact that fear of the U.S. outweighs that of the U.S.S.R.[53]

Yet the recent Cuban military assistance in Central America, coupled with the Soviet turn toward military invasion, raises again the old Caribbean, Central American, and broader Latin American concerns dating back to the late 1960s about Cuban armed intervention. In this regard it must be noted that not only did Jamaica greatly reduce its relations with Cuba after the 1980 elections, but even Cuba's longtime friend, Panama's General Omar Torrijos Herrera, rebuffed El Salvador's opposition leaders who were receiving arms from Cuba in early 1981.[54] And although Columbia, Costa Rica, the Dominican Republic, and Venezuela are not official members of the Nonaligned Movement, their increasing strains with El Salvador's leftists should not go unnoticed, for they are sympathetic to many of the economic and other issues reflected within the nonaligned group.[55] Nor can one lightly dismiss Mexico's second thoughts about the El Salvadoran leftists given its long close association with Cuba and its own image among the Caribbean and Central American countries who belong to the Nonaligned Movement.[56]

Economic restraints also greatly condition Moscow's influence capabilities vis a vis the Third World, a fact of growing significance in Soviet relations with the southern regions of the globe and potentially with Cuba. Many lesser developed countries are increasingly critical of the U.S.S.R. for its poor record in working toward the solution of world developmental problems.[57] Insofar as the Caribbean and Central American countries participate with Cuba in international organizations where indictments against the U.S.S.R. are made, it would be surprising if Cuba's own pro-Soviet posture were to escape more criticism in the future. Added to this situation are the long-run Soviet energy and other economic difficulties which potentially threaten its capability to play the great economic patron of Cuba.[58] Finally, the Soviet encouragement of Cuban militarism is not completely detached from Cuba's own continuing economic difficulties at home. The stress on military spending does not guarantee the best allocation of scarce resources for economic development, especially since much of the manpower is put to work in foreign countries rather than on home soil.[59]

Cuban Capabilities Versus Developmental Needs of the Region

To suggest that Cuba lacks the capability required to meet Caribbean and Central American developmental needs runs the risk of misstating the argument. For certainly Havana demonstrates a keen awareness of the region's educational, health, and social overhead capital problems (including agriculture) as well as the willingness to aid the region with its teaching brigades, construction workers, agricultural technicians, and medical teams -- as underscored in Guyana, Grenada, Jamaica, and Nicaragua during the last half of the 1970s and into the early 1980s. In many ways Havana's foreign assistance programs, emanating from its sense of internationalist responsibilities, are well suited to the types of development that prevail in the region (e.g., low number of doctors per 1,000 of the population, low literacy levels, the need for school construction, etc.).

Yet it seems fair to say that given the area's enormous developmental problems measured against Cuba's own economic performance and capabilities, Havana's ability to move the region into sustained economic growth will be far less than required. Consider first the scope and types of problems faced by the Caribbean and Central America. Both regions face slow economic growth, a result in part of the Organization of Petroleum Exporting Countries (OPEC) oil price rises since 1973. Their economic systems tend to be small in scale, depend on limited types of natural resources for export earnings, carry large external debts (Nicaragua and Jamaica over $1 billion;

Panama over $2 billion), and suffer from structural dualism. By this is meant the coexistence of a high-wage, capital intensive modern sector, much of it usually owned and controlled by foreign-based multinational corporations, alongside a low-wage, labor intensive traditional sector. The former is characterized by mineral extraction, processing industries, and other capital intensive production; the latter by handicrafts, services, and agriculture. The economies tend, under these conditions, to be historically vulnerable to external forces (e.g., the world market price for their natural resources) and in this sense they operate on a high degree of dependency status, which is the type of situation that gives rise to the exploding political leftism in the area.[60] Add to this situation levels of agricultural production generally insufficient to feed adequately hungry populations along with, especially in Central America, the unequal nature of land distribution and national income and the roots of political and social instability become clear. Nicaragua, for example, inherited a $1.3 billion foreign debt and two years after the 1979 Sandinista revolution it was experiencing lagging economic growth and a projected minimum of twenty years' dependence on foreign loans.[61] The economic miracles required to alleviate these conditions simply do not seem available from Cuba.

Continued low rates of economic development are interlocked with other economic pressures. The region is generally plagued by high rates of inflation, unemployment, and low per capita income. Inflation ran at about 20 percent in El Salvador during 1980 with similarly high rates in Nicaragua, while in the Caribbean it averaged between 11 percent (Bahamas) and 35 percent (Jamaica) during the late 1970s.[62] Many of the Caribbean islands have unemployment rates of 25 percent, which is nearer to 50 percent among young people. Urban unemployment in Nicaragua exceeds 35 percent. Gross national product (GNP) per capita is by no means high compared to the United States with its figure of $8,520 in 1977. The comparable figure for Haiti was $230; Honduras, $410; El Salvador, $550; Guatemala, $790; and Jamaica, $1,150.[63]

Social statistics further illustrate the development picture. The population growth rate is high with El Salvador at 2.9 percent; Guatemala, 2.9; Honduras, 3.4; Nicaragua, 3.1; and Panama, 3.1.[64] And much of this population is young as well as unemployed. Illiteracy is a by-product of these conditions, which makes Cuban offers of education assistance attractive, if still insufficient. Central America is especially disadvantaged in this respect, with adult literacy in Nicaragua (late 1970s) running at 50 percent; Guatemala, 45 percent; Honduras, 59 percent; El Salvador, 60 percent; and Panama, 79 percent. Haiti is the lowest of the countries with 23 percent literacy.[65]

Cuba's limited capacity to help these countries develop stems from a number of sources, not least of which is Cuba's own economic deficiencies. As the Second Congress of the Cuban Communist Party (PCC) revealed, the Cuban economy is in trouble. The economic growth rate for the 1976-80 period amounted to 4 percent, which was one-third lower than originally planned. The slowdown in economic growth stemmed in part from the dramatic dip in sugar prices, illustrating Havana's continuing link with the world economy despite Soviet subsidizing of the Cuban economy, and partly from internal conditions. The latter included nagging inefficiency, the absence of production norms, problems with labor discipline, and weaknesses in quality controls accompanied by absenteeism and mismanagement.[66] Here it must be said that Cuban trade is basically with the industrialized countries (socialist and nonsocialist) to which it exports raw materials (sugar, nickel, tobacco, fruits, rum) and from which it imports capital goods and fuel.[67]

While steps are underway to improve the Cuban economic system, including a major energy accord signed with Mexico in January 1981, Cuba's internal economic conditions prohibit it from playing an enormously significant economic role in the Caribbean and Central America.[68] This situation parallels Russia's, whose economic deficiencies constrain its worldwide economic effectiveness among the Third World countries. In fact, Cuban economic and technical aid to the region pales in significance when compared to Western efforts (e.g., United States bilateral programs or aid from the United Nations Development Program, the Economic Commission for Latin America, the World Bank Group, the Inter-American Development Bank, and the International Monetary Fund). Not only do radical leftist states (Nicaragua) and conservative governments (Jamaica) look to these sources for major funding, but they also receive substantial help from other more powerful regional actors such as Mexico and Venezuela.[69] The simple point is that any analysis of Cuban activities in the Caribbean and Central America should avoid overestimating Cuban influence and underestimating the real and potential impact of Western lending agencies.

Internal Political Characteristics of the Caribbean and Central America

How the internal political dynamics of the Caribbean and Central America restrict Cuba's influence seeking is a subject that more befits a book length manuscript than a short essay of this type. The issue is more than simply noting the rising nationalist sentiments among elite decision makers throughout the region such as those which generated Seaga's ire over the Cuban presence in Jamaica during the late 1970s and which make El Salvadoran leftist guerrilla leaders sensitive to Havana's advice and training.[70] Nor is it simply that Cuba's economic limitations translate into political deficiencies, as suggested in the preceding section. What we are after lies more in the domain of political culture and political processes.

In approaching these elements, the <u>differences</u> between the Caribbean and Central Amerian regions first must be stressed. The English-speaking Caribbean inherited systems of legitimate self-government, democratic political traditions, elements of British socialist thought, and trade union organizations. Central America is the home of authoritarian and Hispano-Catholic roots; it lacks the tradition of legitimate self-government, is far more prone to violence in political problem solving, and is much more in tune with the tradition of using bullets rather than ballots. The latter setting suggests why Cuba pursues not only peaceful diplomacy in Central America, but now also supports armed liberation. Yet within both these contexts lie checks to Cuban influence, the more obvious being the democratic tradition in the Caribbean while in Central America it is the difficulty any group has in controlling events over a sustained period of time.

Beyond these broad generalizations, a number of other observations can be made. Central American political culture -- by which is meant the attitudes toward authority and interpersonal behavior within the political system -- suggests the continuation of strong traditional patterns. Personalism (individualism, emphasizing the inner essence of a person; inner dignity; and the need to guard one's inner and unique subjective self), stress on charisma and emotionalism as fulfillment of self, and machismo (male virility and power) characterize much of the culture of politics. These help to generate the major traits of the political process: political fragmentation into groups headed by dominant personalities; lack of cohesive political organizations and unified movements; and a high rate of violence resulting from the translation of political culture into political practice.[71] Individual leaders are not prone toward complete importation of foreign ideologies or subservience to outside leaders; they tend instead to place their own personalist stamp on political thought and internal movements. They resist control by others from inside or outside the political system. For example, middle class opposition in Nicaragua to the Cuban-Sandinista connection has surfaced already[72] and in El Salvador three major left-wing guerrilla groups have anti-Soviet origins, are still distrustful of each other, and retain separate organizational structures.[73] Thus in neither Nicaragua nor El Salvador is the situation especially conducive to Cuban political influence.

In effect, the same aspects of political culture and political processes in Central America that stand as obstacles to political development in the region also impede Cuban external pressures; what prevents domestic grass roots institution building, the emergence of a broadly based developmental consciousness, and the instilling of a sense of legitimate authority in governmental leaders and in the political institutions of the state can also very effectively impede control and direction from the outside. And need it be added that Marxist-Leninist parties are notoriously fragmented here, that ideological pronouncements are often more rhetoric than substantive platforms capable of being implemented, and that once in power political leaders have extreme difficulty in holding their political organization together? Consider also that the Cuban revolutionary model of rapidly socializing the economy with very little left in private hands and creating a single party Marxist system is not likely to be replicated easily in Central America given the different socioeconomic and political conditions, the different stages of development, and the distinct types of evolving leaderships. Certainly the countries with which Cuba has established friendly ties -- Nicaragua, Guyana, Jamaica, and Grenada -- have not replicated the Cuban model.

Caribbean resistance takes other forms. Many of its Marxists do not enjoy broad based popular support while those political leaders with a substantial following are not Marxists. Jamaica's Michael Manley and Guyana's Forbes Burnham are cases in point. Perhaps of greater significance in much of the Caribbean is the deep ethnic-racial cleavages that undermine popular unity and function as another built-in resistance to outside influence seeking. Prime Minister Castro has overcome much of this problem in Cuba after considerable time and financial investment in education, culture, and sports. But elsewhere in the Caribbean ethnic-racial perceptions lie behind political conflict and the difficulty in building a consensus on how to modernize. For instance, the People's Progressive Party (PPP) of Guyana, orthodox communist in ideology, draws its support essentially from East Indian agricultural workers while Forbes Burnham's People's National Congress (PNC) is spokesman for the African community. Politics, including the politics of Marxism-Leninism, in both the Caribbean and Central America, to summarize, marches to its own drummer and Cuban-supported indigenous communists are not likely to assume leadership of the parade.

The Cuban Revolutionary Model: A Waning Image

As one observer recently put it, "The Soviet-Cuban tide in the Caribbean has ebbed" in 1980.[74] Two significant trends lend weight to this argument: first, the declining image of Cuba as a revolutionary model of economic development; and second, the widening network of rifts in Cuba's relations with many of its neighbors. The origins of the first trend lie in the continuing economic deficiencies on the island which became so pronounced during the 1976-1980 period. Add to this the wave of 10,000 Cubans who in April 1980 took refuge on the grounds of the Peruvian Embassy in Havana, followed by an estimated 114,475 Cubans who left the island by boat to the United States later that year, and the recipe for a collapsing public image is complete. Cuban refugees in Costa Rica, moreover, gave accounts of the situation which were televised throughout Central America and the Caribbean to reinforce the profile of something having gone wrong in Cuba.[75] Thus by early 1981, Cuba was no longer being promoted as the revolutionary model by many Caribbean and Central American leftists because of its continued dependence on Moscow, the rigidity of its society, and its economic and political mistakes over the years. Privately it is reported that Prime Minister Castro has advised the

Nicaraguans to avoid making the economic mistakes of Cuba.

Cuba as a revolutionary model began to experience other stresses in its Caribbean and Central American relations as the 1980s began. Panama, as noted earlier, went so far as to offer "friendly warnings" to Nicaragua's leaders about overreliance on the Cubans as they moved into that country after the Sandinista victory. Guyana by 1981 had become disenchanted with the Soviet Union for its political interference and meager economic assistance while a potential rift erupted with Havana over the death of Walter Rodney, leader of the Working People's Alliance (WPA). The Cuban ambassador, Sylvio Gonzalez, attended Rodney's funeral and expressed sympathy with other prominent anti-government WPA leaders, which did not ingratiate him with the Burnham government.[76] Jamaica's new leader, Prime Minister Seaga, entered office in late 1980 with a very clear anti-Cuban posture, leaving no doubt that he intended to wage a struggle against Cuban and Soviet influence in the Caribbean. And these events unfolded on top of the series of elections in Antigua, St. Vincent, Dominica, and St. Kitts-Nevis which brought conservative leaders to power.

Criticism of the Cuban regime is not restricted to the smaller Caribbean and Central American countries. Two large regional actors -- Colombia and Venezuela -- recently demonstrated deep concerns with Cuban foreign policy. While Colombia broke off diplomatic relations over Havana's training of leftist guerrillas on Colombian territory, Venezuela's Foreign Minister, Alberto Zembrano Velasco, blasted the Cuban government in October 1980 for trying to link the Nonaligned Movement with the Soviet Union after its attack on Afghanistan. He went so far as to say that "personality cults regimes such as Cuba's are incapable of understanding democratic principles."[77] Since then the Venezuelan government has supported the El Salvadoran junta which Cuba seeks to help overthrow.[78]

It may well be that these negative reactions to Cuban militant activities in the region encouraged Havana to try with Moscow's support to modify its hostile image. In June 1981 Cuba extended a $3.6 million line of credit to Nicaragua for purchase of spare parts for sugar mills. While this aid was in line with previous Cuban assistance to that country, Havana was known previously not for credits but for manpower aid. Additional economic help arrived in Nicaragua in August 1981 when Moscow extended a $50 million credit line for the purchase of Soviet agricultural and transportation equipment at low interest rates while also agreeing to buy 3,000 tons of coffee and 20,000 tons each of cotton and raw sugar per year.[79] Naturally this type of aid also helped to expand the state rather than the private sector, the latter sponsored more by the incoming administration of President Ronald Reagan.

Changing Regional and International Systems

Much of the analysis thus far has centered on two key dimensions of change. The first is the East-West domain or escalated superpower competition as it affects and is affected by Cuban-Soviet efforts to diminish U.S. power in the Caribbean and Central America by exploiting the anti-American, radical nationalist forces of change, as well as the constraints on those policies. The second dimension is more hemispheric in nature, probing Cuban capabilities in the context of the internal and external economic/political dynamics of the region's countries.

A third dimension of the problem which merits our attention is best understood in today's language as the North-South axis. This arena contains several forces -- essentially economic -- that bear also upon the international politics of Cuba in the Caribbean and Central America. Within the North-South network of interdependent forces lies the potential for economic development which so commands the attention of the Third World, including those countries examined here. That potential is locked into the North-South issues of aid, trade (markets, quotas, tariffs), energy, natural resources, supply and demand, technology transfer, and access for the developing states to decision making in the international lending bodies (e.g., the International Monetary Fund, the World Bank, etc.).

Given Cuba's economic performance, its waning image as a revolutionary model, and the region's other experiences with Soviet aid, trade, and technical assistance, it is unlikely that many of the revolutionary Caribbean and Central American states will look strictly toward Cuba, the U.S.S.R., and Eastern Europe for the capital, technical assistance, and trade outlets required for sustained economic growth.[80] They more likely will continue to search for assistance from developed northern countries, working toward modification of the current international economic system so dominated by the North through their participation in organizations committed to a NIEO. The Caribbean and Central American effort will likely be directed toward trying to improve the terms of international trade with the North, raising the level of available aid and on more favorable terms, strengthening the modes of technology transfer while reducing its associated costs, and widening their access to decision making within the international lending agencies where, it should be added, the Soviets do not participate, thereby limiting their chances to increase their influence in the region.

That his scenario of the future seems likely is strengthened by the continuing role played by the private sector in the Caribbean and Central America. Jamaica's Prime Minister Seaga distinctly endorses the private sector search for northern capital, investment, and trade, but even in revolutionary Nicaragua the economy remains mixed with a private sector role, just as the private sector is very much alive in El Salvador.[81] Yet it is not solely a question of the private sector's continuing links to the international economic system since the entire range of political groups are tied into it. This is vividly illustrated by Cuba's recent efforts to boost its tourist industry by permitting limited foreign investment and to woo American business interests, by Nicaragua's actions to insure the inflow of U.S. aid, and perhaps most clearly by Moscow's grudging acknowledgment that the international economic system is very interlocked and within that interdependent system U.S. capital and aid plays an enormously large part.[82] For the economic and political systems of the Caribbean and Central America to develop, they will require a heavy inflow of capital, concessional financing, and other forms of aid and effective trade outlets from the Northern portion of the global economy. Their needed resources, as it turns out, are simply more available from this section of the globe (in both geoeconomic and geopolitical terms) than from the East.

Among the global economic issues that constrain Cuban influence seeking from this interlocked macroperspective, energy ranks high. The oil price increases of 1973 and the subsequent escalating fuel prices greatly affected the non-oil-producing countries of the Caribbean and Central America. The energy problem has raised the area's debt accumulation, made the development process all the more expensive, and markedly influenced political decision making. Given Cuba's own heavy oil dependence on the U.S.S.R., it simply cannot play an enormously effective role in this domain, especially in comparison to other regional actors such as Mexico and Venezuela. These two countries, for example, have agreed to assist needy Caribbean and Central American states through a joint concessionary facility. Meanwhile, in an effort to cope with their energy and other economic needs, the Caribbean and Central American countries have turned toward supplementing their regional organizations (the Organization of American States and the Latin American Economic System) with strengthened subregional groups. The English-speaking Caribbean states now operate through four distinct organizations of economic cooperation while the Central American states are moving toward a restructuring of the Central American Common Market.

CONCLUSIONS

Cuban foreign policy during the late 1970s and the early 1980s reflects remarkable transformations relative to its activities in the Caribbean and Central America. Havana developed a wide spectrum of economic, educational, health welfare, technical, and political capabilities orchestrated to fit the changing regional settings and in line with its own domestic and international policy objectives. Late in the decade it reemphasized the role of armed struggle, spurred on by the Sandinista victory in Nicaragua in 1979. What one perceives in this portrait of Cuban foreign policy is a high sense of pragmatism as it changed the tactics and strategies it used to maximize its influence as new types of opportunities become available. And as the 1970s unfolded, Havana succeeded in projecting its presence far and wide in the Caribbean and Central America, breaking away from the isolation it had experienced earlier in the 1960s.

Cuban capabilities and objectives, however, are more restrained than appears at first blush. As portrayed in much of the journalistic reporting about the widening Cuban shadow over the region and as implied in recent U.S. government concern about Cuban military support of leftist guerrillas in El Salvador, one would assume substantial Cuban power at work in this arena. But as it turns out, a network of constraints to Cuban influence seeking is generated by its continuing links with the U.S.S.R., its own hemispheric relations, the nature of its economic and political capabilities measured against the region's domestic and external economic/political dynamics, and the North-South forces within the international economic system. This fact should come as no surprise, for the power of all states is relative not absolute, changing not static, applicable only in specific policy contexts, and checked by many internal and external pressures. But in observing Cuba from the United States, these basic facts about comparative foreign policy frequently seem underexamined in the public forum.

This is not the place to go into a detailed study of the consequent implications for U.S. foreign policy. Washington's posture, of course, clearly conditions the trends described above. Its emphasis on the security aspects of a perceived "Cuban threat," for example, may encourage the very trends it wishes to avoid. Heavy military aid, to take one case in point, lends credence to the Cuban stress on American imperialism and its desire for a return to Yankee hegemony. It also tends to crystallize leftist support and opposition to centrist governments on the internal local scene, as in El Salvador, and can also alienate key actors in the region, such as Mexico. Meanwhile protectionist elements in the United States help impede trade and financial programs that might stimulate economic development in the region, thus undermining the Cuban-Soviet appeal. Reduced American aid adds to this generally weakened capacity of the United States to exploit its economic advantages within the North-South setting.

On balance the opportunities for the U.S. and the Northern developed world to bring its economic weight to bear -- not only in ways to help minimize the Cuban quest for influence, but also to enhance the development potential of the region -- are remarkable. Improved trade relations, increased economic assistance, and more attention to the agenda posed by NIEO are elements that could be addressed. On this score the issue turns largely on <u>perception</u> and the analysis here suggests that the U.S. emphasis on Cuba as essentially a security concern, requiring maximum military responses, misses the mark in terms of the central forces now at work in the Caribbean and Central America.[83]

NOTES

1. Useful and important studies of the evolution of Cuban foreign policy in Latin America, the Caribbean, and Central America include the following: Andres Suarez, Cuba: Castroism and Communism, 1959-1966 (Cambridge: The M.I.T. Press, 1969); Edward Gonzalez, Cuba Under Castro: The Limits of Charisma (Boston: Houghton Mifflin Co., 1974); and Jorge I. Dominquez, Cuba: Order and Revolution (Cambridge: Harvard University Press, 1978).

2. It should be stressed that sharp differences in the latest brand of military activities compared to the 1960s exist and it would be inaccurate to assert that Cuba had given up completely a role for military power in its foreign relations over the years. For one thing, Havana does not see armed struggle today as the single principal means to bring down governments hostile to Cuba and to replace them with friendly governments. See Jorge Dominguez, "The Armed Forces and Foreign Relations" in Cole Blasier and Carmelo Mesa-Lago (Eds.), Cuba in the World (Pittsburgh: University of Pittsburgh Press, 1979), pp. 53-86; also H. Michael Erisman, "Cuban Internationalism: The Impact of Nonaligned Leadership and Afghanistan" (Paper prepared for presentation at the 1980 conference of the Latin American Studies Association in Bloomington, Indiana, October 17-19, 1980). For another, Cuban guerrilla activities in Latin America during the 1960s were not tied directly to the role of the Cuban armed forces. See Dominguez, ibid., pp. 60-61.

3. See Tad Szulc, "Confronting the Cuban Nemesis," The New York Times Magazine (April 5, 1981), pp. 36 ff.

4. On these and other aspects of Cuba's military roles in Nicaragua and Grenada, see the testimony of Myles R.R. Frechette, Director of Cuban Affairs, to the Subcommittee on Inter-American Affairs of the House Foreign Affairs Committee on April 17, 1980, Impact of Cuban-Soviet Ties in the Western Hemisphere, Spring 1980, Hearings Before the Subcommittee on Inter-American Affairs (Washington: U.S. Government Printing Office, 1980), pp. 60-73. See also the testimony of Mr. Martin J. Scheina, Analyst for Cuban Affairs, Defense Intelligence Agency, ibid., p. 12. Excellent background reading on the widening Soviet and Cuban military activities in Latin America and

Africa is provided by Robert S. Leiken, "Eastern Winds in Latin America," Foreign Policy, No. 42 (Spring 1981), pp. 94-113.

5. Many scholars on Soviet and United States foreign policy stress this point. See, for examples, George F. Kennan, "Cease This Madness," The Atlantic (January 1981), pp. 25-28; Robert G. Kaiser, "U.S.-Soviet Relations: Goodbye to Detente," Foreign Affairs, Vol. 59, No. 3 (1980 - America and the World), pp. 500-521; and Stanley Hoffman, "The New Orthodoxy," The New York Review, Vol. 28, No. 6 (April 16, 1981), pp. 22 ff.

6. Winston Williams, "Military Spending: Debate Is Growing," New York Times (March 19, 1981), p. D 1.

7. In the early 1960s, Cuba found itself cut off from all of Latin America except Mexico. Today, fourteen Latin American countries have embassies in Havana. On the early period, see Suarez and Gonzalez, op. cit. On later Cuban foreign policy, see various editions of Granma, Granma Weekly Review (in English) and Foreign Broadcast Information Service (Latin America; U.S.S.R.). Also Leon Goure and Morris Rothenberg, Soviet Penetration of Latin America (Miami: University of Miami Press, 1975); Edward Gonzalez, "Cuban Foreign Policy," Problems of Communism, Vol. 26 (November-December 1977), pp. 1-15; and W. Raymond Duncan, "Moscow and Havana in the Third World" in Duncan (Ed.), Soviet Policy in Developing Countries (Huntington, N.Y.: Robert E. Krieger Publishing Co., 1981), pp. 115-144.

8. In addition to the testimony contained in the Hearings, op. cit., see "Assessment of Conditions in Central America," Hearings before the Subcommittee on Inter-American Affairs of the Committee on Foreign Affairs, House of Representatives, Ninety-Sixth Congress, Second Session, April 29 and May 20, 1980; also the full page New York Times appeal by U.S. Congressmen to President Jimmy Carter urging him to not allow "another Cuba" in Nicaragua at the time Anastasio Somoza was under siege by the Sandinistas, New York Times (June 18, 1979).

9. New York Times (March 19, 1981). Secretary of State Alexander Haig's observations were in testimony before the House Foreign Affairs Committee on March 18th.

10. Leiken, op. cit., p. 101.

11. See Joseph C. Harsch, "U.S., U.S.S.R. Agitated About Tiny, Troublesome Neighbors," Christian Science Monitor (February 20, 1981). On the Cuban-Venezuelan rift over the Venezuelan government's acquittal of four people accused of dynamiting a Cuban plane which killed 73, see Paris Radio Broadcast, October 1, 1980, Foreign Broadcast Information Service (FBIS).

12. Mr. Seaga, moreover, resolved to wage a struggle against communism in the Caribbean region to prevent it from becoming under "Soviet influence." See Caribbean Contact, Vol. 8, No. 8 (December 1980), pp. 8-9.

13. Conversation with James Nelson Goodsell, Latin American editor, Christian Science Monitor, March 18, 1981.

14. Alan Riding, "Reagan and Latin America," New York Times (February 13, 1981), p. A8. And as Fidel Castro acknowledged in his report to the Second Congress of the Communist Party on December 17, 1980, the economic plan of the First Congress had not been carried out in full. Castro cited the fall in sugar prices, worldwide inflation, and the deterioration in trade relations as causes for Cuba's problems. See Granma Weekly Review in English (December 28, 1980), p. 6.

15. See Dominguez, "The Armed Forces and Foreign Relations," op. cit., pp. 53-54; also Erisman, op. cit., p. 3.

16. See W. Raymond Duncan, "Nationalism in Cuban Politics" in Jaime Suchlicki (Ed.), Cuba, Castro and Revolution (Coral Gables: University of Miami Press, 1972), pp. 22-43; James D. Therberge, The Soviet Presence in Latin America (New York: Crane, Russak & Co., Inc., 1974); Leon Goure and Morris Rothenberg, Soviet Penetration of Latin America (Coral Gables: Center for Advanced International Affairs, 1975); Dominguez, op. cit.; and Gonzalez, op. cit.

17. Duncan, "Nationalism in Cuban Politics," op. cit.; also Duncan, "Problems of Cuban Foreign Policy" in Irving Louis Horowitz (Ed.), Cuban Communism (New Brunswick, N.J.: Transaction Books, 1977), p. 45.

18. On the importance of the Caribbean and Central America as lying in America's "strategic rear," see V. Vasilyev, "The United States 'New Approach' to Latin America," International Affairs (June 1971), p. 43;

and S. Mishin, "Latin America: Current Trends of Development," International Affairs (May 1975), pp. 54-55. It should be noted that Cuba's primary role in Latin America and the Caribbean as the leader and catalyst of "profound progressive changes" is frequently cited in radio broadcasts and other Soviet media. See, for example, V. Yakubov, "Behind the Screen of the 'New Approach' (of the United States - W.R.D.)", Moscow Pravda, March 7, 1978 (FBIS).

19. Consider that Moscow extended many types of economic help to Cuba after 1960, including direct subsidies for Havana's trade deficits with Moscow, payment for Cuban sugar above the prevailing world market price, lowered prices for Soviet petroleum products, supplies of military equipment, and direct credits for economic development. By the late 1970s, Soviet aid to Cuba had risen from an estimated $3 million per day during the 1960s to approximately $9 million per day. See Jorge Dominguez, "Cuban Foreign Policy," Foreign Affairs, Vol, 57, No. 1 (Fall 1978), p. 90. A new trade agreement with the Soviet Union for the 1981-1986 period called for a 50 percent increase in trade to $8 billion per year according to Havana Radio Broadcast, October 30, 1980.

20. Edward Gonzalez offers a penetrating analysis of the distinct interpretations of Cuban foreign policy in his "Complexities of Cuban Foreign Policy," Problems of Communism, Vol. 26 (November-December 1977), pp. 1-15. See also Jiri Valenta, "The Soviet-Cuban Alliance in Africa and the Caribbean," The World Today (February 1981), pp. 45-53; and A.M. Kapcia, "Cuba's African Involvement: A New Perspective," Survey (London), Vol. 24, Nos. 106-109 (1979), pp. 142-159.

21. On Cuba as a surrogate of the U.S.S.R., see Strategic Survey 1978 (London: International Institute for Strategic Studies, 1979), pp. 1-2, 44.

22. Gonzalez, "Complexities of Cuban Foreign Policy," op. cit.; also Gregory F. Treverton, "Cuba After Angola," The World Today, Vol. 33, No. 1 (January 1977), pp. 17-27; and Kapcia, op. cit.

23. Testimony of Randolph Pherson, Analyst, Office of Political Analysis, National Foreign Assessment Center, Central Intelligence Agency, before the House Committee on Foreign Affairs, Sub-committee on Inter-American Affairs, Impact of Cuban-Soviet Ties in the Western Hemisphere, op. cit., p. 46. The Cuban

teachers in Nicaragua began to return home in July 1980, but new groups returned to Nicaragua in September 1980. See Managua Radio Broadcast, July 1, 1980; and Havana Radio Broadcast, September 18, 1980.

24. Frechette, op. cit., p. 2.

25. W. Raymond Duncan, "Caribbean Leftism," Problems of Communism (May-June 1978), pp. 55-56; and testimony of Martin J. Scheina, Analyst for Cuban Affairs, Defense Intelligence Agency, Impact of Cuban-Soviet Ties in the Western Hemisphere, op. cit., p. 13.

26. St. George Radio Broadcast, September 3, 1980.

27. Szulc, op. cit., p. 36.

28. See H. Michael Erisman, "Cuba's Struggle for Third World Leadership," Caribbean Review (Summer 1979), pp. 8-12. See also Granma (September 16, 1979), p. 16.

29. Cubans made up two-thirds of the 51,000 Communist military advisers, instructors, technical personnel, and troops posted in the Third World by 1979. See Central Intelligence Agency, National Foreign Assessment Center, Communist Aid Activities in Non-Communist Less Developed Countries, 1979 and 1954-1979, p. 1.

30. Scheina testimony, op. cit., p. 12. See also testimony by Lt. Col. Rafael E. Martinez-Boucher, Chief, Latin American Branch, Defense Intelligence Agency, Impact of Cuban-Soviet Ties in the Western Hemisphere, op. cit., p. 28.

31. Ibid., p. 29.

32. Ibid., p. 37.

33. United States Department of State, Communist Interference in El Salvador, Special Report No. 80 (February 28, 1981), Bureau of Public Affairs, 8 pgs.

34. Ibid. As to agreement by other Latin American governments, this conclusion is based upon the observations of James Nelson Goodsell, Latin American editor, Christian Science Monitor, conversation, March 18, 1981. The Wall Street Journal and Washington Post later criticized the State Department Report, but the State Department argued that their

articles were "inaccurate". See Department of State Response (June 17, 1981); and Christian Science Monitor (June 25, 1981), p. 5.

35. See Duncan, "Caribbean Leftism," op. cit.

36. On the earlier conflict, see D. Bruce Jackson, Castro, the Kremlin, and Communism in Latin America (Baltimore: Johns Hopkins Press, 1969).

37. See Duncan, Soviet Policy in Developing Countries (Waltham, Massachusetts: Ginn-Blaisdell, 1970), Introduction.

38. See Soviet Policy and the United States Response in the Third World, a Report prepared for the Committee on Foreign Affairs, U.S. House of Representatives, by the Congressional Research Service, Library of Congress (Washington: U.S. Government Printing Office, March 1981), Chapter Two.

39. Communist Aid Activities in Non-Communist Less-Developed Countries, 1979 and 1954-79, op. cit., p. 15.

40. Ibid.

41. Scheina testimony, op. cit., p. 12.

42. Ibid., p. 12. Other observers debate this point. See testimony by William M. LeoGrande, Impact of Cuban-Soviet Ties in the Western Hemisphere, op. cit., p. 105 where LeoGrande states that the Cuban support for the Sandinistas was truly of marginal consequence in the outcome of that insurrection.

43. United States Department of State White Paper, p. 2. See also Robert S. Leiken, "Eastern Winds in Latin America," Foreign Policy, No. 4 (Spring 1981), p. 100.

44. Communist Aid Activities, 1979, op. cit., p. 39.

45. Ibid., p. 21.

46. Ibid.

47. Soviet Policy and United States Response in the Third World, op. cit., pp. 124-125.

48. The pattern of unsuccessful Soviet attempts to be influential over the years, which suggests the possibility of potential similar outcomes in Cuba's expanded military interventionist presence in the Caribbean and Central America, is reflected in a number of Soviet-Third World cases (e.g., Indonesia, Ghana, Algeria, Mali, Sudan, and Egypt). The reasons for these failures are many: inability of the U.S.S.R. to supply sufficient technical and organizational assistance; heavy-handed meddling in the domestic affairs of host countries; and disillusionment with the Soviet model of economic development. See Alvin Z. Rubinstein (Ed.), Soviet and Chinese Influence in the Third World (New York: Praeger Publishers, 1975); also Soviet Policy and United States Response in the Third World, op. cit., pp. 126 ff; and Duncan, Soviet Policy in Developing Countries (1981), op. cit., Introduction.

49. See H. Michael Erisman, "Cuban Internationalism: The Impact of Nonaligned Leadership and Afghanistan," op. cit., p. 28.

50. On the "natural ally" thesis, see Erisman, ibid., pp. 41-42. Also Rozita Levi, "Cuba and The Nonaligned Movement" in Blasier and Mesa-Lago, op. cit., p. 149.

51. Ibid., p. 35.

52. Ibid., pp. 29 ff.

53. Ibid.

54. Alan Riding, "Latin Neighbors Reconsider Policy Following Failure of Offensive," New York Times (February 16, 1981), p. 1.

55. Colombia, for example, suspended relations with Cuba in March 1981 and the Colombian president, Julio Cesar Turbay Ayala, stated that Cuba is widening "the geographical orbit" of its "offensive" beyond Central America and the Caribbean by training guerrillas to be used against the Colombian government. See James Nelson Goodsell, Christian Science Monitor (March 25, 1981), p. 3.

56. See James Nelson Goodsell, Christian Science Monitor (January 21, 1981), p. 4.

57. Roger D. Hansen, Beyond the North-South Stalemate (New York: McGraw-Hill Book Co., 1979), pp. 5-7.

58. See Theodore Shabad, "Russia Faces an Energy Shortage," New York Times (February 22, 1981), p. 8F.

59. Use of Cuban manpower in the Angolan conflict produced discontent among some economic decision makers at home who, in the words of one student, obstructed "the withdrawal of personnel from their production tasks. This was the first time the government has acknowledged substantial elite civilian unwillingness to contribute to military activities." See Jorge Dominguez, "The Armed Forces and Foreign Relations," op. cit., p. 63.

60. For an excellent analysis of "dependency" perceptions, see Richard R. Fagen, "A Funny Thing Happened on the Way to the Market: Thoughts on Extending Dependency Ideas," International Organization, Vol. 32, No. 1 (Winter 1978), pp. 287-300.

61. Christian Science Monitor (July 23, 1981), p. 9.

62. See International Monetary Fund, International Statistics (Washington, D.C.: June 1978).

63. See World Development Report, 1979 published for the World Bank by Oxford University Press (Washington, D.C.: 1980), pp. 126-127.

64. Ibid., pp. 164-165.

65. Ibid., pp. 170-171.

66. See Fidel Castro's main report to the 2nd Congress of the Communist Party of Cuba, December 17, 1980, Granma Weekly Review (December 28, 1980), pp. 6-16. Cuba's agricultural sector was especially hard hit during the 1976-1980 period by the fall in sugar prices, mildew in the sugarcane industry, blue mold blight in the tobacco harvest, and African swine fever in the hog industry. See ibid., p. 6.

67. See Latin American Weekly Report (February 20, 1981), pp. 9-10; also Carmelo Mesa-Lago, "The Economy and International Economic Relations" in Blasier and Mesa-Lago, op. cit., pp. 179-191.

68. The Mexican energy agreement calls for broad assistance to Cuba in oil and gas exploration, refinery construction, acquisition of oil equipment, sale of propane gas, and training of petroleum workers.

69. Mexico, for example, signed an agreement in April 1981 to supply Nicaragua with 25,000 tons of sugar a year and to import manufactured goods from Nicaragua and other Central American republics at preferential rates. In addition, Mexico has extended very favorable terms to Nicaragua for Mexican oil purchases, apparently feeling that not squeezing Nicaragua is the best way to prevent another Cuba. See Latin American Weekly Review (April 10, 1981), p. 4; and Daniel Southerland, Christian Science Monitor (April 3, 1981), p. 1; also Managua Radio Broadcast, July 1, 1980 (FBIS). One-half of Nicaragua's oil needs will be met by Mexico; the other half by Venezuela.

70. Lt. Col. Rafael E. Marrinez-Boucher, Chief, Latin American Branch, Defense Intelligence Agency, testified that, "The Salvadorans have made it abundantly clear that they neither seek nor will accept any leadership other than their own." See Impact of Cuban-Soviet Ties in the Western Hemisphere, op. cit., p. 29.

71. W. Raymond Duncan, Latin American Politics: A Developmental Approach (New York: Praeger Publishers, 1976), Chapters 2, 5 & 6. See also Ronald C. Newton, "On 'Functional Groups,' 'Fragmentation,' and 'Pluralism' in Spanish American Political Society," Hispanic American Historical Review, Vol. 50, No. 1 (February 1970), pp. 1-29; also Viron P. Vaky, "Hemispheric Relations: 'Everything is Part of Everything Else,'" Foreign Affairs issue of America and the World 1980, Vol. 59, No. 3 (1981), pp. 618-625; and Russell H. Fitzgibbon & Julio A. Fernandez, Latin America: Political Culture and Development (Englewood Cliffs, N.J.: Prentice-Hall, Inc., 1981), Chapters 1, 3, & 6.

72. Leiken, op. cit., p. 103.

73. Ibid.; see also Viron P. Vaky, op. cit., pp. 620-622.

74. Leiken, op. cit., p. 101.

75. Ibid., p. 108.

76. Paris Radio Broadcast, July 12, 1980 (FBIS).

77. Paris Radio Broadcast, October 1, 1980 (FBIS).

78. Buenos Aires Radio Broadcast, October 9, 1980 (FBIS).

79. Managua Radio Broadcast, August 4, 1981. The Soviet Union also donated $16 million to the Nicaraguan Agricultural Development and Agrarian Reform Industry, although the precise terms of the "donation" were not made clear. Managua Radio Broadcast, August 15, 1981.

80. Nicaragua's Minister of the International Reconstruction Fund, Haroldo Montealegre, reported in July 1981 that his country had received $1.23 billion in loans and donations since July 1979. Of this amount the U.S. had contributed 14 percent; Latin America (Mexico, Panama, and Venezuela), 20 percent; Western Europe, 34 percent; and the United Nations 13 percent with lesser amounts coming from elsewhere. The socialist countries contributed 22 percent, of which Cuba's portion was 14 percent. Managua Radio Broadcast, July 15, 1981.

81. Leiken, op. cit.

82. See Robert Legvold, "The U.S.S.R. and the World Economy: The Political Dimension," in The Soviet Union and the World Economy, paper prepared by the Council on Foreign Relations, September 1979; see also Elizabeth Kridl Valkenier, "The U.S.S.R., the Third World, and the Global Economy," Problems of Communism, Vol. 28 (July-August 1979), pp. 17-33.

83. By mid-1981 the United States had not developed a totally coherent policy for the Caribbean and Latin America, although the elements were beginning to fall into place. U.S. economic aid to El Salvador, for example, remained at more than three times its military aid and the Reagan administration recognized the need to work with other key regional actors, notably Canada, Mexico, and Venezuela. Economic problem solving had come into focus, with stress on increasing the region's productive capacity through foreign investment, increased trade, more tourism, and help from Europe, Japan and the international financial institutions. Yet Washington resisted being drawn into a global discussion of North-South developmental issues, as Mexico, Cuba, and many Caribbean countries wished, and was at odds with France and Mexico over their joint declaration in August 1981 recognizing El Salvador's guerrilla-led left wing opposition Democratic Revolutionary Front as "a representative political force." Secretary of State Alexander Haig, in contrast, characterized the Front as one of "straight terrorism." See the Christian Science Monitor, August 31, 1981.

4
Ideology and Oil: Venezuela in the Circum-Caribbean

John D. Martz

> "We want the Caribbean to be a zone of peace, to be off-limits to the hegemonic appetites that so often have taken the world to the brink of war. The Caribbean, as a zone of peace, must be a guarantee that the scandalous arming of interests alien to Latin American destiny will be confronted by a sturdily effective wall."
>
> President Luis Herrera Campins, Santo Domingo, October 7, 1980[1]

Appeals for regional peace and condemnations of military armaments are stock in trade for chiefs of state and, standing alone, often merit minimal attention. For a Venezuelan president standing on Dominican soil, however, the event is meaningful, underlining as it does the recent surge of attention and commitment to the Caribbean and the shores it washes. The potential impact of Venezuelan policy, moreover, has magnified suspicions over the intentions and objectives of Caracas. Indeed, President Herrera's predecessor had already been taxed by Trinidad-Tobago's Prime Minister Eric Williams with undertaking a "recolonization of the Caribbean."[2] Within the past decade, Venezuelan foreign policy has directed increasing attention to Caribbean affairs, projecting its political and ideological preferences through petroleum-based diplomacy. This in turn has constituted a characteristic manifestation of Venezuela's ascending foreign policy interests during its post-1958 era of democratic politics. Moreover, the turbulence which gripped Central America by the 1980s has encouraged an ever-stronger Venezuelan presence throughout the circum-Caribbean, the ramifications of which have become increasingly a subject for partisan debate inside the country. Efforts by the Reagan administration to elicit more direct and active participation from influential Latin American powers have further heightened both the magnitude and the relevance of Venezuelan foreign policy throughout the region.

THE EMERGENCE OF VENEZUELA'S CIRCUM-CARIBBEAN PRESENCE

Since the 1958 removal of Marcos Perez Jimenez and the initiation of elected civilian government, Venezuela has steadily and progressively augmented its role in hemispheric affairs. As I wrote previously, it was "the circumstantial confluence of several events, most importantly the massive rise of petroleum earnings, which provided the opportunity...[and] the emergence of Latin America's most vigorously competitive political system."[3] During the Betancourt administration (1959-1964) the ideological rivalry between Cuban socialism and Venezuelan democratic reformism as developmental models was acute, and the latter became an ardent advocate of democracy and civilian rule in opposition to authoritarianisms of Left and Right. Besieged by both Cuban-supported revolutionary violence and by destabilization efforts of the Dominican dictator Trujillo, Venezuela constructed its foreign policy on the cornerstone of the Betancourt Doctrine, which denied diplomatic recognition to unconstitutional regimes. As later enunciated by his successor and fellow member of Accion Democratica (AD), Raul Leoni, Venezuela chose to "maintain our principles, often alone, such as the repudiation of government by force and the usurpation of governments by violence."[4] This unequivocal commitment to the championing of democratic government has remained a hallmark of Venezuelan policy, both in the Caribbean and throughout Latin America.

With the subsequent administration of Rafael Caldera (1969-1974) for the rival Social Christian party COPEI, Venezuela moved to what was termed "ideological pluralism." As Caldera employed his considerable personal stature on behalf of ever-increasing Venezuelan influence, he insisted upon "the establishment of relations with countries of political organization and ideology different from ours, for their presence in the world and their influence on economic relations cannot be ignored."[5] Yet policy toward the circum-Caribbean was not primary, and Venezuela was more preoccupied with its perceptions of Brazilian expansionism and with policy in South

America. Given the perceived diminution of the threat from Cuba which had been so pronounced in the first half of the 1960s, Venezuela did not identify the region as one bearing high priority among its foreign policy objectives. This was to change with the return to power of Accion Democratica in 1974 under Carlos Andres Perez and with further alterations has continued under the present copeyano administration of Herrera Campins.

Perez entered office at the moment when Venezuelan oil prices had just quadrupled over a twelve-month period and thus enjoyed the economic wherewithal to support his tempermental proclivity toward a greater assumption of international responsibility. In the Caribbean he employed both subregional and bilateral approaches. Following up on Venezuela's 1973 entry into the Caribbean Development Bank (CDB) as its first non-English speaking member, he promptly paid the membership share allotment of $3 million, also granting a loan of $10 million to the Bank's Special Development Fund (SDF). In August 1975 the Fondo de Inversiones de Venezuela (JFIV) negotiated with the CDB a $25 million trust fund designed to enhance Caribbean integration and agroindustrial development. The Perez administration joined the new eighteen-nation Caribbean Tourism Association in 1974 and through its Banco Industrial de Venezuela (BIV) extended a loan of $5 million that same year to bail out the bankrupt regional airline LIAT Ltd., which provided service to the smaller members of the Caribbean Community and Common Market (CARICOM).[6]

A series of bilateral agreements further augmented the Venezuelan presence, as well as arousing Caribbean apprehension over possible hegemonic ambitions in Caracas. Perhaps most notable were the discussions with Jamaica, whose Prime Minister Michael Manley enjoyed a warm friendship with President Perez. During an April 1975 visit to Caracas Manley solicited Venezuelan and Mexican participation in a projected aluminum smelter in Jamaica, accompanied by an agreement to sell specified quantities of aluminum and bauxite annually for a decade. Perez pledged the sale of petroleum under cash-loan terms such as already granted to Central America, reducing payment to half the international price with the remainder to be reinvested locally for developmental purposes. Perez and Manley also agreed to increased cultural, scientific, and technical exchanges and a joint declaration called for closer Caribbean cooperation with Venezuela.

Among the biproducts of these negotiations was vocal opposition from Eric Williams, who feared the smelter project would jeopardize existing plans for a CARICOM aluminum plant. He thereby withdrew Trinidad-Tobago's support for the latter, additionally charging that Venezuela was dragging its feet in talks over the perennially disputed fishing rights in the Gulf of Paria contiguous to the two countries. Such criticisms of the Venezuelan role under Perez were not publicly shared by other Caribbean leaders, several of whom had themselves drawn closer to Caracas. Thus Barbados had secured cash-loan terms for the purchase of Venezuelan oil and financial assistance of various types was promised to Grenada's Eric Gairy, Robert Bradshaw of St. Kitts-Nevis, and Antigua's George Walter.

In the Spanish-speaking countries the Venezuelan presence was initially more problematic. President Joaquin Balaguer of the Dominican Republic alleged at a meeting of the Inter-American Development Bank that Venezuela was intruding unjustifiably into the affairs of its Caribbean neighbors. This, however, reflected both an initial reluctance by Venezuela to include the Dominicans among those enjoying cash-loan terms for the purchase of oil and most particularly the undisguised sympathy of Carlos Andres Perez and the ruling Accion Democratica for the Partido Revolucionario Dominicano (PRD) and its leader Antonio Guzman. When President Balaguer was defeated in his bid for a fourth term in summer 1978, Perez was among the most vocal in publicly denouncing the abortive efforts by security forces to annul the results and continue Balaguer in power. Even today there is resentment on the part of the Balaguer forces for what they view as unwarranted intervention, while those who benefitted have upheld the Venezuelan posture as consistent with its commitment to democracy and the sanctity of the ballot.

With the Cuban case, attitudes had gradually softened in the wake of the collapse of armed rebellion in Venezuela and the gradual extension of amnesty by both the Leoni and Caldera governments. While Perez as Betancourt's Minister of Interior had once been a fierce critic of Fidel Castro, he took the initiative in 1974 to restore diplomatic relations. Expressing views more similar to Caldera than to his former mentor Betancourt, Perez argued that Venezuela "must accept ideological differences if we are to join together in the common quest for independent decision-making. And by helping to solve political problems in Latin America, we also create conditions in which democracy may become the system of government all over Latin America."[7] In keeping with his hemispheric ambitions, Perez led the drive for the reincorporation of Cuba into the American family of nations. When Venezuela failed to secure a lifting of OAS sanctions against Cuba at the November 1974 consultative meeting of foreign ministers in Quito, the foreign minister was discredited and soon replaced. In July of 1975 Venezuelan influence was important in a vote by foreign ministers meeting in Costa Rica to leave OAS members free to treat the Havana regime as they preferred.

An historically ironic exchange of <u>abrazos</u> between Perez and Castro in either Caracas or Havana, which many anticipated, was rendered academic in early 1976 with the news of Cuban military activity in Angola. The fact that Cuban troops had been ferried to Africa through Guyana, with whom Venezuela was disputing their mutual border, further soured the relationship. Perez took the lead in cancelling the projected sesquicentennial celebration of the 1826 Congress of Panama, at which Castro was to meet with other chiefs of state. The cooling of ties was encouraged by the politically powerful colony of Cubans in Caracas, whose sentiments were illustrated by the machine-gunning of the embassy from a passing vehicle. In short, the empathy toward Cuba which marked the early years of the Perez government had diminished substantially when he left office in March 1979.

By that time, Venezuela under Perez had also moved more actively into Central American affairs. The President, while publicly praised as "my number one adviser on Latin America" by Jimmy Carter, had evolved a close friendship with the late Omar Torrijos of Panama, playing a strong role in helping to guide US-Panamanian negotiations over the Canal. Similarly, the Perez administration openly encouraged the Sandinista-led struggle against the Somoza dynasty in Nicaragua, funnelling small arms through Panama to the insurgents and hailing their virtues in the battle against the long-enduring Somoza dictatorship in Managua. As noted later, Perez after leaving office remained a vocal enthusiast for the new revolutionary government in Nicaragua and, as civil war spread in El Salvador, also denounced that country's government and espoused the cause of the Frente Democratico Revolucionario (FDR) in that conflict.

THE SOCIAL CHRISTIANS IN POWER

In December of 1978 for the third consecutive time, the government party was voted out of office.[8] Luis Herrera Campins defeated AD candidate Luis Piñerua by a margin of 46-43 percent and during the campaign, like his opponent, had promised to reduce the <u>carlosandresista</u> concentration on foreign affairs. Citing the primacy of domestic problems, Herrera suggested that Venezuela's hemispheric profile would be lowered. In practice, however, he has proved only slightly less peripatetic than his predecessor, travelling abroad frequently while entertaining a succession of foreign dignitaries in Caracas. As detailed later, he has combined the continuing emphasis on democratic values and traditions with a vigorous drive to promote Christian Democratic interests. This has been manifested throughout the Caribbean and Central America; thus it is important to recall the ideological tenets of the current President and of COPEI toward international affairs.

Rafael Caldera, both founder of the party and the leading intellectual spokesman of Christian Democratic thought in the hemisphere, had first conceived of International Social Justice as a logical extension of previous theorizing.[9] Both internationally and domestically, as he put it,

> There is a social justice which obligates the stronger with regard to the weaker; it demands from the richer an obligation with regard to the poorer; it demands duties which can neither be figured by machines nor the mathematics of communitive justice. There is a social justice which establishes inequality of duties to reestablish fundamental equality among men; that social justice, which exists in the name of human solidarity, imposes whatever is necessary for the common good.[10]

Such was the basis for the "ideological pluralism" of the Caldera foreign policy. It has been reflected also in the views of COPEI's unsuccessful 1973 candidate, Lorenzo Fernandez,[11] and was echoed by Herrera as well. While sharing COPEI's gradual shift to the political center under the impetus of papal encyclicals and progressive European theoretical currents, Herrera himself had spent years as a principal party representative to both international and Latin American Christian Democratic congresses.[12] This had notably included service as secretary general of the Organizacion Democrata Cristiana de America (ODCA). Personally acquainted with many leaders of the movement and familiar with their political problems and circumstances, Herrera has been a conscious and conscientious supporter of such sister hemispheric movements.

At the time of Herrera's inauguration in March 1979, the role of hemispheric Christian Democracy, with Venezuela a leading spokesman, appeared on the rise. The recent election of Rodrigo Carazo Odio as Costa Rican president had been strongly supported by Christian Democracy; with the July collapse of Somoza, Christian Democratic forces sought their place within the new revolutionary government; in August a new civilian government in Ecuador included as vice-president the Christian Democratic intellectual Osvaldo Hurtado; and Peru's Partido Popular Cristiano (PPC) entered the new ruling coalition of Fernando Belaunde Terry in Lima. For Venezuela, the time appeared favorable for yet greater activism in the circum-Caribbean. Inspired in no small measure by the intellectual tutelage of Aristides Calvani, formerly Caldera's foreign minister, the Herrera government sought the leadership of anti-communist forces in the region while stimulating democratic regimes in which Christian Democrats might be influential.

In Nicaragua, where the Sandinistas had enjoyed both official encouragement and clandestine arms support from the Perez administration, Herrera worked to enhance the political role of Christian Democrats. He continued the economic assistance initiated by Carlos Andres Perez, which soon totalled $120 million. In due course, however, continuation of aid was implicitly conditioned on Nicaraguan acceptance of Christian Democratic leaders into the highest governmental circles. With the gradual solidification of Sandinista leaders and the marginalization of Christian Democrats, the herrerista enthusiasm waned. By the close of 1981, Venezuela had become deeply apprehensive over Nicaragua's apparent shift toward Cuba and the flow of aid was consciously diminished. While official attitudes towards Nicaragua thus cooled rapidly, Christian Democratic allegiances produced a strong commitment to the government of El Salvador.

When the struggling provisional junta was reorganized cosmetically in December 1980 with the

Christian Democrats' Jose Napoleon Duarte named civilian president, Duarte's old friend and associate in Caracas--where Duarte passed the 1972-1979 years in exile--promptly reinvigorated Venezuelan assistance. An estimated $20 million was swiftly dispatched to the floundering regime and in January 1981 agreement for a renewed loan of $31 million was extended through Venezuela's Central Bank. Charges by government critics that Venezuelan military aid, advisers, and National Guardsmen were also being sent to El Salvador were hotly denied and constituted undocumented attacks from Venezuelan leftists. At the same time, repeated "private" flights to San Salvador by Aristides Calvani--explained by reason of Calvani's position as secretary general of ODCA, of which Duarte was president--did little to diminish the obvious Venezuelan interest.

As Calvani himself told interviewers, "If a Marxist regime installs itself in El Salvador, it will represent a profound unbalance in the area. It is most important for international Marxism to triumph in El Salvador, because it permits them to establish the beginning of a bridge. They intend to have a Marxist government in Nicaragua, too."[13] While this perspective clearly mirrors the herrerista perception of Salvadoran affairs, COPEI itself has been far from united on the policy. There are doubts as to the political viability of the junta and especially of Duarte's survival as junta president. Moreover, party divisions stimulated by President Herrera's opposition to Rafael Caldera's bid for a second presidential term beginning in 1984 have further contributed to internal dissent. Nonetheless, the broad herrerista orientation towards the circum-Caribbean dictates a continuing presence in El Salvador. For the Venezuelan government the opportunity for regional leadership, etched by policy lines easily distinguishable from those of Carlos Andres Perez in Central America, suggests the desirability of such expanded commitments and economic assistance programs.

Oil has continued to provide an important political and diplomatic tool, as Perez had found earlier. In 1975 an agreement had included Central America and Panama as beneficiaries of a cash-loan arrangement whereby payment at much reduced prices would permit the recipients to finance their own development projects with loans from the unencumbered funds. Before Perez left office both Jamaica and the Dominican Republic had also been included. Under Herrera, Venezuela further increased its economic support, extending the terms and conditions of various and diverse commitments. Despite a distinctly unenthusiastic view of the Manley government in Jamaica, which Perez had warmly embraced, the copeyano government in mid-1980 extended a $10 million line of credit for the purchase of food, fertilizer, and agricultural equipment. By that date an estimated $100 million had been provided to Jamaica. With the November 1980 electoral victory of Edward Seaga, the Herrera government promptly sent advisors to Kingston to discuss Jamaican needs and Seaga gratefully acknowledged that emergency shipments of Venezuelan rice had immeasurably aided thousands of destitute Jamaicans.

Meanwhile, the Venezuelan-Mexican friendship which had blossomed between Presidents Perez and Echeverria--including their central role in the creation of the Sistema Economica Latinoamericana (SELA)--was further elaborated by Herrera and Mexico's Jose Lopez Portillo. On August 3, 1980 the two nations signed an agreement in San Jose, Costa Rica whereby they would jointly supply petroleum at preferential prices for several Central American and Caribbean countries. Venezuela and Mexico collectively promised up to 160,000 barrels per day; credits would be granted equal to 30 percent of the cost of oil purchases for a five-year period at 4 percent interest annually. If a recipient could demonstrate the use of the loan for internal energy development, the repayment period would be stretched over twenty years with the interest rates halved to 2 percent.[14] The accord, while bestowing international prestige on Venezuela and Mexico, also promised measurable assistance to the recipients who, even in the event of sharp price increases, would be favored by such easy loans, by the security of supply, and by modest shipping costs.

By the close of 1981, the agreement had been extended to Costa Rica, Nicaragua, Honduras, El Salvador, Guatemala, Panama, Barbados, Jamaica, Haiti, and the Dominican Republic, with Belize soon to follow. Trinidad-Tobago had received a similiar offer, to which Eric Williams had not responded when he died in March 1981. Given longstanding problems between Trinidad and Venezuela, the new government of George Chambers may opt to remain outside terms of the accord. In the meantime, plans were afoot to cope with technical complications attendant upon the agreeement. Construction of a new refinery in Costa Rica or Panama, to be owned jointly by all participating countries, would aid in the processing of oil appropriate to the needs and facilities of the recipients. And in January 1981 the Dominican government agreed to equal quantities from both Venezuela and Mexico, but with 14,000 barrels per day of Venezuelan crude to be reconstituted so that it then might be mixed with the lighter Mexican oil in order to be processed in the Dominican refinery.

This adjustment whereby Venezuela reduced its daily consignments to the Dominican Republic by 50 percent had followed on the heels of President Herrera's historic October 1980 visit to Santo Domingo to formalize the Venezuelan-Mexican program of oil pricing. Even at the outset, it was expected to save the Dominican Republic approximately $100 million for 1981 alone. During the same trip, Herrera and President Antonio Guzman also proclaimed their desire to broaden economic, financial, commercial, and cultural cooperation.[15] Notwithstanding the presumed displeasure of Guzman, Herrera and his advisors also paid a courtesy call of fraternity to national Christian Democratic leaders. Be that as it may, by 1981 Venezuelan assistance to the Dominican Republic included some $64 million for a hydroelectric project and subsidiary housing along with $2.3 million for an alcohol distillery. Aid for agricultural services were also negotiated. Meanwhile, Venezuelan interests were sometimes being enhanced by initiatives from the private sector. Since September 1980, for example, the privately financed Comarvenca Shipping Corporation has operated four ships on four separate Caribbean routes. With a capacity of 600 to 1200 tons each--ideal for the Caribbean market--ports in Haiti, the Dominican Republic, Jamaica, Trinidad, Puerto Rico, the Virgin Islands, and St. Lucia are visited every fifteen days. The Venezuelan Exporters Association (AVEX) operates the service and is developing new agreements for the creation of local distribution centers.

Fundamentally, however, it has been the government which has stood at the center of efforts to extend the Venezuelan presence, with bilateral diplomacy retaining high priority. To cite a few illustrations, the Bishop government in Grenada was supplied a new radio beacon for its airport; an asphalt plant in tiny St. Lucia was financed by $400,000 from Venezuela; talks with the Netherlands Antilles opened mutual exploration of the latter's energy needs; and in August 1980 Venezuelan representatives flew to the Bahamas to lay the groundwork for the establishment of diplomatic relations between the two. Then in March 1981 Barbados' Prime Minister Tom Adams visited Caracas, stressing the need for a Caribbean community free from foreign influence. Luis Herrera Campins, ignoring the possible inclusion of Venezuela as a potential source of such penetration from the outside, responded with a call for "ideological pluralism and self-determination" for the region. Even the recent high-level review of administration foreign policy--discussed below--holds little likelihood of any significant reduction in such Venezuelan approaches to the islands of the Caribbean.

While the Herrera government has thus continued to promote its role in Central America and the Caribbean, the Cuban connection has deteriorated gravely. Although having already cooled in the latter years of the Perez government, that president had sought a stabilization and regularization of relations. Cuban exiles carrying Venezuelan passports had been implicated in the October 1976 sabotage of a Cuban airliner which crashed off Barbados at the cost of 73 lives. Perez sent Castro a sympathetic message of regret and four men suspected of involvement were jailed in Venezuela soon after. The disposition of the case later became a major source of friction between the Herrera administration and Havana. In fact, the increasingly ardent anti-Marxist thrust of Herrera's policies in Central America and the Caribbean has been an ideological factor of considerable significance in the worsening of relations between Caracas and Havana.

Simmering mistrust and mutual suspicion flared dramatically in early 1980 over the status and treatment of disenchanted Cubans who had gained refuge in several Latin American embassies in Havana, including the Venezuelan. Cuba pronounced such persons to be common criminals lacking the right to seek diplomatic asylum. Venezuelan authorities considered them political dissidents and thereby eligible for guarantees of safe conduct off the island. As the conflict deepened, the Venezuelan embassy was among the most active in attending to the needs of the erstwhile exiles and seeking to obtain their safe departure from Cuba. In April of 1980 both Caracas and Havana called home their respective ambassadors. The following months saw Cuba launch a series of verbal attacks on the Herrera government, especially condemning the latter's support of the Salvadoran junta. It charged that the COPEI administration was engaged in untoward intervention in Central America, working in conjuction with North Americans as a surrogate for Washington's policies.

Relations approached their nadir in late September when a Venezuelan military tribunal voted to acquit the four men charged with complicity in the 1976 attack on the Cuban airliner. Fidel Castro publicly accused the Herrera government of ordering the absolution of the four men, attacking it as sharing responsibility for the "monstrous crime." Cuban diplomatic personnel were withdrawn as Venezuelan authorities surrounded and mounted barricades about embassy grounds--as Cuba had already done with the Venezuelan embassy in Havana. President Herrera retorted that the Cuban government, for two decades the perpetrator of a police state, was incapable of comprehending a system based upon laws and due process. He rejected the charge that executive directives to the military court had been issued or that any diplomatic provocation had been planned. From the Casa Amarilla came a communique in which the Foreign Ministry insisted,

> The government of Venezuela has observed with serene responsibility the aggressive and defiant conduct of the Cuban government. The Government of Venezuela has limited its replies to those indispensable to the demands of national dignity, an attitude which does not correspond to that of Cuba.[16]

Contrary to expectations, this renewal of verbal hostilities did not lead the two countries shortly to a formal break in diplomatic relations. The former was reluctant to take such action while twenty-one Cuban refugees remained housed in its embassy and the ambassador's residence in Havana. Cuba apparently concluded that the moment was not yet propitious for a total rupture. Yet the mutual antagonism was severe. In mid-October Venezuela had permitted the convening of 300 anti-Castro exiles headed by Huber Matos for a congress in Caracas. The gathering adopted a ten-point plan to promote "the subjective and objective conditions for an uprising" against the Castro government, with an office to be opened in Venezuela.[17] Officials of COPEI were in attendance at the meeting. Moreover, the head of the advisory committee on foreign policy, copeyano deputy Jose Rodriguez Iturbe, noted that a diplomatic break would imply the cessation of Venezuelan oil shipments to Cuba. And COPEI Secretary General Eduardo Fernandez, a confidante of Rafael Caldera, told newsmen that Cuba was using the dispute to distract attention from domestic difficulties. In response, Cuban officials periodically issue new attacks on the Herrera government, frequently from the pages of Granma. There seems little if any possibility of rapprochement during the life of the Herrera government, given the mutual aggravation of the relationship and the prevailing ideological abyss between Caracas and Havana.

By the summer of 1981, prodded by the hostility toward Cuba and a rising preoccupation with marxist encouragement of Central American insurgencies, the Herrera government underwent a reexamination of its foreign policy. COPEI's own reassessment had been initiated earlier in the year with the party urging upon the President an increasingly hard line, especially in the cases of Nicaragua and El Salvador. There was growing skepticism that events in the former might be influenced in favor of democratic pluralism; with the latter, misgivings over the role and power of Duarte were blended with heightening alarm over the rising death toll and the apparent durability of anti-junta revolutionary forces. Foreign Minister Jose Alberto Zambrano Velasco spoke publicy of the need for a "new global strategy for Latin America" consistent with the desire to maintain a sharp profile in international affairs.

While the Christian Democratic preoccupation with the circum-Caribbean had not diminished, the foreign ministry envisaged a greater involvement and heavier diplomatic interchange with other Latin American countries. By the close of the year both Herrera and Zambrano had paid separate visits to Mexico, Brazil, and Argentina, in every instance projecting a greater Venezuelan role in both regional and global affairs. The evident cordiality of ties with the new North American government lent a further coat of internationalist veneer to herrerismo. Yet the very preoccupation of the Reagan administration towards Central America and the Caribbean, in conjunction with Venezuelan concern over marxist activism, assured an enduringly high priority for the region. And notwithstanding sensitivity to partisan charges of serving merely as a surrogate for Yankee interests, the Herrera government remained basically consistent to the patterns outlined when it first took office.

POLICY INTERESTS

At least four intricately interrelated strands of interest are woven into the fabric of Venezuelan policy toward the Caribbean: (a) the ideological; (b) the geopolitical; (c) the economic; and (d) the domestic partisan. While none exist in isolation from the others, analytic clarity suggests the value of treating them individually. At the broadest level of generality, none is more crucial than the ideological, which in the Venezuelan context reflects the country's role as a defender and proponent of democracy, electoral competition, constitutionality, and civilian rule. It is a theme writ large in the post-1958 experience and one that is shared by the national political leadership, most importantly the *copeyanos* and *adecos*. Even the multitude of small leftist parties pay at least lip service to democratic procedures and values, while public opinion is unequivocal. For notwithstanding negativism toward professional politicians and government officials, Venezuelans have clearly demonstrated their preference for elected government and the expression of political choice in selecting and periodically renewing the leadership.[18]

When party leaders returned from years of exile in 1958, they had concurred on the necessity of building a democratic system resistant to pressures from all forms of authoritarianism. They negotiated the Pact of Punto Fijo, whereby a multiparty coalition government would be established following elections, with compromise and conciliation stressed as a means of assuring the survival of the system. As the years have seen the growing hegemony of the AD and COPEI, a succession of governments has promoted democracy throughout the hemisphere. For Betancourt it included the struggle against both leftist and rightist extremes, typified by the Betancourt Doctrine which was continued by Leoni. Caldera's advocacy of "ideological pluralism," an important departure, was nonetheless so applied as to enhance Venezuela's continental democratic profile.

By the 1970s, Venezuela was among a very small number of democratic regimes, islands in a veritable sea of authoritarianism. While reasonably confident of the internal viability of their system, Venezuelan leaders looked askance at the prevalence of dictatorships in the hemisphere. At least one of the propelling forces behind the activism and high international visibility of Perez was that of encouraging democratic forces. It also fueled his drive to strengthen the ties among nations. Addressing a gathering of Latin American intellectuals on May 3, 1976, he insisted,

> The history of all our countries confirms and reaffirms the conclusion that we cannot develop or progress without uniting. The fortune of each and every one of us cannot be a matter of indifference to the others. The doctrine and action of the Government over which I preside is adjusted to these sincere convictions of solidarity, of integration,...strengthening the ties and links of the Latin American community.[19]

It was with a latent Bolivarian vision that he attempted further to project Venezuelan democracy outwardly, to restore Cuba's inter-American legitimacy, and to bring newly independent English-speaking Caribbean countries into hemispheric decision-making circles.

Both Perez and Herrera were especially sensitive to the implications for democracy of domestic political events elsewhere in Latin America. Both were frank in their distaste for Chile's military authoritarianism, kept their distance from Argentina, and sporadically demonstrated skepticism toward the alleged liberalization of the Brazilian regime. The succession of military <u>golpes</u> and counter-<u>golpes</u> in Bolivia have been criticized; and the restoration of elected governments in Ecuador and Peru were eulogized--President Herrera was among the guests at the August 1979 inauguration of the late Jaime Roldos Aguilera in Quito. Albeit less openly or flamboyantly, Herrera continued Perez' frequent consultations with the elected leaders of Colombia and Costa Rica. He also attended the commemoration in Riobamba of the 150th anniversary of the signing of Ecuador's first constitution. Joining the chiefs of state of Costa Rica, Panama, Colombia, and Ecuador, he signed the Carta de Conducta enshrining the observation of human rights and the consolidation of Latin American democracy.

On September 11, 1980 the signatories agreed on their mutual obligation to defend "human, political, economic, and social rights," adding that collective action on their behalf was not contrary to the principles of nonintervention. They reaffirmed a determination to support and encourage democracy and social justice and made clear their opposition to the July 17, 1980 Bolivian <u>golpe</u> against the democratic electoral process. In Herrera's view, "the despotism and the violence organized in portions of our continent where liberty had previously flamed, can only postpone sine die the democratic normalization of countries of humans...."[20] For so long as Venezuelan democracy endures, this abiding concern with democracy and individual freedoms will remain a cornerstone of its foreign relations. Whether manifested in friction with the Castro government, denunciation of conditions in Haiti, concern over the character of the regime in Grenada, or condemnation of an abortive military golpe in Santo Domingo, policy toward the states of the Caribbean remains ineluctably influenced by Venezuela's democratic vocation.

Concrete evidence of the pro-democratic, antimarxist ideological orientation has already been cited in the variegated forms of economic and military aid extended to Venezuela's neighbors. In terms of sheer foreign aid, a total of $5.8 billion had been provided from 1975 through 1979, some 80 percent of which was channelled through such multilateral lending agencies as the World Bank, the Inter-American Development Bank, the Caribbean Development Bank, and agencies of the Andean Pact. Herrera further elaborated upon the Perez commitments, providing $500 million in 1980 alone, and by the close of 1981 Venezuelan aid constituted some 3 percent of the nation's total output of goods and services. Despite the intermittent accusations of seeking hegemonic domination in the circum-Caribbean, the thrust of foreign policy priorities remained evident. As the influential Minister of Energy and Mines Humberto Calderon Berti put it, "We don't want to interfere in the internal affairs of these countries, but we hope that our help in solving their problems will contribute to democracy and stability."[21]

Running parallel to this ideological orientation is the perception of geopolitical national interests. Given the prevalence of authoritarian regimes to the south, accompanied by Caracas' uncertainty and doubts over the quality of its relations with Brazil, it is logical to look instead to the Caribbean and to Central America. As early as 1971, Foreign Minister Aristides Calvani of the Caldera administration told a North American scholar that Venezuelan activities in the Caribbean were intended in considerable part to offset growing Brazilian power and influence.[22] As that administration was projecting Venezuela into the region, Calvani's 1973 annual report to Congress was illustrative, in which he noted "resumption of our diplomatic relations with the Republic of Haiti; the Joint Declaration subscribed to by the minister of agriculture of Venezuela with the ministers of Dominica and Barbados; the visit to Barbados of a Venezuelan delegation to negotiate an agreement of technical cooperation in matters of housing and urbanization and, finally, the visit to Venezuela of a group of advisors and professionals of Trinidad and Tobago to exchange ideas about investments, tourism, education, and communication."[23]

Thus the movement toward the Caribbean initiated under Caldera and expanded by his successors provided a geopolitical outlet for influence and involvement which was not readily available to the south. It permitted an opportunity to counter marxist encroachments from Havana and even broadened the arena within which to compete as well as collaborate with Mexico. It also offered the promise of enlarged markets for Venezuelan products, which related to the third area of policy interest--the economic. There was obvious benefit to accrue from a diversification of customers for oil. Even before the January 1, 1976 nationalization of oil,[24] Venezuela had sought to extend and to broaden its clientele and the new state-affiliated Petroleos de Venezuela assigned high priority to the effort. Caribbean markets would minimize transportation costs while cash-loan arrangements and related transactions could be linked with other sectors of the Venezuelan economy.

Among other considerations, it was hoped that further openings to the Caribbean would encourage the traditionally conservative and cautious private sector in Venezuela to expand its activities. This indeed appears to be occurring, although less extensively than suggested by those who are criticizing Venezuelan imperialism. In such areas as construction, textiles, light industry, and to a degree technological transfer, the availability of greater Caribbean markets is viewed in Caracas as economically desirable. While much of the output of Venezuela's burgeoning heavy industry may find only limited demand in much of the Caribbean, its food processing sector and such petrochemical products as fertilizers and synthetics may well be marketable. In addition, without for a moment overstressing disinterested or charitable motivations, it is true that Venezuela is not unaware of the economic and political burdens entailed by international oil prices. Having failed thus far to prod its fellow OPEC members into creating a special fund and aid program for impoverished non-oil producers, Caracas can assuage its conscience and increase its influence through the cash-loan arrangements.

Finally, the impact of domestic interests and partisan politics cannot be discounted. The competition for power and perquisites has centered on COPEI and Accion Democratica for a decade and is unlikely to be challenged seriously by other parties in the near future. In terms of international outlook and external linkages, this translates into the broader competition between Christian Democracy and Social Democracy. COPEI stands as the hemisphere's leading Christian Democratic movement.[25] The Chileans and Eduardo Frei have been marginalized by General Pinochet and therefore it is to Venezuela that Latin American Christian Democracy looks for support and strength. Under President Herrera the effort has been not only to sustain an anti-marxist front in the Caribbean and Central America, but to give it the coloration of copeyano green. Aristides Calvani, the present ODCA secretary general, has not been bashful in urging the use of Venezuelan oil diplomacy to further the ideological movement and Herrera's trips in 1980 to Managua, San Jose, and Santo Domingo testified to that effort.

What seems implicit is a Venezuelan approach whereby oil-related assistance would be conditional for governments of an ideological outlook uncongenial with Christian Democracy. Contracts and commitments may be negotiated only for a short term, subject to periodic review and reassessment in Caracas.[26] Such an outlook has not only stirred animosity in some recipient countries, but has fanned the flames of opposition within Venezuela. While foreign affairs are frequently regarded in a nonpartisan fashion, the injection of Christian Democratic objectives has precipitated predictable criticism from the AD as well as domestic marxist organizations. An important element has been the concomitant charge that current Venezuelan policy toward El Salvador, Nicaragua, Jamaica, the Dominican Republic, and Cuba is perilously similar to that of the United States, stirring allegations that Herrera is serving as a virtual sword carrier for Washington in the region.

The advent of the Reagan administration in the United States has indirectly politicized even further the foreign policy of Venezuela's Christian Democratic government. Washington's hard line toward the Soviet Union, Cuba, and Nicaragua, combined with an inability or unwillingness to distinguish between marxist and non-marxist opponents of the status quo in Central America and the Caribbean, has inevitably implied Venezuelan collaboration. When Herrera sent his Interior Minister Rafael "Pepi" Montes de Oca to Washington soon after Reagan assumed power--a measure intended in part to add luster to the Minister as a potential alternative to another Caldera presidential candidacy--the congruence between Caracas and Washington was evident. When Secretary of State Alexander Haig subsequently met in July 1981 at Nassau with his counterparts from Venezuela, Mexico, and Canada, this became even more evident. North American plans for an ill-defined "mini-Marshall Plan" of economic assistance in the circum-Caribbean seemingly drew the two administrations even closer, although Venezuela joined with Mexico in insisting that political and ideological preconditions for potential recipients would be unacceptable. Negotiations for the sale of F-16 planes to Venezuela further emphasized the symbiotic character of the two nations' outlook towards the region.

However superficial the convergence of Venezuelan and North American policies toward an economic and political package for the region, it provoked further partisan disputation over foreign policy inside Venezuela. After two decades of relative accord, this growing divergence constitutes a significant departure from previous patterns. Aside from the more opportunistic and self-serving allegations of opponents that Herrera is serving United States interests, there are increasingly sharp divergences in perceptions of the circum-Caribbean. For the opposition Accion Democratica, long active in Social Democratic circles and internationalist by conviction, *copeyano* initiatives run counter to its own analysis of political events. Carlos Andres Perez remains sympathetic to the Sandinista government in Nicaragua and, when Herrera disapprovingly rejected an invitation to attend the July 19, 1980 anniversary celebration in Managua, received enthusiastic acclaim at his own appearance, fierily attacking potential imperialist intervention. Perez' friendship with Jamaica's Manley has already been mentioned and the AD position toward El Salvador criticized the junta which Herrera firmly supports. Representatives of Salvador's Frente Democratico Revolucionario (FDR) have been warmly received by AD leaders in Caracas.

The contradictions in domestic partisan views have also been underlined by the AD leadership among

Latin American members of the Socialist International. In the summer of 1979 its international conference was hosted in Venezuela, with the sessions chaired by AD party president Gonzalo Barrios. Romulo Betancourt himself appeared to cast his blessings. September of 1980 saw the Latin America/Caribbean branch of the Socialist International gather in Caracas to prepare an agenda for the forthcoming conference in Madrid. A communique was issued condemning the Bolivian golpe; attacking repression in Haiti, Paraguay, and Uruguay; and declaring solidarity for Manley's People's National Party (PNP). The Salvadoran junta was characterized as a military dictatorship supported by Christian Democrats and Perez, who chaired the conference, accused European governments of abetting the escalation of armed conflict in Latin America.[27]

As 1980 drew to a close, and in response largely to apprehension over the implications of the Reagan victory for future United States policy in the region, the Socialist International sponsored the creation of a committee for the defense of the Nicaraguan revolution, with Perez the Latin American member of a distinguished group of Social Democratic leaders and statesmen. All of this added to the partisan dissensus over foreign policy in Venezuela, promising a level and intensity of debate and conflict which has customarily been restricted to domestic affairs. Thus the dimension of partisan politics has become a more significant factor for Venezuelan foreign policy, further complicating an already intricate concatenation of interests and perspectives. It remains to evaluate these within the context of Venezuelan capabilities and resources as a means of examining the nation's future role in Central America and the Caribbean.

THE LIMITS AND EFFECTIVENESS OF OIL DIPLOMACY

Venezuela will unquestionably continue to seek a maximization of its role and influence in the circum-Caribbean, whatever the partisan stripe of its government. After 300 years as a neglected backwater of the Spanish colonial empire and another century-and-a-half as a minor power in Latin America, it can be expected to continue its pursuit of hemispheric leadership. The basic foundation stones will be the democratic morality and legitimacy of its political system accompanied by the diplomatic muscle of its oil economy. Despite its petroleum reserves and a host of other rich subsoil deposits, however, there are clear constraints and limitations on its range of actions.

Its capacity to shape Central American and Caribbean politics is finite and the effectiveness of its future foreign policy is dependent upon a wide array of factors.

In the most general ideological terms, Caracas will continue to operate from a position of strength. Presuming for the near future a prolongation of Castro's rule in Cuba, the predominance of authoritarian regimes in the hemisphere, and the survival of the present Venezuelan system, any Caracas government will continue to enjoy a degree of prestige and legitimacy which is lacking in many neighboring states. The conviction over the importance of advocating and encouraging free governments is not at issue between COPEI and AD. Similarly, the antimarxist commitment is equally strong and will be manifested in approaches toward political events throughout the area, including the case of Cuba. Thus a deeply-rooted consensus among political elites--excepting only the small if vocal marxist left in Venezuela--can be expected to provide continuing regional leadership in promoting democratic government and resisting the incursions of international communism. Furthermore, whether or not working in tandem with the United States government, the basic preoccupation will be less that of global East-West conflict than the internal health and well-being of Venezuela's immediate neighbors.

But on a narrower level, the differing ideological perspectives of the two major parties will affect the configuration of specific policies such as, for example, those concerning El Salvador and Nicaragua. Attitudes and assessments towards these and other countries are at variance. As already noted, for instance, perceptions and policies concerning the respective Manley and Seaga governments in Jamaica have been divergent when viewed alternatively through the Christian Democratic and Social Democratic prisms. Personal friendships and past relationships between Venezuelan and Caribbean leaders will also mirror the distinctions between partisan ideological and programmatic orientations. The posture of President Herrera, notwithstanding the overpublicized "reassessment" of foreign policy in 1981, is not expected to change dramatically toward the circum-Caribbean. Since he is constitutionally ineligible to succeed himself, however, elections will bring to power a new chief of state in March 1984.

At this writing, two years in advance of national elections, the implications cannot be clearly defined. The continuation in power of COPEI under a second Caldera presidency would mean that the hemisphere's most eminent Christian Democrat would be in office. Yet the deep animosity between calderistas and herreristas, in conjunction with the long experience of Caldera in foreign affairs and his deep sensitivity to diplomatic nuances and subtleties, suggest that priorities might be reordered. For the opposition Accion Democratica, presently rent by countless cross-cutting internal disputes and a party leadership best characterized as a shifting and impermanent group of warring tribal chieftains, the anticipated candidacy of Jaime Lusinchi does not lead to meaningful conclusions about an AD foreign policy. Whether or not the avowedly Social Democratic activism and worldview of Carlos Andres Perez would dominate the thinking of an AD administration is totally unclear at this early date. In short, the element of partisanship may well endure in the next few years of Venezuelan foreign affairs, although the details must await later events.

Future governments may therefore lack bipartisan support for specific regional policies. Furthermore, the country's available human resources place constraints on their effectiveness of action. As a middle-sized Latin American country with an estimated population of only some 15-16 million, Venezuela is dwarfed by Mexico, Brazil, and of course the United States. In qualitatiave terms, its diplomatic service is decidedly uneven, although the level of professionalization is being slowly upgraded. Indeed, the Herrera government has been plagued by conflict between the Foreign Ministry and the Ministry of Energy and Natural Resources, with the latter attempting to place its own representatives in key positions at embassies for the negotiation of oil contracts. As a military power, moreover, Venezuela's level of training and equipment, while adequate for needs at home, is presently insufficient to permit the significant exercise of authority in the Caribbean or Central America. The country can funnel arms to another state--as in the case of the anti-Somoza struggle in Nicaragua--but is not in an effective position to send substantial numbers of either military or civilian advisers elsewhere, as Cuba is capable of doing. In addition, the limited numbers of teachers and technicians sent in recent years to the circum-Caribbean can in no sense compete professionally or politically, quantitatively or qualitatively with their Cuban counterparts.

Human resources, in brief, will limit Venezuela's capacity to advance rapidly its Caribbean role. Even its wealth of natural resources cannot support a quantum leap forward. To be sure, the presence of enormous oil deposits in the Orinoco Tar Belt promise a continuing flow of petroleum for at least a century. However, the level of production cannot be swiftly altered. In the past decade three successive governments have prudently followed the course of conservationist policy. The present output of some 2.0 million barrels per day will not be dramatically increased. Domestic consumption is rising vertiginously, threatening a noticeable reduction in exports. Venezuela is slowly but progressively increasing its sales to Brazil, whose oil-hungry industrial machine has been even further cramped by the disruption of shipments from Iraq, customarily its major supplier. Granted a continuing effort further to diversify its markets, Venezuela does not anticipate a possibility of massive increases of sales--whatever the pricing and payment terms--to the Caribbean.

Geopolitically the situation is complex. Mexico has been flexing its muscles as Jose Lopez Portillo seeks to strengthen his nation's role as an independent force in world politics. This may well continue after his departure from office in late 1982, although the exaggerated optimism over its oil bonanza has been shattered by the many problems Mexico has encountered. In any event, however, Mexican oil production will continue at a level well above the Venezuelan, whatever the shape of relations between the two countries. The oil-sharing arrangement now in effect has contributed to closer collaboration between Mexico City and Caracas, although Herrera and Lopez view Caribbean and Central American politics rather differently. Herrera's April 1981 visit to Mexico City produced a vague joint communique of little real substance, with the Venezuelan calling for greater political collaboration while obliquely minimizing the disparate views of events in El Salvador, Nicaragua, and elsewhere.

As for the United States, the relatively cordial relationship between the Reagan and Herrera administrations is largely circumstantial. While Perez was personally close to Jimmy Carter and Herrera was not, we have seen that with the advent of the Reagan administration, policies of Caracas and Washington have dovetailed. It cannot be assumed that this will endure indefinitely, whatever the course of political events and regardless of the outlook of Herrera's eventual successor. For the present, Caracas' interest in purchasing new and sophisticated fighter planes from the United States, accompanied by a willingness to discuss possible multilateral aid programs with Washington, Ottawa, and Mexico City, implies a harmony for the near future.

This is not to suggest necessarily either a convergence of opinion or a breakdown of consensus between Caracas and Washington over the Caribbean. There are presently no glaring problems in the direct bilateral relationship, thus few obvious obstacles to a common outlook exist. However, the similarity of views cannot be automatically assumed as a given in the equation. Notwithstanding long speculation over the outlines of the Reagan foreign policy toward the Caribbean and Central America, it is still necessary to await further developments. At this time many politically knowledgeable Venezuelans, not without some cause, share the basic view of the late Romulo Betancourt. Speaking with the experience of fifty years as participant and observer, the grand old man of Accion Democratica on the eve of North American elections told an audience in Madrid, with characteristic directness and candor,

> There is a difference between Carter and Reagan which we Latin Americans readily appreciate. Whenever the Republican Party has governed the United States, the White House and the Department of State have favored dictatorial regimes.[28]

A final dimension to the limitations of Venezuelan oil diplomacy lies in the long unresolved border disputes with its two immediate neighbors, Colombia and Guyana. With the former, a renewed effort at negotiation of the dispute was badly mishandled by President Herrera. First calling for a "national" and nonpartisan approach, he then insisted that it would be solely the product of his own administration, thus guaranteeing a lack of domestic support. An agreement was drafted in secret, little effort was made to explain the terms or inform the Venezuelan people, and the predictable outcry of opposition drove him into embarrassed retreat and a refusal to negotiate further with disillusioned Colombian officials. To Venezuela's east, the sizeable Essequibo area "<u>en reclamacion</u>" only engendered worsened relations after a brief 1981 visit to Caracas by Guyana's Forbes Burnham, who ended by denouncing alleged Venezuelan invasion plans to seize nearly two-thirds of Guyanese territory. Both Foreign Minister Zambrano and Hilarion Cardozo, Herrera's ambassador to the Organization of American States (OAS), travelled through the Caribbean and even to Europe in search of international support in 1981, to little effect. Should either frontier dispute become more acute, Venezuelan activities in the Caribbean and Central America would lose some of their immediacy, at least for a time.

That the Venezuelan presence in the circum-Caribbean will be maintained, even despite such problems, can be treated as a given. Its wealth of natural resources will remain a factor while Venezuelan government officials, technicians, representatives of the private sector, and ordinary tourists will be in evidence. Caribbean resentments over the aggressive, Spanish-speaking _criollos_ can also be expected, with the former feeling themselves only infrequently treated with the appropriate degree of sensitivity and understanding. It is to be remembered that as such things are measured, Venezuela is a relative newcomer to active participation in foreign affairs and certainly to its relationship with the Caribbean. Despite the 1979 change from Perez to Herrera in Miraflores Palace, "the substance of Venezuela's new assertiveness has not changed...Venezuela's promotion of a new economic order and a north-south dialogue also reflects her need to reform the method through which necessary technological innovations flow to the third world."[29]

It is to be remembered, in short, that Venezuelan activism and penetration into the circum-Caribbean, at least on a sizable scale, is a rather new and recent component to its foreign policy. Especially with the English-speaking islands, Venezuela is neither fully knowledgeable of local traditions and attitudes nor is it yet wholly accepted. In view of the breach with Cuba, moreover, its only natural ties in the islands are with the Dominican Republic. As for the Central American isthmus, its presence and involvement in some sense are also relatively new, with past experience limited in character and predating the advent of the 1973 oil price increases which initiated the era of oil diplomacy and the leverage of _petrobolivares_. There are real and potential limits to the exercise of regional influence and in the long run the Venezuelan presence will most likely be neither hegemonic nor imperialist, but rather supportive of pluralistic democracy, political freedom, and socioeconomic progress. For this to evolve, a greater degree of mutual trust and understanding will be the minimal requisite to effective and cooperative partnership. The lesson has not yet been fully learned, but there can be no basic reversal of Venezuelan projections into the region.

NOTES

1. Luis Herrera Campins in "Viaje del Presidente a la Republica Dominicana," SIC (Caracas), no. 429 (Noviembre 1980), p. 414.

2. From a speech of Williams' Peoples National Movement. The text was reported in the Venezuelan press following its mid-1975 delivery.

3. John D. Martz, "Venezuelan Foreign Policy Toward Latin America" in Robert D. Bond (Ed.), Venezuela and Its Role in International Affairs (New York: New York University Press for the Council on Foreign Relations, 1977), p. 161.

4. For an English version of Leoni's full statement, see Venezuela Up-to-date, 12 (Winter 1968-69), p. 8.

5. Rafael Caldera, Discurso a la nacion (Caracas: Imprenta Nacional, 1969).

6. These included Antigua, Dominica, Grenada, Montserrat, St. Kitts-Nevis-Anguilla, St. Lucia, and St. Vincent.

7. "Interview with President Perez" reproduced in Venezuela Now, p. 23.

8. For an overview of the electoral setting plus analyses of the COPEI and AD campaigns, see the respective chapters by John D. Martz, Donald L. Herman, and David J. Myers in Howard Penniman (Ed.), Venezuela at the Polls (Washington: American Enterprise Institute, 1980), pp. 1-30, 133-54, and 91-133.

9. For a brief synthesis of Caldera's thought, see Miguel Jorrin and John D. Martz, Latin-American Political Thought and Ideology (Chapel Hill: University of North Carolina Press, 1970), pp. 415-21.

10. Rafael Caldera, El bloque latinoamericano (Santiago: Editorial del Pacifico, 1961), pp. 25-26.

11. An analysis of Fernandez' campaign program is found in John D. Martz and Enrique A. Baloyra, Electoral Mobilization and Public Opinion: The Venezuelan Campaign of 1973 (Chapel Hill: University of North Carolina Press, 1976), pp. 134-42.

12. The most extensive examination of COPEI is Donald L. Herman, Christian Democracy in Venezuela (Chapel Hill: University of North Carolina Press, 1980).

13. The Washington Post (January 17, 1981).

14. George W. Grayson, "The Mexican Oil Boom" in Susan Kaufman Purcell (Ed.), Mexico-United States Relations (New York: The Academy of Political Science, 1981), p. 153.

15. SIC, no. 429 (Noviembre 1980), p. 414.

16. Zeta (Caracas), no. 343 (Octubre 5, 1980), p. 10.

17. El Nacional (Caracas) (Octubre 19, 1980).

18. Baloyra and Martz, Political Attitudes in Venezuela; Societal Cleavages and Political Opinion (Austin: University of Texas Press, 1979).

19. Resumen (Caracas) (Mayo 16, 1976), p. 14.

20. SIC, no. 428 (Septiembre-Octubre 1980), p. 370.

21. The New York Times (November 23, 1980).

22. Herman, op. cit., p. 186.

23. Oficina Central de Informacion, Cuenta Ante El Pais (Caracas: Imprenta Nacional, 1973), p. 71.

24. Analysis of partisan discussions over the terms of nationalization appears in John D. Martz, "Policy-Making and the Quest for Consensus: Nationalizing Venezuelan Petroleum," Journal of Inter-American Studies and World Affairs, XIX-4 (November 1977), 483-509.

25. The single overarching treatment of the hemispheric movement is Edward J. Williams, Latin American Christian Democratic Parties (Knoxville: University of Tennessee Press, 1967).

26. Latin American Weekly Report, #30 (August 1, 1980), p. 5.

27. Latin American Weekly Report, #37 (September 19, 1980), p. 11.

28. El Nacional (Octubre 31, 1980), p. D-1.

29. David Eugene Blank, "Oil and Democracy in Venezuela," Current History, #454 (February 1980), p. 74.

5
Mexico's Central American Policy: Revolutionary and Prudential Dimensions

Edward J. Williams

INTRODUCTION

As Central America burns, a number of international and domestic actors have evolved policies and programs designed to feed the flames of rapid change or to dampen the conflagration. The list of interested parties is rather long and tends to shift somewhat according to time and place, but two general propensities are sufficiently crystallized to permit definition. Recognizing variations of commitment and degree, one group seeks to moderate the revolutionary blaze or to scotch it altogether. This alliance is headed by the United States and includes Venezuela, Costa Rica, the Christian Democratic International, the established governments of the area (excluding Nicaragua), and the semi-independent right-wing terrorists operating in several Central American nations. The other group of actors has no clearly defined leader intimately involved in the day-to-day drama of the region, but includes Cuba, Nicaragua, the Social Democratic International, the Soviet Union, other Eastern bloc nations, and, of course, the left-wing revolutionaries.

Most commentary in the United States places Mexico in the second category of nations. A fairly typical description of Mexico's Central American policy proposes that it "has consistently supported leftist guerrilla movements in El Salvador and Guatemala and has sought close ties with Nicaragua's revolutionary government, which includes Marxists."[1] As far as it goes, that description of Mexico's policy is fairly accurate but it gets to only one part of the complex. Not surprisingly, the larger perspective implies a rather different vista characterized by competing propensities, disparate proclivities, and contradictory initiatives pertaining to the formulation and implementation of its policy toward Central America.

The purpose here is to describe and analyze Mexico's Central American policy. The several foci of the effort include a documentation of Mexico's importance to and interest in the region and a discussion of two differing (and contradictory?) propensities typified as "the revolutionary dimension" and "the prudential dimension." In the process, it is argued that Mexico's policy is less committed to the revolutionary left than it appears at first blush and, concomitantly, that it contains a strong dose of calculating prudence, a characteristic so well defined in Mexican domestic policy formulation.

MEXICO'S IMPORTANCE TO AND INTEREST IN CENTRAL AMERICA

Mexico's potential for influencing the currents of change in Central America is clear enough. With the exception of the United States, it is the largest, richest, and most powerful nation intimately involved in the region. Officially defined as a "middle income" nation, Mexico counts a population of about 70 million and a gross domestic product of more than $150 billion, calculated at current prices. It ranks among the top twenty wealthiest nations in the world. Compared with its combined Central American neighbors, Mexico is well over three times more populous and about eight times wealthier.[2]

Mexico is also fairly highly industrialized and its enormous petroleum holdings imply the stuff of political power in the contemporary world. The distribution of its gross domestic product (GDP) attests to its relatively high level of industrialization. According to 1978 data, the nation's industrial sector accounted for 37 percent of its GDP, with services contributing another 52 percent. By way of comparison, the industrial sector contributes significantly less to the economies of the Central American nations. The figures range from 21 percent in El Salvador to 27 percent in Costa Rica. As of early 1981, furthermore, Mexico claimed the fifth largest proved hydrocarbon reserves in the world and ranked fourth in production, behind only the Soviet Union, Saudi Arabia, and the United States.[3]

As a state bordering upon Central America with some history of special relations, Mexico has a particular interest in the evolution of its neighbors. Although Mexican ideologues on the contemporary scene make too much of the historical ties between their nation and Central America, geographic propinquity is obvious enough and certainly contributes its part to Mexico's designs to influence change in the volatile region.

All of these factors have combined to catapult Mexico into a leading role in interpreting the events of the Central American drama and in suggesting appropriate policy stances in response to them. Although Mexico has not assumed a singular leadership position among the coalition of powers and interests in the area, it has exerted significant influence.[4]

Mexico's present interest in Central America evolves from the confluence of two larger trends, both initiated in the 1960s. One of them concerned Central America quite specifically; it was sparked by economic interests. The other trend was more broadly conceived geographically and involved both political and economic implications.

The first featured a concerted drive by Mexico to diversify its trading partners and increase its export earnings. As its trade balance began to assume serious negative proportions in the mid-1960s and as the Central American Common Market (CACM) began to take on some coherence, Mexico's decision makers set out a new policy to strengthen and increase relations with its immediate neighbors to the south (really the southeast!). On different occasions they broached proposals to affiliate with (and dominate) the CACM and/or to merge the Latin American Free Trade Association (LAFTA), to which Mexico belonged, and the CACM.

Mexico failed in both attempts, but in 1964 a trade commission initiated a more successful campaign to increase commercial contacts without formal economic integration. In its footsteps, President Gustavo Diaz Ordaz (1964-1970) launched in early 1966 the first goodwill tour of the Central American nations ever undertaken by a Mexican chief of state.[5] From that beginning, the die was cast. In early 1971, President Luis Echeverria (1970-1976) encountered "an unprecedented crisis in the Mexican balance of payments" and responded by meeting with the chief executives of Costa Rica, Guatemala, and Nicaragua to "explore the possibilities of increasing the exportation of manufactured products to Central America."[6] Shortly after his accession to power, President Jose Lopez Portillo (1976-1982) followed the lead of his predecessors in conducting a series of bilateral meetings with his Central American counterparts looking to ongoing growth in Mexican exports.

Mexico's involvement in Central America in the late 1970s and the 1980s goes much beyond the interests crystallized by that process. Nonetheless, it is one of the elements of the larger picture and it establishes a series of initiatives tying Mexico to Central America and running for well over a decade before the present turmoil struck the Central American region.

In the same vein, the second trend in the unfolding of Mexican foreign policy pertains to the present Central American nexus in offering evidence of a more broadly conceived expansion of Mexican interests leading to increased prestige and influence in global politics. Although certainly not encompassing unilinear development, the first steps toward a more open and dynamic foreign policy were taken by President Adolfo Lopez Mateos (1958-1964). Amid zigs, zags, and backsliding, the evolving policy was marked by several significant commitments, including a specific decision to affiliate with the Latin American Free Trade Association (LAFTA), a more implicit bid for expanded influence in Latin American affairs, and a move toward an increased role in Third World politics through sponsorship of the Charter of the Economic Rights and Duties of Nations. In even more definite and theatrical form, President Echeverria initiated a conscious campaign for Mexican world leadership which included such measures as his appearance at numerous conferences, his visits to even more numerous Third World, socialist, and European nations, and his regime's establishment of diplomatic relations with sixty-five new governments.[7]

While President Lopez Portillo backed off his predecessor's flamboyant theatrics, he continued to pursue an active foreign policy after a short respite when he was concentrating on Mexico's domestic economy. Parlaying Mexico's newly found petroleum power, Lopez Portillo negotiated with leading states in both the developed and less developed world and definitively established Mexico as a voice to be reckoned with in the larger global arena. Mexico's acceptance of a seat on the United Nations Security

Council in 1980 symbolized both the direction and the success of the new policy launched by Lopez Mateos in the 1960s and pursued by Lopez Portillo in the 1980s. By the time the Central American caldron began to heat up in the late 1970s, Mexico could lay claim to some global prestige to couple with its peculiar regional competence. Logically enough, the two trends have combined to contribute to its stellar role in the international politics of Central American change.[8]

THE ELEMENTS OF MEXICO'S CENTRAL AMERICAN POLICY

The official rhetoric of the Mexican decision-making elites declares a posture of "nonintervention" in Central America, but the facts of the matter are not so simple. Along with a half-dozen or so other powers, Mexico is wheeling and dealing in the area and will continue to influence events in Central America. The crux of the matter is not whether nations are intervening, but rather how, why, and to what ends their intervention obtains.

Mexico's policies and programs in the region are easy enough to identify, but more difficult to analyze. Indeed, they are characterized by a solid strain of inconsistency. One set is consciously designed to aid and abet the forces of revolutionary change; another group of measures is far more prudent to the point of helping the established governments in the area. The first set of initiatives, "the revolutionary dimension," is composed of a series of diplomatic, economic, and political initiatives confected to assist and/or encourage revolutionary forces in Nicaragua, El Salvador, and Guatemala. Conversely, other policies and programs have the opposite effect or the potential to impede the progress of the revolutionary forces in Central America. These include ongoing diplomatic relations with the established regimes; significant economic aid to those governments resulting from cheap loans in the context of oil sales; and the modernization of the Mexican military.

The Revolutionary Dimension

A survey of recent relations between Mexico and the Central American nations makes several points. It offers good evidence of programs to comfort and assist the revolutionary movements, especially in Nicaragua. It likewise suggests that Mexico has assumed a cool, if not hostile, stance toward the established governments in El Salvador and Guatemala. Finally, in anticipation of some reservations to be drawn below, the record also demonstrates differing strategies applied to the several nations.

Mexican-Nicaraguan relations offer the fullest exemplification of the revolutionary dimension of Mexico's Central American policy. In both word and deed, politically and economically, Mexico has consistently supported the Sandinista revolutionaries. Political support began as early as September 1978 when Mexico's Managua embassy welcomed hundreds of political refugees fleeing an abortive insurrection. Mexico also took a leading role in blocking a United States attempt to facilitate the intervention of the Organization of American States in Nicaragua before the fall of Anastasio Somoza. Most importantly, in May 1979 it joined Costa Rica in breaking diplomatic relations with the Somoza regime and recognizing the belligerency of the Sandinista revolutionaries. That decision lent legitimacy to the Sandinista cause and was crucial in mustering international support for the revolutionaries. After the Sandinistas assumed power, moreover, words of praise continued to emanate from the highest reaches of the Mexican political system. In his Fourth State of Nation message delivered in 1980, President Lopez Portillo proudly referred to Mexico's role in "assisting in Nicaragua the birth of a society pledged to respect pluralism and seeking to bring about liberty and justice." Foreign Minister Jorge Castañeda has been equally generous and supportive in characterizing the Sandinista government as "a pluralistic regime which respects human rights.[9]

Beyond political succor, Mexico has offered generous economic assistance to revolutionary Nicaragua. Of all the financial aid received by the Sandinista government through early 1981, it supplied fully 16 percent, more than twice the amount coming from any other Latin American nation. It donated oil drilling equipment and is training Nicaraguan technicians. The Lopez Portillo government joined Nicaragua in establishing a company for the exploitation of forestry products. As discussed below, Nicaragua also benefits from ongoing concessionary oil prices offered to the Caribbean and Central American nations by Mexico and Venezuela. Finally, Mexico's Finance Ministry offered valuable advice to the Sandinista government when it renegotiated its foreign debt with private banks. In view of that economic assistance in tandem with important political support, it is perfectly reasonable that a leading publication has dubbed Mexico as Nicaragua's "chief external patron."[10]

An analysis of Mexican-El Salvadoran intercourse adds some additional credence to Mexico's revolutionary diplomacy in Central America, but the evidence is not nearly so strong as in Nicaragua. From one perspective the rhetoric and some policy decisions of the Mexican leadership have implied opposition to the ruling junta and support of the revolutionary left. During a meeting in Costa Rica, for example, President Lopez Portillo refused to agree to a communique stating support for the El Savadoran government. Foreign Minister Castañeda has "deplored the constant, massive, and flagrant violation of human rights in El Salvador and taken notice of the growing incapacity of the authorities to stop the violence." In another message, the Foreign Minister appeared to imply tacit approval of the El Salvadoran left in noting that some peoples in the Caribbean and Central America were struggling "to free themselves from tyrannies" and to "modify obsolete economic and social structures." The Mexican government pushed that line a half step further in mid-1981 when it joined France in declaring recognition of the left in El Salvador as a "representative political force." Mexico's official party, moreover, has expressed open sympathy with the revolutionary left and worked to isolate El Salvador's Christian Democratic Party from a new organization of Latin American political parties founded in 1979. It is also noteworthy that Mexico withdrew its ambassador to El Salvador in mid-1980.[11]

The tone of Mexican-Guatemalan relations parallels the Mexican-El Salvadoran equation. The Mexican government has been consciously cool toward the dictatorship of Romeo Lucas Garcia. On the other hand, it has certainly eschewed any endorsement of the left-wing revolutionaries in Guatemala. Indeed, relations between the Guatemalan and Mexican military establishments suggest an intriguing possibility of potential cooperation.

The unfriendly perspective is illustrated by several stances. President Lopez Portillo has indefinitely postponed a visit to Guatemala mandated by diplomatic protocol. Mexico has received many Guatemalan political refugees. The two governments have been at odds over procedures to investigate the kidnapping of a famous journalist who was residing in Mexico. Most importantly, Mexico has alienated the Lucas Garcia government by opposing the Guatemalan claims to Belize. On the contrary, Mexico has offered strong support for Belizean independence. One source has reported that Mexico has gone so far as to be a party to a putative multinational defense force to protect Belize should Guatemala threaten the small nation.[12]

The evidence from Nicaragua, El Salvador, and Guatemala, in short, lends some credence to the charge that Mexico has aligned with the "leftist" forces in support of guerrilla warfare. The record is especially clear in the case of Nicaragua. The facts of the Mexican-El Salvadoran relationship also indicate a strong strain of revolutionary diplomacy, although some nuances of prudence characterize that scenario. Regarding Guatemala, the contention is valid enough in the sense that Mexico clearly opposes the Lucas Garcia government, but the Mexican-Guatemalan relationship also suggests caution in pushing the argument too far. The reservations about Mexico's revolutionary diplomacy that pertain to the El Salvadoran and Guatemalan equations, moreover, combine with the "prudential" dimension of Mexico's Central American policy to contribute to a far less radical overall posture.

The Prudential Dimension

If it is true that Mexico's recent Central American policy implies disapproval of the established order and some measure of support for revolutionary change, it is equally clear that other elements of the larger picture suggest a rather different conclusion. These initiatives include the fact of Mexico's ongoing relations with the government of El Salvador. They also involve continuing formal relations with Guatemala and some intriguing hints of cooperation between the two nations' military establishments. In another extrapolation, the established governments of the area also receive important assistance from the Mexican-Venezuelan petroleum supply program. Finally, there are the implications of the Mexican military's modernization program. To be sure, none of this suggests a "conservative" or "rightist" foreign policy, but it certainly indicates an alternative panorama and hints at a much more prudent and cautious stance designed to respond to varying alternatives in the outcome of the Central American drama.

Mexico's relations with Guatemala and El Salvador provide intriguing case studies for the above conclusion. While the Lopez Portillo government has certainly assumed a cool posture toward Guatemala, several contextual factors need consideration. In the first instance, Mexican-Guatemalan relations are traditionally fragile, not unlike the United States-Mexican situation and for many of the same reasons. Mexico's relative wealth and power lend a certain arrogance to its posture and, conversely, Guatemala's inferior position leads to a touch of paranoia. However, with the Belizean conundrum evolving toward a final settlement, thorny issues between Mexico and its neighbor to the south may assume less divisive significance. Finally, as noted previously, some indications point to a cooperative spirit between the two nations' armed forces. In the late 1960s, for example, the Mexican military contributed a major effort in the capture and eventual demise of Marco Antonio Yon Sosa, a leading Guatemalan guerrilla leader. More recently, in 1980, high-ranking Guatemalan military officers participated in Mexican military maneuvers in the nation's southeastern states. It may be a matter of significance that these exercises were conducted in states bordering on Guatemala and were described by the Mexican defense minister as "the most important military maneuvers of the last 50 years."[13]

In a somewhat different way, bilateral intercourse between Mexico and El Salvador also makes the point that Mexico is pursuing a cautious policy. Even though Mexico has urged recognition of the Salvadoran left as a "representative force," both President Lopez Portillo and Foreign Minister Castañeda have played their cards close to the vest. A journalistic account of the Lopez Portillo meeting with Fidel Castro in 1980 illustrates the President's prudent posture.

> During the Lopez Portillo visit, Castro several times offered the Mexican leader a chance to comment on El Salvador, at one time practically putting the words in his mouth, saying "It can never be said of Mexico...(ellipsis in orginal) that it supports genocidal governments such as that of El Salvador."
>
> Lopez Portillo, however, refused repeatedly to take the bait. The final communique signed by the two leaders noted only that both condemned "the constant and systematic violations of human rights in El Salvador," and supported the "right of the

> Salvadorean people to decide their own destiny without foreign intervention."
>
> This careful stance, hard for anyone to argue with, came at a time when the junta is holding its own in El Salvador, despite a virtual civil war in that country. In other words, the issue is still very much in doubt, and Mexico showed it preferred for the moment to wait and see what happens but to make sure all of its bridges are in good repair.[14]

In an interview addressing "The Attitude of Mexico before El Salvador," Castañeda was equally circumspect and captured the judicious bent of the Mexican policy several times. While admitting that "there is a large sector of Mexican public opinion that is demanding the breaking of relations," the Foreign Minister set out a series of apologies arguing against such a move. Unlike the Nicaraguan experience, he explained that the El Salvadoran opposition controlled no territory. Hence, Mexico could not recognize the belligerency status of the nation's left in the process of breaking relations. Moreover, he continued, the Mexican government had received word from the Salvadoran left that it opposed Mexico's breaking relations for the time being.

Most significant, however, he dwelled several times on the political calculations attendant to the problem. In one instance he noted that the move to discontinue relations was "a question of opportunity;" later he proposed that "it is a question of seeking the opportune moment." Even more to the point, the Foreign Minister cautioned that "there is no general rule which indicates to us what we ought to do; it is partly a question of political intuition. The conduct of international relations does not relate exclusively to moral considerations.[15]

When looking at Mexico's relations with Guatemala and El Salvador, then, its policy and the larger scenario combine influence with attitudes suggesting moderation and caution. The Mexican military tie with its Guatemalan counterparts and the evolving resolution of the Belizean controversy counter the aura of coolness in official relations. In the same vein, the stresses and strains of Mexico's intercourse with El Salvador are balanced by clear indications of calculating prudence in Mexico's behavior.

Mexico's decision to join Venezuela in supplying petroleum at cut-rate prices to Caribbean and Central American nations offers even more salient proof of the nation's moderate policy in the region. Launched in mid-1980, the arrangement authorizes a credit of 30 percent on the market price. The credit, in turn, is provided in low-interest, long-term loans for developmental projects of the recipient nation's choosing. General developmental projects are funded at the rate of 4 percent and energy programs at the even more negligible rate of only 2 percent for as long as 20 years. Mexico supplies 80,000 barrels of oil per day (b/d), or one half of the total obligation assumed by the two nations; Venezuela ships the other half. The recipient nations include Barbados, Costa Rica, the Dominican Republic, El Salvador, Guatemala, Haiti, Honduras, Jamaica, Nicaragua, and Panama. The Bahamas are being considered for inclusion in the arrangement and Foreign Minister Castañeda has made it clear that Cuba is also eligible.[16]

The significance of the program emanates from two facts; it involves rather large sums of financial aid and is applied to the nations of the area without discrimination. The aid is apportioned equally to Mexico's supposed friends and putative enemies. Calculating from a price of $35.00 per barrel and 80,000 b/d, Mexico's financial assistance to Central American and Caribbean nations totals $300 million per year.[17]

Even more cogent for this analysis, considerable sums in financial aid are being apportioned to nations which support a conservative position on Central American change and therefore are, supposedly, at odds with what many assume to be Mexico's policy. The ruling junta in El Salvador, for instance, is receiving 7,500 b/d in cut-rate petroleum from Mexico and the loan arrangement could transfer to El Salvador nearly $29 million during 1981. The same amount could go to Guatemala and even larger amounts to Jamaica and other nations. Indeed, the nations opposed to at least some elements of revolutionary change in Central America or experiencing strained relations with Mexico for some other reason receive the lion's share of its largess. The list of those includes Costa Rica, the Dominican Republic, El Salvador, Guatemala, Haiti, Honduras, and Jamaica. Those seven nations account for more than 70 percent of the benefits--58,500 of the 80,000 b/d and almost $225 million of the approximately $300 million freed for financial assistance under the scheme.[18]

Other measures within the context of Mexico's petroleum diplomacy in the Caribbean and Central America teach the same lesson. Pemex is assisting nations supportive of revolutionary change in the region, but it is also aiding nations opposing the revolutionary strategy or at least some aspects of it. Mexico's state-owned petroleum monopoly is exploring for oil in Nicaragua and has signed an oil cooperation agreement with Cuba. Despite Costa Rica's stance in favor of the Salvadoran junta, on the other hand, Pemex has a wide-ranging program in that nation including exploration, the training of technicians, and possible drilling. Pemex has also initiated negotiations with the Dominican Republic and Panama.[19]

From one perspective, Mexico's petroleum diplomacy in Central America and the Caribbean invites accolades for its unselfish refusal to attach political conditions to its financial assistance. More to the point of this analysis, the policy also evokes admiration for its political perspicacity in consciously maintaining its options as the winds of change refashion the political panorama of the region. Despite opposition from the left on the Mexican domestic political scene, the nation's policy makers have continued to offer assistance to El Salvador and other nations. In clear and dramatic fashion, those decisions form part of an overall policy package emanating from a calculating position designed to maximize flexibility and minimize the risk of alienating potential winners in the struggle.[20]

The modernization of the Mexican military is the final element of Mexico's prudential posture on Central America. It differs from the strictly defined foreign policy stances discussed above and is germane to the Central American region more by future implication than present reality. Its significance is so profoundly important, however, that even an indirect and future connection to the scenario demands description and analysis.

Although the military's modernization program had begun before that time, the new stance was crystallized during the celebrations for Mexico's Independence Day in September 1980. A first-hand account of the military parade captures the unfolding drama.

> Dressed in new combat uniforms and wearing green, red, and blue berets, about 8,000 soldiers ran the four mile length of the parade to prove their fitness. And behind them came hundreds of newly painted military vehicles, including some carrying small rockets, never before seen in Mexico.[21]

A short time later, the modernization program was explained and advocated in a rare interview granted to Proceso by Mexico's Defense Minister, General Felix Galvan Lopez. The Defense Minister waxed insistent about the necessity for the modernization effort and spoke glowingly of the armed forces' role in guaranteeing the security of the nation. Overall budgetary allocations for the military and its activities during 1980 and 1981 indicated the military's commitment and success in pushing its programs. Budgetary comparisons between 1980 and 1981 show important increases for the military sector. From 1980 to 1981, overall governmental spending increased 38.6 percent, but projected allocations for the military ministries far surpassed that figure. The Ministry of National Defense was scheduled for an increase of 86.3 percent and the Navy Ministry for 59.2 percent.[22]

Armed with these additional resources, Mexico's military began to upgrade its capabilities. The nation's cavalry regiments traded in their horses for reconnaissance vehicles. Mexico bought from West Germany the license to manufacture G3 automatic rifles. The nation's naval secretary purchased six patrol boats from Spain; Spain also received an order for "an undetermined number" of military transport planes. After having decided against Israeli Kfir fighters, the Mexican air force convinced the United States to deliver "at least a dozen" supersonic F5 jet fighters. As part of the deal, U.S. advisors also consulted with the Mexican armed forces about necessary modifications to its air fields to handle the F5's.[23]

The Mexican military's modernization is certainly important and may well have implications for both domestic and foreign policies, but it is important to keep it in perspective. Even with the measurable increases channeled to the military ministries in the 1981 budget, the relative amounts are still small and Mexico's military expenditures are among the lowest in the world. A calculation extrapolated from the 1981 document shows that military spending accounts for only 1.4 percent of total governmental expenditures and 2.3 percent for general government spending, which does not include allocations for Mexico's decentralized organizations and state enterprises. It is clear enough, furthermore, that the nation's military is sorely in need of updating. One report, for example, describes a foreign analyst as noting that its military relies on pre-World War II tanks, airplanes, and artillery pieces "only seen in front of veterans' halls." As massive new financial resources are made available by Mexico's burgeoning petroleum industry, it is logical enough to see the armed forces as having a reasonable claim to some of them, just as other sectors have vied for their share of the new riches.[24]

With that salient reservation duly noted, it is also important to plumb the significance of the Mexican military's modernization program within the context of recent trends, contemporary events, and future projections. In the first instance, several initiatives in recent years clearly exemplify the military's readiness to defend the Mexican system. Two of these, furthermore, are experiences germane to counterinsurgency capabilities. The 1968 slaughter of protesting students at Tlatelolco serves as horrifying evidence of the armed forces' readiness to employ force. Although that shocking episode does not quite relate to the present scenario in terms of strategy and tactics, it may well have some applicability as proof of the military's willful commitment to utilize extreme measures in the face of destabilizing opposition. The eradication of Lucio Cabañas' guerrilla movement in Guerrero in the 1970s contributes to the same point and also involved valuable experience in responding to the type of struggle now characterizing the Central American region. The military's fairly successful campaign against drug production and trafficking in Sinaloa and Durango beginning in the mid-1970s teaches the same lesson.

Beyond such specific cases, the Mexican military has struck literally hundreds of times over the years in intervening against recalcitrant sindicatos, rebellious peasants, upstart students, and dissident members of the middle class. A sense of that omnipresent role is captured by commmentary on the war games conducted in the nation's south during 1980. However the military leadership may have characterized the exercises, an opposition source saw them as designed to "intimidate the popular movements that are evolving in the rural zones [of the area] and, for that reason, [the military leadership] selected places where there existed important peasant political activity."[25]

All of these initiatives form the outline for an evolving scenario characterized by several elements that imply potential applicability to Mexico's Central American policy. At the highest level of strategic thinking the Mexican elites have begun the formulation of a national security policy. Afforded wide diffusion by Defense Minister Galvan's interview, the incipient policy debate is mightily concerned with the implications of the country's new role as a petroleum power. As oil resources become increasingly crucial for national prosperity, even survival, Mexico's national security is intimately bound to them and a modernized military is necessary for their protection.[26]

The location of the new petroleum reserves is especially salient to Central American policy. The fields are located in the southeastern states of Chiapas and Tabasco. Both states border on Guatemala and some of the fields are less than 100 miles from the frontier. The spectre of the contagion effect from the germs of revolutionary change sweeping Central America is part of the motivation informing the discussion of national security policy and part of the impetus for the nation's military modernization program. Though less frequently noted, an additional strategic consideration in the south is the transisthmian rail line, which is in the process of being upgraded and refurbished and is destined to be in competition with the Panama Canal before mid-decade.[27]

The dimensions and directions of the Mexican military's modernization program adds the final element of analytical evidence applicable to the Central American scenario. The selection of the southeastern states as the locale of the military exercises is significant. The Navy's commitment to upgrade its patrol boat capacity may stem from its increasing responsibilities flowing from the expansion of Mexico's territorial waters, but that added capacity is also relevant to countering guerrilla activity spreading from the south. The entire panoply of new hardware, moreover, implies a defense capacity designed to do more than maintain domestic order, the traditional role of the Mexican military.[28]

CONCLUSION

The major elements of description and analysis have been well drawn here and thus require only brief reiteration and re-emphasis. In the first place, Mexico is the second most important exogenous political actor intimately involved in Central American change. Its power and influence are exceeded only by the United States. Its intrusion into the Central American cauldron logically flows from two long-range evolutionary trends in its foreign policy posture. One trend centers on increasing cognizance of its Central American neighbors; another is composed of a series of steps designed to increase Mexico's political standing in the larger global arena. Both have been capped in the contemporary period by the nation's emergence as one of the world's leading petroleum powers and have matured at about the time of the ignition of the Central American conflagration.

Opinion in the United States posits that Mexico's foreign policy has favored the cause of the revolutionary left in Central America. One nuance of policy lends credence to that conclusion, but an equally salient strain of policy and other events in Mexico give pause in accepting it. The revolutionary dimension of Mexico's Central American stance is best exemplified by its relations with Nicaragua. From the outset, Mexico's policy makers have offered political and economic succor to Nicaragua's Sandinista revolutionaries. Regarding Mexico's position on revolutionary change in El Salvador, the scenario tends to fog up a bit, but it also contains measures designed to discredit the ruling junta and encourage the left. With reference to Guatemala, the picture is again ambiguous, but some aspects of Mexico's policy have certainly been critical of the ruling dictatorship, if not quite supportive of its revolutionary opposition.

Conversely, a careful examination of Mexico's recent policy also reveals an important prudential dimension. Although relations are strained with El Salvador, they continue to be formally correct. Both President Lopez Portillo and Foreign Minister Castañeda, furthermore, have assumed measured tones in policy declarations on El Salvador calculated to maintain options as the uncertain struggle evolves. Turning to bilateral relations with Guatemala, the contemporary stress is in no way extraordinary and the easing of the Belizean crisis may well signal their improvement.

Mexico's formulation and implementation of its petroleum supply arrangement with the Caribbean and Central American nations offers even stronger evidence of a prudential stance. The cornerstone of Mexico's policy for the area, the arrangement sends cut-rate petroleum to friend and foe alike, including the established governments of El Salvador and Guatemala. Indeed, nations opposed to revolutionary change in Central America are receiving the largest share of Mexico's financial assistance. All are in debt to Mexico and its partner in the program, Venezuela.

Finally, the modernization of its armed forces connotes obvious implications for Mexico's stand on Central American revolutionary change. Although it is sparked by more than a contagion effect from the southeast, the modernization effort is partly a reaction to that concern. But regardless of what the immediate motivation may be, a stronger and better equipped military establishment is clearly a factor in the larger equation of Mexico's response to the area's turmoil. Given the location of its petroleum wealth in the southeast, military preparedness has a special significance for the larger scenario.

The existence of these factors engenders a solid dose of calculating prudence as Mexico analyzes events in Central America. They indicate not an unequivocal commitment to the revolutionary left, but rather a measured position designed to maximize advantages as the drama unfolds.

NOTES

1. The quotation is from Guy Gugliotta, "U.S.-Mexican Policies on a Collision Course?," Miami Herald (February 19, 1981), Information Services on Latin America (ISLA) 524. For similar commentary and analysis, see Constantine Christopher Menges, "Current Mexican Foreign Policy and United States Interests" (Washington, D.C.: mimeographed, 1980); Alan Riding, "Lopez Portillo to Reagan on Central America: Don't," New York Times (January 4, 1981), ISLA 19; Marlise Simons, "U.S.-Mexican Ties Getting New Test," Washington Post (January 25, 1981), ISLA 20; and "All Roads Lead to Mexico City," Latin American Weekly Report (January 16, 1981), pp. 3-4.

Although the title and organizational foci of this article are rather similar to an effort by Professor Olga Pellicer de Brody, neither have been inspired by it. See her "Pragmatismo y tradicion revolucionaria en la politica exterior de Mexico," *Proceso* (August 28, 1980), pp. 13-14.

2. The data is extrapolated from the World Bank, *World Development Report, 1980* (New York: Oxford University Press, 1980), p. 111; and Banco National de Mexico, *Mexico Statistical Data, 1970-1980* (Mexico, D.F.: Banco Nacional de Mexico, 1981), p. 6.

3. The data on the distribution of the gross domestic product are from the World Bank, op. cit., p. 115. The figures on petroleum reserves and production are in "XLII Aniversario de la Industria Petrolera Nacional" (The annual report of the Director General of Petroleos Mexicanos), *El Mercado de Valores* (March 23, 1981), p. 303.

4. The Menges paper, op. cit., supports this claim.

5. For the discussion and analysis, see Ramon Medina Luna, "Proyeccion de Mexico sobre Centroamerica" in Centro de Estudios Internacionales, *Mexico y America Latina: La Nueva Politica Exterior* (Mexico, D.F.: El Colegio de Mexico, 1974), especially pp. 15-20.

6. Olga Pellicer de Brody, "El Acercamiento de Mexico a America Latina" in James W. Wilkie et. al. (Eds.), *Contemporary Mexico* (Los Angeles: University of California Press, 1976), p. 449.

7. For some recent analyses of Mexican foreign policy, see George W. Grayson, "Mexican Foreign Policy," *Current History* (March 1977), pp. 97ff; William H. Hamilton, "Mexico's New Foreign Policy: A Re-examination, *Inter-American Economic Affairs*, Vol. 29, No. 3 (Winter 1975), pp. 51-58; Errol D. Jones and D. La France, "Mexico's Foreign Affairs Under President Echeverria: The Special Case of Chile," *Inter-American Economic Affairs* Vol. 30, No. 1 (Summer 1976), pp. 45-78; and Guy E. Poitras, "Mexico's 'New' Foreign Policy," *Inter-American Economic Affairs* Vol. 28, No. 3 (Winter 1974), pp. 59-77.

8. On the foreign policy of President Jose Lopez Portillo, see Kevin J. Middlebrook, "Energy and Security in U.S.-Mexican Relations" (Cambridge, Mass.: Department of Government and Center for International Affairs, Harvard University, n.d. [1980?]); and Pellicer de Brody, "Pragmatismo y tradicion revolucionaria...," op. cit., pp. 13-14.

9. See "Condena a los asesinatos; petroleo a El Salvador, pero tambien a Cuba," Proceso (December 8, 1980), p. 26; "Cuarto Informe Presidencial," El Mercado de Valores (September 8, 1980), p. 884; Menges, op. cit., pp. 25-26; and Alan Riding "Mexico Pursues Role of Leader for Caribbean Region," New York Times (August 20, 1980), ISLA 536.

10. See "Aiding Democracy," Latin America Regional Report: Mexico and Central America (February 15, 1980), p. 4; "Breaking the Economic Stranglehold," Latin American Weekly Report (March 27, 1981); "Proyecto Industrial entre Mexico y Nicaragua," El Mercado de Valores (December 1, 1980), pp. 1185ff; and Riding, "Mexico Pursues Role...," op. cit.

11. See "Central America: A Key Feature of the President's Latest Grand Tour," Latin American Weekly Report (July 18, 1980), p. 6; "Condema a los asesinatos...," op. cit., p. 28; "Difficulties with El Salvador," Comercio Exterior (September 1980), p. 320; "Mexico/President's Travels," Latin America Weekly Report (August 1, 1980), p. 12; Miguel Angel Granados Chapa, "Castañeda el la ONU: Del analisis a las posiciones," Razones (October 6-19, 1980), p. 21; Menges, op. cit., p. 28.; and Alan Riding, "Salvador Rebels Gain New Support," New York Times (August 29, 1981), p. 1.

12. See "Belize," Latin America Regional Report: Mexico and Central America (February 13, 1981), p. 3; Central America Report (January 24, 1981), p. 31; and "Copatrocina Mexico la independencia, mientras Guatemala insiste en la anexion," Proceso (November 3, 1981), pp. 24-25.

13. See "Belize: Locking Horns with Opponents of Independence Movement," Central America Report (March 28, 1981), p. 97; and "Mexico/Army," Latin America Weekly Report (December 19, 1980), p. 12. On the Mexican part in the Yon Sosa affair, see Milton H. Jamail, Guatemala 1944-1972: The Politics of Aborted Revolution, Unpublished Ph.D. dissertation (Tuscon, Arizona: University of Arizona, 1972), p. 78.

14. Guy Gugliotta, "Mexico is Flexing its New Muscle," Miami Herald (August 31, 1980), ISLA 538.

15. Carlos Fazio, "Explica Castañeda la actitud de Mexico ante El Salvador," Proceso (December 15, 1980), pp. 8-9.

16. The agreement is contained in "Program de Cooperacion Energetica," El Mercado de Valores (August 11, 1980), pp. 761ff. President Lopez Portillo described it in his 1980 presidential message; see "Cuarto Informe Presidencial," El Mercado de Valores (September 8, 1980), p. 883. The Foreign Minister's Statement is found in "Condena a los asesinatos...," op. cit., p. 29. Some confusion about the inclusion of Guatemala and El Salvador arose during the initial announcement of the petroleum supply arrangement. El Salvador was questioned on what appeared to be political grounds and Guatemala because it was nearing self-sufficiency in petroleum. As of this writing (early May 1981), it seems that both are partners to the arrangement. For the story, see Eduardo Amador and Guillermo Fernandez, "Mexico y Venezuela suscriben aqui plan de ayuda financiera al istmo," La Nacion (San Jose; August 4, 1980), p. 4A.

17. As of December 23, 1980, Petroleos Mexicanos set prices on Maya grade at $34.50 per barrel and Isthmus grade at $38.50 per barrel. See "Increases In Export Price of Oil and Gas," Comercio Exterior (January 1981), p. 11.

18. The list of recipient nations and their respective amounts are from Petroleos Mexicanos as reported in "Pemex Cuts Dependence On U.S. Market," Latin America Regional Report: Mexico and Central America (February 13, 1981), p. 8. The addition of the Dominican Republic is reported in Alan Robinson, "Pemex Inks Oil Pacts with Four Countries," Journal of Commerce (December 9, 1980), ISLA 2360. If other reports on the amounts being shipped to several nations are correct, the figures would be even higher for Guatemala, Haiti, and Jamaica. See American Chamber of Commerce of Mexico (AMCHAM), Mexico Update (February 1981), p. 9; "Mexico Widens Its Crude Markets," Financial Times (December 15, 1980), ISLA 2368; and "Jamaica/Finance," Latin America Weekly Report (November 28, 1980), p. 12.

19. See "Pemex Wins Out Over Oil Majors," Latin America Regional Report: Mexico and Central America (November 28, 1980), p. 4; Robinson, "Pemex Inks Oil Pacts...," op. cit.; and short notes in the Latin America Weekly Report (November 7, 1980), p. 5, (January 30, 1981), p. 7, and (March 13, 1981), p. 5.

20. For a short discussion of the left's opposition to the petroleum accord, see "Pemex Cuts Dependence...," op. cit., p. 8.

21. The quotation is from Alan Riding, "Mexican Army, Parading Pride Raises Concern," New York Times (October 5, 1980), ISLA 1371.

22. For the Galvan interview, see Roberto Vizcaino, "La seguridad del pais: fin primordial del Estado," Proceso (September 22, 1980), pp. 6-8. The budgetary data are extrapolated from AMCHAM, Quarterly Economic Report (January 1981), p. 23.

23. See "Mexico/Arms," Latin America Weekly Report (January 30, 1981), p. 11; "Mexico Modernizes Army as Revolution Spreads," Miami Herald (October 17, 1980), ISLA 1370; Sam Moriarity, "Spain, Mexico Ratify Joint Industrial Projects," Journal of Commerce (October 30, 1980), ISLA 1402; Riding, "Mexican Army...," op. cit.; Marlise Simons, "U.S. Said to Approve Jet Sale for Mexico's Military Buildup Plan," Washington Post (February 24, 1981), ISLA 531.

24. The data on the budget are from AMCHAM, Quarterly Economic Report (January 1981), pp. 23-25. The quotation is taken from "Mexico Modernizes...," op. cit.

25. "Simularco de guerra," Proceso (December 8, 1980), p. 29.

26. For some elements of the national security discussion, see Rene Herrera Zuñiga, "De cara al sur: Mexico ante Centroamerica," Nexos, III, No. 28 (April 1980), pp. 3-10; Olga Pellicer de Brody, "La Seguridad Nacional en Mexico: Preocupaciones Nuevos y Nociones Tradicionales" (Paper presented in a seminar of the Program on U.S.-Mexican Studies, University of California, San Diego, September 1980); and Vizcaino, "La seguridad del pais...," op. cit., pp. 6-8.

27. See Herrera, "De cara al aur...," op cit., p. 3; and "Mexico Modernizes Army...," op cit. On the Tehuantepec peninsula project, see "Land Bridge May Hit Legal Snag," Latin America Regional Report: Mexico and Central America (May 1, 1981), p. 3.

28. See Simons, op. cit. Mexico's military modernization program and the putative contagion effect from Central America also have important implications for Mexican domestic politics. For some commentary on two of those implications, see Pellicer de Brody, "La Seguridad Nacional en Mexico...," op. cit., pp. 11-12; and Riding, "Mexican Army..., op. cit.

6
Some Central American Perceptions and Positions in the Face of Big and Middle Power Politics in the Caribbean

Neale J. Pearson

INTRODUCTION

The Central American nations and Panama are of substantial interest to Washington due to their geographic proximity to and economic interdependence with the United States as well as the common cultural/ethnic heritage which they share with many U.S. citizens. Since the turn of the century, the United States has been the dominant economic and political power in the area, but with the flight into exile of Anastasio "Tachito" Somoza DeBayle on July 19. 1979 and the outbreak of civil war in both El Salvador and Guatemala, its position has been challenged (as Michael Erisman notes in Chapter One). With these events, American policy makers have rediscovered the Caribbean region--as has happened on several other occasions since World War II. While the rhetoric of Jeane Kirkpatrick in describing Central America as "the most important place in the world for the U.S." was probably extreme,[1] it was not much more so than some of the statements coming out of the White House, the Congress, or the media when Fidel Castro came to power in 1959 or the efforts of Secretary of State John Foster Dulles and his brother Allen, Director of the CIA, to paint Col. Jacobo Arbenz Guzman of Guatemala as a Soviet tool and threat to the hemisphere in early 1954.

Given this legacy, this chapter will discuss: (1) some of the common problems facing the relatively poor and developing Central American nations and Panama; (2) the broad spectrum of ideologies and personalities in the area as well as examples of complex conspiracies aimed at protecting or increasing the power and influence of different individuals and parties, especially Somoza, Jose Figueres Ferrer of

Costa Rica, and Omar Torrijos of Panama; (3) the wide range of diplomatic contacts and alliances of the Central American nations and Panama compared to those of Mexico and Venezuela; (4) the numerous contacts by politically disparate Mexican presidents which generated an awareness that Mexico was not supporting one ideological line consistently; (5) Honduran efforts to play off Mexican and Venezuelan desires for increased influence in order to improve her economy; (6) Costa Rica's reduction in 1981 of her relations with the Soviet Union and Cuba as an indicator of Central American abilities to understand and withstand outside efforts to manipulate internal domestic matters; and finally (7) some remarks about the need to encourage long-term Central American institutional development and stability apart from short-term ideological victories.

SOME OF THE INTER-RELATED COMMON PROBLEMS

Among the inter-related problems affecting the region are: (1) per capita incomes that are among the lowest in Latin America with accompanying malnutrition, poor health, insufficient housing, and illiteracy; (2) concentration of land ownership and wealth in the hands of small minorities; (3) monopolies of political power by the wealthy that frequently have used army and police violence to put down efforts to organize worker and peasant groups or new political parties rather than accepting them into a pluralistic system; (4) rural-urban migration into capital cities by peasants and small town inhabitants seeking better economic and educational opportunities for themselves and their families; and (5) dependent, underdeveloped economies reliant upon the export of a few agricultural crops generally controlled by multinational corporations like United Fruit or Castle and Cooke, the firm controlling the Dole and Standard Fruit interests.

Tables 1-5 show some of the characteristics of these small nations that are the size of South Carolina and Tennessee. Statistics for Cuba, Mexico, and Venezuela are also included for comparative purposes.

The bulk of the population of Central America (see Table 1) lives in the highlands where coffee is the key crop, with the exception of Panama where most people live near the Canal Zone. The Caribbean coastal lowlands of Costa Rica, Guatemala, and

TABLE 6.1

POPULATION AND AREA

NATION	EST. 1979 POPULATION	AREA IN SQ. MILES	% URBAN POP. 1960	1975
Costa Rica	2,168,000	19,575	34	40
El Salvador	4,364,539	8,260	38	40
Guatemala	7,050,000	42,042	33	37
Honduras	3,639,000	43,277	23	32
Nicaragua	2,485,000	50,193	40	50
Panama	1,862,000	29,209	41	51
Mexico	67,500,000	761,602	51	63
Venezuela	14,539,000	352,143	67	80

Sources: The Europa Yearbook, 1979 and International Bank For Reconstruction And Development, World Development Report, 1979.

TABLE 6.2

AGRICULTURALLY ACTIVE POPULATION AND THE ROLE OF PRIMARY COMMODITIES AND MANUFACTURES IN EXPORTS

NATION	% POP. IN AGRICULTURE		PRIMARY COMMODITIES % OF EXPORTS		MANUFACTURES AS % OF EXPORTS	
	1960	1977	1960	1975	1960	1975
Costa Rica	51	30	95	74	5	26
El Salvador	60	47	94	71	6	29
Guatemala	67	57	97	75	3	25
Honduras	70	63	98	89	2	11
Nicaragua	62	44	98	83	2	17
Panama	51	30	100	?	0	?
Mexico	55	34	88	48	12	52
Venezuela	35	21	100	99	0	1

Source: World Development Report (1978, 1979)

Honduras are crucial economically because this is the location of the important banana and sugar plantations. Bananas, sugar, and cotton are grown in the Pacific coast lowlands of all six Central American nations. Also, cattle raising for export to the United States has become increasingly significant in the past ten years. For instance, in 1978 Honduras exported $32.3 million of meat to the U.S. while Nicaragua's total was $67.7 million.[2]

Although agriculture is still the primary source of employment and foreign exchange, as can be seen in Table 2, all of the countries have tried to diversify their economies by replacing imports with domestically-produced manufactures and have appealed to the U.S., Mexico, Venezuela, and international institutions such as the Inter-American Bank for help in this respect. Costa Rica and Guatemala have been perhaps the most successful in this effort since the creation of the Central American Common Market in 1965.

All of the Central American nations are relatively poor compared to the United States, Western Europe, or Japan while El Salvador, Guatemala, and Honduras are also poor compared to Costa Rica, Panama, Mexico, and Venezuela (see Table 3). And because of inflation and a deteriorating economic situation, it is even possible that Costa Rica's per capita GNP will have dropped to less than $1,000 by the end of 1981. Cuba's declining per capita income and the exodus of thousands of Cubans to the United States via the port of Mariel in 1979 or through asylum in Latin American embassies and consulates in Havana in 1980-1981 have dimmed its luster for most people in Central America and Panama, although it still appeals to many socially-concerned individuals in the region because of its literacy and rural economic development programs. Also, Havana's willingness and ability to send 2,000 school teachers to Nicaragua in 1979 to participate in the Nicaraguan Literacy Campaign--as opposed to the unwillingness or inability of the U.S. and other nations, although Costa Rica and Panama made a few teachers available--has scored many propaganda points for Castro's regime in Nicaragua and elsewhere.

While health care has improved in the Central American and Caribbean countries since World War II, especially with respect to the distribution of physicians and nurses among the population and the increased percentage of people having access to safe drinking water, infant mortality and death rates are

TABLE 6.3

PER CAPITA INCOME AND EDUCATION IN CENTRAL AMERICA, CUBA, MEXICO, AND VENEZUELA

NATION	PER CAPITA GNP 1960	1976	1978	ELEM. AGE %/POP. IN ELEMENTARY SCHOOL 1975	% ADULT LITERACY 1975
Costa Rica	$540	$1040	$1540	109	83
El Salvador	n.a.	490	660	71	49
Guatemala	n.a.	630	784	62	39
Honduras	260	390	480	89	57
Nicaragua	325	750	840	85	57
Panama	437	1310	1290	124	96
Cuba	n.a.	860	810	126	96
Mexico	n.a.	1090	1290	112	76
Venezuela	n.a.	2570	2910	96	82

Sources: World Development Report (1978-1980)

TABLE 6.4

SELECTED HEALTH INDICATORS IN CENTRAL AMERICAN/CARIBBEAN REGION

NATION	LIFE EXPECTANCY 1975	POP. PER PHYSICIAN 1977	% POP. WITH ACCESS TO SAFE WATER, 1975
Costa Rica	70	1580	72
El Salvador	61	900	60
Guatemala	57	2490	40
Honduras	57	3420	46
Nicaragua	55	1670	70
Panama	70	1260	79
Cuba	72	1100	?
Mexico	65	1820	60
Venezuela	66	930	62

Source: World Development Report (1978, 1980)

high (except in Costa Rica) when compared to Cuba, Mexico, Panama, and Venezuela. (See Table 4).

None of the Central American states is rich in mineral resources, especially petroleum and natural gas (although Guatemala is now exporting small amounts). Large hydroprojects are being developed in all countries to provide more electricity for industry and rural areas as well as to reduce the outlay for imported fuel.

All the Central American nations are facing deficits in their balance of payments because the costs of petroleum imports, machinery, and consumer goods have increased while the prices for their primary agricultural and mineral products have generally not risen as fast or, in the case of coffee and sugar, have declined since 1978. (See Table 5).

As can be seen in Tables 6 and 7, the United States is the principal trading partner of the Central American nations with Guatemala also important to all except Panama, which has not joined the Central America Common Market (CACM) and for whom shipping costs by land to the region are higher than those to the U.S. or Venezuela. Venezuela has become their most important Caribbean associate outside of the CACM because of petroleum imports. Costa Rica and Nicaragua did not buy very much there before 1978, but are now importing much of their oil as a consequence of the Mexican-Venezuelan pact to supply petroleum products to Caribbean nations at reduced prices for developmental purposes. Nevertheless, the Mexicans refused to make additional shipments to Costa Rica in December 1981--after apparently supplying it on a loan basis for six months--until San Jose made arrangements with the International Monetary Fund to restructure its foreign debt payments, which amounted to at least $521 million for the last quarter of 1981 even after generous adjustments were made by IMF experts. It is not known if the Mexican decision was also influenced by Costa Rica's oblique criticism of the Franco-Mexican declaration in August 1981 that the Salvadoran Democratic Revolutionary Front ought to be recognized as a "representative political force."

Cuba, Mexico, and Venezuela have not been significant customers for Central American products--a fact that many Central American businessmen and governments are trying to correct; and unless the middle-level powers like Mexico and Venezuela are able to import more from their small neighbors, there will

TABLE 6.5

FOREIGN TRADE INDICATORS OF CENTRAL AMERICA, MEXICO, AND VENEZUELA 1976 (Millions of Dollars)

NATION	EXPORTS	IMPORTS	1970-1976 AVG. ANNUAL GROWTH EXPORTS	1970-1976 AVG. ANNUAL GROWTH IMPORTS	MOST IMPORTANT EXPORTS
Costa Rica	$584	$714	4.0%	1.5%	Coffee Bananas
El Salvador	718	720	3.3	6.2	Coffee Cotton
Guatemala	782	982	3.5	6.7	Coffee Cotton
Honduras	392	453	1.4	-2.0	Bananas Coffee
Nicaragua	543	532	5.2	4.5	Cotton Sugar
Panama	227	838	3.8	6.3	Bananas Sugar
Mexico	2043	3578	2.9	5.5	Coffee Sugar
Venezuela	9149	6086	-10.0	12.5	Oil Coffee

Sources: World Development Report (1978, 1979) and Statesman's Yearbook, 1981-1982

TABLE 6.6

IMPORTS FROM PRINCIPAL TRADING PARTNERS, CENTRAL AMERICA, 1977-1979 (millions of dollars)

		USA	FED REP GERMANY	JAPAN
Costa Rica	1977	$342.0	$55.6	$136.4
	1978	270.8	124.7	6.7
El Salvador	1977	276.5	54.3	104.4
	1978	312.1	53.5	122.2
Guatemala	1977	405.9	88.4	122.1
	1978	382.6	108.2	136.1
	1979	480.4	107.2	122.9
Honduras	1977	248.7	20.6	63.3
	1978	292.8	24.3	61.8
	1979	368.8	27.6	59.6
Nicaragua	1977	219.5	51.4	77.1
	1978	186.0	32.3	41.2
	1979	90.9	14.0	13.6
Panama	1977	230.2	12.1	33.1
	1978	299.4	20.9	37.4
PERCENTAGE OF IMPORTS FROM PRINCIPAL TRADING PARTNERS				
Costa Rica	1977	33.6%	35.4%	13.4%
	1978	23.2	10.9	5.8
El Salvador	1977	29.8	5.8	10.2
	1978	30.4	5.2	11.9
Guatemala	1977	38.8	8.5	11.7
	1978	29.8	8.4	10.5
	1979	34.2	7.6	8.6
Honduras	1977	42.8	3.5	10.9
	1978	42.1	3.5	8.9
	1979	44.8	3.3	7.2
Nicaragua	1977	34.5	8.1	12.1
	1978	28.8	5.0	6.4
	1979	16.1	2.5	2.4
Panama	1977	29.7	1.6	4.3
	1978	35.4	2.5	4.4

Sources: Europa Yearbook, Vol. II (1980) and The Statesman's Yearbook, 1981-1982

UNITED KINGDOM	MEXICO	VENEZUELA	GUATEMALA	WORLD TOTAL
$25.4	----	----	$58.6	$1021
2.5	----	----	61.6	1166
28.9	18.3	74.1	128.0	2323
23.7	25.6	77.9	150.0	2568
33.5	42.9	83.9	----	1045
32.0	48.4	94.3	----	1284
31.4	----	110.3	----	1403
14.4	14.2	33.3	32.9	581
18.4	17.2	42.7	44.0	696
19.6	21.0	69.8	53.2	832
144.9	----	----	52.3	637
150.9	----	----	50.6	646
179.8	----	----	36.3	567
10.4	9.7	69.7	----	776
13.4	10.7	56.9	----	845
				TOTAL
2.3%	----	----	5.7%	90.4%
2.1	----	----	5.3	47.3
3.1	2.0	8.0	13.8	72.2
2.5	2.8	7.6	14.6	75.0
3.3	4.0	8.0	----	74.3
2.5	3.7	7.3	----	62.2
2.2	----	7.9	----	60.5
2.5	2.4	5.7	5.7	73.5
2.6	2.5	6.1	6.3	72.0
2.4	2.5	8.4	6.4	75.0
22.8	----	----	8.2	85.7
23.2	----	----	7.8	71.2
31.2	----	----	6.4	56.6
1.3	1.3	9.0	----	47.2
1.6	1.3	6.7	----	51.9

TABLE 6.7

EXPORTS TO PRINCIPAL TRADING PARTNERS, CENTRAL AMERICA, 1977-1979 (millions of dollars)

		USA	FED REP GERMANY	JAPAN
Costa Rica	1977	$247.7	$106.8	$69.9
	1978	374.4	59.2	156.7
El Salvador	1977	317.4	59.4	61.2
	1978	194.4	154.0	54.9
Guatemala	1977	381.8	158.5	90.3
	1978	316.3	135.8	72.6
	1979	368.2	108.4	98.7
Honduras	1977	251.0	93.1	26.8
	1978	337.9	78.6	14.9
	1979	395.9	71.0	35.0
Nicaragua	1977	144.9	85.4	69.8
	1978	150.1	91.1	56.1
	1979	179.8	54.7	30.4
Panama	1978	102.4	28.7	----
	1979	133.7	23.0	----
PERCENTAGE OF EXPORTS TO PRINCIPAL TRADING PARTNERS				
Costa Rica	1977	29.9%	12.9%	8.5%
	1978	43.3	6.9	18.2
El Salvador	1977	32.6	6.1	6.2
	1978	22.9	18.2	6.5
Guatemala	1977	32.4	13.5	7.7
	1978	29.0	12.4	6.6
	1979	30.2	8.9	9.0
Honduras	1977	48.9	18.1	5.2
	1978	55.7	12.9	2.5
	1979	47.6	8.5	4.2
Nicaragua	1977	22.7	13.4	11.0
	1978	23.2	14.1	8.7
	1979	31.7	9.7	5.4
Panama	1978	41.9	11.7	----
	1979	23.6	7.9	----

Sources: Europa Yearbook, Vol. II (1980) and The Statesman's Yearbook, 1981-1982

UNITED KINGDOM	MEXICO	VENEZUELA	GUATEMALA	WORLD TOTAL
$20.2	----	----	$53.4	$828
27.4	----	----	71.3	864
----	2.2	----	121.8	972
----	----	----	144.5	848
4.1	----	.5	----	1179
9.9	----	1.5	----	1092
15.7	----	.5	----	1221
1.7	----	6.6	26.6	513
5.8	----	6.6	25.7	607
7.3	----	10.2	30.5	832
1.8	----	----	34.7	636
2.1	----	----	34.3	646
1.9	----	----	21.5	547
----	----	----	----	244
----	----	----	----	291
				TOTAL
2.4	----	----	6.4	60.1%
3.2	----	----	8.3	79.9
.2	----	----	12.5	57.6
----	----	----	17.0	64.6
.3	----	.1	----	54.0
1.0	----	.1	----	49.1
1.3	----	.1	----	49.5
.3	----	1.3	5.2	79.0
1.0	----	1.0	4.2	77.3
1.0	----	1.2	3.7	66.2
.3	----	----	5.4	52.8
.3	----	----	5.3	51.6
.3	----	----	3.8	50.9
----	----	----	----	53.6
----	----	----	----	31.5

be limits to the amount of influence they will be able to develop.

THE IMPACT OF REGIONAL COMMODITY AND ENERGY AGREEMENTS

Central American and Caribbean nations have created various commodity agreements covering bananas, bauxite, and sugar to supplement the CACM, but their success as cartels has been modest so far and does not provide much hope for the future.

The Latin American Energy Organization (OLADE) was founded in 1975 to coordinate the development, conservation, and expansion of regional energy resources.[3] Both Mexico and Venezuela appear to have ignored the organization, presumably because the costs of paying for collective goods and services were judged inconvenient and greater benefits could be achieved through bilateral agreements.

Mexico and Venezuela did, however, help to create SELA, the Latin American Economic System, in 1975 (which included Cuba and excluded the U.S.), but one reads little about its plans for or success in developing the regional food production schemes, telecommunications, and other infrastructure projects and their financing that it originally was going to focus upon.[4]

THE HETEROGENEITY OF POLITICAL CULTURES

Central America and the Caribbean Basin cannot be viewed as having homogeneous political cultures, although the nations with an English heritage have developed parliamentary procedures and elections for voters to judge the stewardship of office-holders to an extent much greater than their Spanish-speaking colleagues. Indeed given the wide spectrum of ideological positions not only in Central America but also in Mexico and Venezuela, it is not surprising that there is little agreement on how to change internally to achieve both economic development and broader participation in the political process. Generally Central America has a history of political and business leaders engaged in conspiracies with their counterparts in other countries to either obtain political power or to protect it, sometimes in cooperation with the U.S. government. But many times a Somoza, a Castro, or other individuals have acted on their own for reasons which were not always ideological.

Furthermore, political, trade union, peasant, and university student leaders are involved in a variety of regional and international organizations aimed at sharing information and improving their power positions domestically or abroad as well as creating the personal contacts so necessary to politics anywhere in the world, but especially in Latin America. Christian Democrats, Liberals, Social Democrats, and Communists all have formal hemispheric organizations linking groups in different countries. For example, the Popular Liberal Alliance faction (ALIPO) of Honduras participated in 1979-1980 in a hemispheric grouping of Liberal parties--including the PRI of Mexico--and also was involved with Social Democrats of the Revolutionary Party of Guatemala, the National Liberation Party of Costa Rica, the Dominican Revolutionary Party of the Dominican Republic, and Democratic Action of Venezuela in meetings of the Socialist International. Trade union and peasant leaders of the reformist left or social democrats are linked in the Inter-American Regional Organization of Workers (ORIT) to which the AFL-CIO, the Mexican CTM, the Venezuelan CTV, and the Aprista-oriented CTP of Peru belong. Unfortunately, outside of these AFL-CIO ties to Latin American trade unions and peasant associations, there are few formal ideological links between U.S. and Latin American political parties, trade unions, peasant groups, and universities.

Two examples involving Costa Rica and Panama in recent years should suffice to show not only the *personalismo* of Latin American politics briefly discussed by Duncan in Chapter Three as an impediment to regional unity, but also the fact that ideology alone is not always adequate for understanding policy actions.

INTERNATIONAL LINKS AND THE 1948 COSTA RICAN REVOLUTION

In 1948 Jose (Pepe) Figueras, leader of the Social Democratic Party (later transformed into the Party of National Liberation or PLN), spearheaded a successful revolt of civilians when incumbent conservative President Calderon Guardia refused to recognize the election of another conservative, Otilio Ulate, as President. Figueras, aided by the governments of Juan Jose Arevalo (the self-proclaimed "spiritual socialist") in Guatemala and Carlos Prio Socarras in Cuba and followers of Juan Bosch in exile from the Dominican Republic, defeated the forces of Calderon

Guardia which were aided not only by Costa Rican Communists, but also by the governments of Anastasio "Taco" Somoza Garcia of Nicaragua and Tiburcio Carias Andino of Honduras. Under an interim junta headed by Figueras, a new constitution was drafted, the army abolished, the Communist Party outlawed from running candidates, all banks nationalized, and a career civil service system based on merit established. With Ulate's assumption of office on November 8, 1949, Costa Rica started a tradition of peaceful transfer of power from one party or coalition to another, a practice developed later in Venezuela by followers of Romulo Betancourt (Democratic Action) and Rafael Caldera (COPEI, who also spent time in exile in Costa Rica in the 1950s).

PANAMANIAN FOREIGN RELATIONS UNDER TORRIJOS

Panama under Omar Torrijos developed into an important actor in Third World politics between 1968 and 1979, especially in Central America and the Caribbean, as a consequence of efforts to change Canal Zone arrangements. "Anti-American" positions--supported by the Communist People's Party of Panama (PDP) and its ancillary Federation of Workers of the Republic of Panama (FSTRP) and the Federation of Students (FES)--neutralized leftist and nationalist criticism of the civilian-military regimes that have dominated Panama since 1968 when Colonel Torrijos and the National Guard ousted the government of civilian Arnulfo Arias Madrid after a hotly-disputed election. On the other hand, Torrijos followed policies which in many respects were more accommodating than those of Mexico in attracting U.S. and other multinational banks and corporations to the country and the Colon Free Trade Zone.[5] For example, the Labor Code of December 31, 1976 (Ley 95) included provisions allowing business firms to dismiss workers and union leaders without having to inform the Ministry of Labor.[6]

Torrijos' support for Cuban and Soviet positions, which irritated many American conservatives such as Representatives John Murphy (D-New York) and Larry McDonald (D-Georgia) and Senator Barry Goldwater (R-Arizona), did not exist when he assumed the position of Chief of State in 1968 because in May 1959 eighty Cubans led by Major Cesar Vega landed at Nombre de Dios on the Atlantic Coast in an effort to regain power for the Roberto and Arnulfo Arias families which had been ousted in the early 1950s. Although after the Vega forces were captured Fidel Castro claimed that he had nothing to do with the invasion and said that the Panamanian regime was not a dictatorship like Nicaragua's, diplomatic relations were nevertheless severed in December 1961 after he referred to Panama as a government of "traitors" and "accomplices of the imperialist Yankees." The break remained complete until April 1973 when Cuban Foreign Minister Raul Roa backed Torrijos' demand for a new canal treaty at a United Nations Security Council meeting in Panama and Panamanian diplomats reciprocated by calling for an end to Havana's diplomatic and economic isolation from the hemisphere, something which Martz notes in Chapter Four that Carlos Andres Perez--also a friend of Torrijos--was doing in Venezuela. Since 1975 Cuba has purchased goods in the Colon Free Trade Zone not directly available elsewhere in Latin America. Torrijos' support for the Sandinista Liberation Front in Nicaragua before 1979 paralleled Havana's because: (1) both Castro and Torrijos disliked the Somozas who supported the Bay of Pigs invasion in 1962; (2) Congressman John Murphy, a member of the Panama Canal Subcommittee of the House of Representatives and a long-time Somoza friend, sought to convince Howard Hughes and Daniel Ludwig to finance construction of a new sea-level canal through Nicaragua; and (3) the Nixon administration, principally E. Howard Hunt and his anti-Castro Cuban exile "plumbers", contemplated assassinating Torrijos.

Even though a 1970 U.S. government study supported construction of a second canal through Panama, Murphy and other conservatives argued that the political safety of a Nicaraguan route made it more acceptable than a Panamanian one! It is therefore not surprising that Torrijos viewed Somoza with alarm and Castro as a potential ally. Thus he supplied the Sandinista guerrillas with Cuban arms and with weapons purchased in Miami, Florida and permitted 40-45 Panamanians to join the Victoriano Lozano Brigade--named after an "Indian" Liberal Party general who was executed in 1902 by the Colombian garrison--which trained at a Panamanian government penal colony on the island of Coiba.[7]

Nevertheless, despite this "support" for causes backed by Cuban and other communist states, Panama does not have diplomatic relations with either the Soviet Union or the People's Republic of China. In fact, Cuba and Poland were the only Eastern bloc countries with embassies or consular sections in Panama City in 1980 and relations with Castro were at their lowest in many years in early 1981 due to his regime's solidarity with M-19 guerrillas trying to topple Luis Turbay Ayala's government in Colombia and its obstruction of the efforts of Cubans to obtain asylum in Costa Rican, Panamanian, Peruvian and other diplomatic offices in Havana. Panama recognized Czechoslovakia, Hungary, Rumania, and Albania, but they do not maintain an embassy or consulate in Panama City. It does not recognize either East Germany (the German Democratic Republic) or Bulgaria, which raises some interesting questions about its recognition policy.

Table 8 shows the embassies and consulates found in the capitals of the Central American nations, Panama, Mexico, and Venezuela.

MEXICAN ATTEMPTS TO COURT DIFFERENT CENTRAL AMERICAN REGIMES

Williams notes in Chapter Five that a Mexican trade commission in 1964 sought to increase commercial contacts without formal integration after relatively unsuccessful efforts by Mexico to join (and dominate) the Central American Common Market and the Latin American Free Trade Association. He notes that President Gustavo Diaz Ordaz (1964-1970) "launched the first goodwill tour of the Central American nations ever undertaken by a Mexican Chief of State." Since that time, every Mexican president has frequently hosted Central American and Panamanian leaders with little regard for their ideology or relations with one another and also has gone to see them.

For example, Diaz Ordaz called on conservative Joaquin Trejos in Costa Rica January 18-20, 1966 and Trejos returned the visit June 5-11, 1967. Luis Echeverria Alvarez invited "Pepe" Figueras, the social democratic PLN successor, to Mexico City May 20-25, 1971 along with the conservative, if not reactionary, Colonel Arana Osorio of Guatemala and "Tachito" Somoza (Figueras' old enemy) to "explore the possibilities of increasing the exportation of manufacturing products to Central America."[8] Echeverria also invited Honduras' General Melgar Castro to Mexico in 1975-1976.

Also, Lopez Portillo received Daniel Oduber, the PLN successor to Figueras, in Cancun February 23-24, 1977 and Mexico City January 10-11, 1978.[9] When conservative businessman Rodrigo Carazo Odio replaced

TABLE 6.8

EMBASSIES AND CONSULATES IN THE CAPITALS OF CENTRAL AMERICAN NATIONS, PANAMA, MEXICO, AND VENEZUELA, 1980-1981, WITH EASTERN BLOC REPRESENTATION LISTED SEPARATELY

NATION	NO. OF EMBASSIES OF NON-BLOC STATES INCL. YUGOSLAVIA	EASTERN BLOC COUNTRIES
Costa Rica	28 (5 consulates)	Bulgaria, Czechoslovakia, Rumania, and the USSR.
Cuba	48	Albania, Bulgaria, People's Republic of China (PRC), Czechoslovakia, German Democratic Republic (GDR), Hungary, Kampuchea, Democratic People's Republic of Korea (DPRK), People's Republic of Yemen (PRY), Poland, Rumania, and USSR.
El Salvador	22	
Guatemala	30	
Honduras	22 (3 consulates)	
Mexico	51	Albania, Bulgaria, PRC, Czechoslovakia, GDR, Hungary, DPRK, Poland, USSR, PRY, and Cuba.
Nicaragua	22	Bulgaria, Cuba, GDR, Hungary, Poland, USSR, and DPRK.
Panama	34	Cuba and Poland
Venezuela	50	Bulgaria, PRC, Cuba, GDR, Hungary, Poland, Rumania, and USSR.

Source: Compiled from data in *The Statesman's Yearbook, 1981-1982* and the San Jose and Tegucigalpa telephone directories.

Oduber as Costa Rican president, he came to Cancun May 20, 1979 and on July 25-27, 1980 Lopez Portillo reciprocated by going to San Jose. While there are substantial Mexican investments in Costa Rica now--and Mexican movies and television programs are part of the cultural fare of Costa Ricans as well as other Central Americans--those investments and foreign trade are still modest if one looks at the data in Tables 6 and 7.

HONDURAN EFFORTS TO MANIPULATE MIDDLE POWERS

While Mexico and Venezuela are working to increase their influence in Central America, small nations such as Honduras are also attempting to attract trade and investment from these countries with varying results. Honduras is profiled in this case, but other examples could also be cited.

On September 20, 1980, Ruben Mondragon, Honduran Minister of Economy and Commerce, went to Mexico City to "try to obtain...a large supply of oil and technological cooperation to install a steel mill" in Honduras. Honduran Ambassador to Mexico Lopez Villamil noted at the time that the trade balance between the two countries was more "favorable to Mexico and that the cooperation programs are not subject to the political or economic situation, but respond to a genuine desire for bilateral participation."[10]

On September 14, 1981, Honduran President General Policarpo Paz Garcia returned from Mexico after a 28-hour official visit. As a result of the trip, a $4 million credit agreement was signed with the National Bank of Mexico to help stimulate the further expansion of the Honduran Cement Company's plant at Piedras Azules in Comayagua Department--a firm originally started with Venezuelan credits granted as a consequence of personal relationships established between Honduran President Melgar Castro and Venezuela's Carlos Andres Perez in a Washington, D. C. meeting and subsequently maintained by telephone conversations between the two.[11] Honduras also sought more credit from Mexico to construct additional roads in its heavily-forested eastern regions, but Mexico only promised to study this request (which would be channelled through the Inter-American Bank if granted). Mexico pledged to train Honduran personnel in administering petroleum taxes and refining crude oil, thus giving Honduras some political and technical leverage over the one refinery in the country owned and operated by Texaco at Puerto Cortes. Mexico also agreed to open its markets to Honduran exports at a tax rate of only 25 percent. "In the case of products that must be taxed at 100 percent, the remaining 75 percent will revert to Honduras," according to a report by Armand Cerrato which did not indicate which products were taxed at 25 percent and which ones at 100 percent.[12] How these tax concessions compared to the favorable rates given to Nicaragua which are noted by Williams in Chapter Five is not known. Nothing, however, was announced relating to Honduras' desire to obtain credits (which it had been seeking ever since the period 1957-1963 when Ramon Villeda Morales was president) to build a steel mill. Furthermore the ACAN news agency in Panama reported that "Honduran officials also managed to clear up the Mexican media's confused image of Honduras" (without saying what that image was) and went on to state that "the Mexicans said that they admire Honduras' electoral process and recognize the country's social stability."[13]

It is not known if Mexico's desire to "help" Honduras was affected by the August 24-26, 1981 visit of Paz Garcia, his Cabinet, and leaders of all four parties nominating presidential candidates for the November 29, 1981 elections to Caracas where they were going to ask for at least $27 million in assistance. It is most likely that Mexico wanted to respond in some way to the very large Venezuelan package offered Honduras as well as the symbolic support rendered by the Herrera Campins regime to the elections that resulted in the victory of Roberto Suazo Cordova of the Liberal Party by a clear majority over Ricardo Zuñiga Agustinius of the National Party and two minor party candidates of the Christian Democrats and the Party of Innovation and Unity (PINU). Venezuela extended the following aid: (1) $23 million to build a gasahol plant and $2.5 million for petroleum storage tanks on the Pacific Coast; (2) $81.5 million to expand the El Cajon hydroelectric power project, including capital goods and labor costs; (3) $5.5 million for further construction at the Puerto Castilla docks from which lumber is exported to Venezuela, the U.S., and other countries; and (4) $1 million to stimulate the production and export to Venezuela of black beans (frijoles-caraota) which was advertised as being something of direct benefit to the Honduran peasantry.[14]

While the Paz Garcia regime was obtaining economic aid and new or potentially new markets in Mexico and Venezuela, Foreign Minister Cesar Elvir Sierra was not having as much success doing so in

Argentina, Brazil, and Chile, although he did receive political support from those governments for transferring power from the military to an elected civilian regime and perhaps the assistance of military instructors (who would join the U.S. and a few rumored Venezuelan advisors already on site) in strengthening the professional skills of the Honduran army in its occasional exchange of artillery and small weapons fire with Sandinista troops on the unstable Honduran-Nicaraguan border.

THE POTENTIAL IMPACT OF CUBAN, MEXICAN, AND VENEZUELAN POLICIES

The rivalry between Cuba, Mexico, and Venezuela for influence in the Caribbean Basin has been referred to by other authors. It seems obvious that Caracas' greater capacity to lend money--as illustrated in the Honduran example--might give it more leverage than Cuba or Mexico. However, it is problematic whether the total aid given by Venezuela (some $5 billion versus $250 million by Mexico and significantly less by Cuba) will result in that much more influence in the long run.[15] Still, it is quite likely that Caracas' greater financial assistance was influential in the support immediately rendered by the Dominican Republic and Honduras as well as the governments of Argentina, Bolivia, Chile, Guatemala, and Paraquay to the September 2, 1981 declaration by President Herrera Campins and Turbay Ayala of Colombia condemning as "intervention" an August Franco/Mexican announcement recognizing the Farabundo Marti National Liberation Front (FMLN) and the Revolutionary Democratic Front (FDR) as "representative political forces" in El Salvador with whom the Duarte regime ought to negotiate a political settlement.[16]

One unidentified U.S. State Department source told Ricard Chavirra of the Copley News Service:

> (I)t's quite possible that what irked the Venezuelans is that the Mexicans went outside the [Latin American] region. That's why they used the word intervention.[17]

Herrera Campins also criticized France and Mexico indirectly in a September speech to the United Nations General Assembly:

> Unfortunately...in recent times some democratic countries have committed the

> error of trying to give undeserving respectability to groups engaged in terrorism.[18]

A meeting at the United Nations between Herrera Campins and Mexican Foreign Minister Jorge Castaneda to defuse the conflict was unsuccessful.

While U.S. political influence in the Caribbean Basin has declined in some respects in recent years, Mexico's position on El Salvador has not gained many adherents, as illustrated in the surprising 22-3 vote at the Santa Lucia meeting of the Organization of American States (December 7, 1981) on a resolution supporting Salvadoran elections scheduled for March 1982 and repudiating violence, terrorism, and other acts of foreign intervention there. Mexico was joined only by Grenada and Nicaragua in opposing the resolution while four small nations (Trinidad-Tobago, Panama, Santa Lucia, and Suriname) abstained. Costa Rica, Guatemala, and Honduras joined Venezuela, the United States, and all of the South American republics in backing it. It is possible that Lopez Portillo has failed to recognize the extent to which Central American and Caribbean governments other than Nicaragua are worried about Cuban/Soviet subversion in their countries.

SOME CONCLUDING REMARKS

Civilian and military leaders in Central America are linked to the United States even more than they are to Mexico and Venezuela by their business and education ties. The goals of all regimes include economic development, although the distribution of expanded income varies from an egalitarian model in Costa Rica to a more traditional pattern in Guatemala. Also, not all governments support expanded literacy and freedom of choice in political as well as economic decisions. It is apparent that civilian and military elites in Honduras and Panama have accepted the idea of change and are willing to ride its waves in much the same ways as have the civilian elites of Costa Rica and Venezuela. But their counterparts in El Salvador and Guatemala have not been willing to do so. Such reluctance to allow the participation of new groups in politics and the economy or to give up some political power while still retaining economic and social power led, of course, to Somoza's downfall.

The U.S. has valid economic and military security interests in the region. But it has frequently frustrated long-range internal economic and political stability and development by undermining the growth of local institutions to deal with local problems, as exemplified by its initial misgivings about the banking reforms of the 1948 Figueras-led junta in Costa Rica and by the Eisenhower administration's unhappiness with trade unions and agrarian reform in Guatemala during the Arevalo/Arbenz period that were modelled after Mexican prototypes of the 1920s and 1930s.

Central American political leaders are sophisticated in many respects about the implications of Marxist theory and of ties with Cuba and Russia. Costa Rica, for example, closed its consulate in Havana in May 1981 and formally renounced a 1977 Technical and Economic Cooperation Agreement with the Soviet Union.[19] The closure of the Havana consulate came after: (1) several Costa Rican Ministry of Security officials were indicted for embezzlement, bribery, and illegal enrichment for issuing visas permitting Cubans to enter the country enroute to the United States; (2) the arrest of four terrorists after an April 20 shootout in the Zapote neighborhood; (3) the discovery of at least two safehouses in April in the San Jose area; (4) a bazooka attack on a U.S. embassy car carrying Marine guards and the bombing of the downtown offices of the Honduran embassy in San Jose on March 17; (5) Major Luis Alvarado Saravia, a Salvadoran rebel defector, told San Jose's Radio Reloj on April 27, 1981 that many Costa Ricans were receiving four-month training courses in Cuba along with guerrillas from El Salvador, Chile, Colombia, and Guatemala; and (6) the February 17 resignation of two top Security officials after newspaper disclosures that Ministry personnel reportedly sold Cuban arms to Salvadoran leftists which were originally part of shipments to the Sandinistas, but which were supposedly "stockpiled" in Costa Rica for "police use" in case Somoza's National Guard invaded in retaliation for the Carazo regime's granting of safe haven to the Sandinistas.[20] Costa Rica's unhappiness with the Cubans was intensified by their opposition in November/December 1980 to its candidacy for a two-year term on the United Nations Security Council, a seat ultimately won by Panama. Contributing to the renunciation of the Costa Rican-Soviet agreement was the involvement of three Cubans, one Russian, one Yugoslav, and one Bulgarian (all of whom were later expelled) in a December 1979/January 1980 strike on banana plantations operated by subsidiaries of United

Fruit and Castle and Cooke/Dole, especially since the agreement provided for training in the Soviet Union of Costa Ricans in labor relations!

The Reagan administration's resurrection of the Dulles approach that nations would be considered "against the U.S." if they did not show their support for Washington demonstrates a lack of sensitivity to political realities in Central America and the Caribbean, as Will notes in Chapter Seven. While Cuba has funneled arms to guerrilla and terrorist groups through Nicaragua and local communist parties, American military aid should nevertheless come only as part of a package that encourages open political systems. Relations with regimes that seek to prevent opposition parties and interest groups from playing meaningful roles in the political process should be kept formally correct, but cool. The package also needs to promote economic development that benefits those in the lower strata of society by supporting: (1) long-range financial commitments by the U.S., Canada, Mexico, and Venezuela to bilateral and multilateral aid efforts; (2) initiatives to improve the management of Washington's loan and grant programs since the institutional capacity of many governments to administer such projects is limited and is sometimes open to corruption; (3) continued educational exchanges of scholars and students under the Fulbright programs as well as the training of democratic union and peasant leaders by the American Institute for Free Labor Development (AIFLD) and other U.S. groups as part of the continuing ideological struggle in the region; and (4) Latin American efforts to stabilize prices for their agricultural and mineral exports, which Vice President George Bush unhappily discovered was more important to leaders in the Dominican Republic and Colombia than "the dangers of Cuban and Soviet expansionism" during an October 1981 visit.[21] Furthermore, in a symbolic gesture laden with unmistakable policy implications, Reagan should send delegations with high level administration and congressional figures to presidential inaugurations in nations such as Costa Rica and Honduras which select public officials through competitive elections and allow a free press. Conversely, in cases such as installing a successor to the Lucas Garcia regime in Guatemala, the U.S. party should be composed of lower level personnel unless there is evidence that the new government is not going to permit the intimidation or indiscriminate murder of its critics nor distort the political process so as to prevent opposition groups from playing a meaningful role. Finally, Washington must increase its backing for the OAS and regional institutions such as the Central American Court of Human Rights and must get its budgetary house in order. Worldwide recession is linked to downturns in the American economy. Heavy military spending that leads to deficits and federal borrowing that contributes to high interest rates restricts the ability of Latin American nations and enterprises to borrow money to expand business opportunities and thereby reduce unemployment.

In a classified background paper circulated in December 1981 to American diplomatic missions, Secretary of State Haig apparently was sincere in saying that Guatemala's only problem was one of "extremist groups", supported and encouraged by Cuba, engaged in terrorism. Phillip Gevelin of the Washington Post noted that the Haig memorandum also said:

> This study does not attempt to explain why violent indigenous movements may develop, nor does it attempt to explain why militant radicals who are self-proclaimed nationalists accept foreign guidance and assistance as readily as the evidence suggests.[22]

The administration's thinking as reflected in this memorandum shows little understanding of the complexities of Latin America and what the U.S. might do in the long run about the causes of indigenous violence.

NOTES

1. "Storm Over El Salvador," Newsweek (March 16, 1981), p. 34.

2. The Statesman's Yearbook, 1981-82 (New York: St. Martin's Press, 1981), pp. 580 and 924.

3. Guy Poitras, "Latin America in the Changing Global System," (Paper presented at the Southwestern Social Science Association, Dallas, Texas, April 7-10, 1976), p. 15.

4. Ibid.

5. Perhaps the best discussion of the difficulties of separating "the rhetoric of revolution from the reality" of Panamanian politics in recent years is

the article by Steve C. Ropp, "Cuba and Panama, Signalling Left and Going Right?" *Caribbean Review*, Vol. IX, No. 1 (Winter 1980), pp. 15-20 ff. Ropp's article is drawn upon for much of the information in this section.

6. "Ponencia sobre la ley 95," *Revista Sindical Inter-Americana* (Enero-Febrero 1979), pp. 12-16.

7. Ropp, op. cit., p. 17.

8. Olga Pellicer de Brody, "El Acercamiento de Mexico a America Latina" in James W. Wilkie et al., *Contemporary Mexico* (Los Angeles: University of California Press, 1976), p. 449.

9. "Una Amistad de Siempre," *La Nacion* (San Jose) (July 25, 1980) is the principal source of information on the dates of the presidential visits.

10. Madrid, Radio EFE in Spanish as quoted in Foreign Broadcast Information Service (FBIS), *Daily Report, Latin America* (September 22, 1980), p. M1.

11. "Planta Cementera Piedras Azules Configura Vigoros Impulso Al Desarrollo Industrial," *El Heraldo* (Tegucigalpa) (August 31, 1981), pp. 20-21 notes that the dedication ceremonies for the plant the previous Saturday (August 28) were conducted by President Paz Garcia and that the ASLANDZ firm of Spain and C. ITOH/KAWASAKI of Japan played important roles in the construction and supply of machinery for the INCEHSA plant. An interview with General Melgar Castro (August 30, 1981) in Tegucigalpa is the source of information on his personal relationships with Carlos Andres Perez of Venezuela.

12. Armando Cerrato, Panama City ACAN (September 15, 1981) as reported by FBIS, *Latin America Daily Report* (September 17, 1981), p. P7.

13. Ibid., p. P7.

14. "Todo El Gobierno en Venezuela," *La Prensa* (San Pedro Sula) (August 25, 1981), p. 32; and Illsa Diaz Zelaya, "Asi Vimos a Venezuela," *Tiempo* (San Pedro Sula) (August 31, 1981), p. 14.

15. Ricardo Chavira, Copley News Service, "Rivalry Between Mexico and Venezuela Grows," *The Brownsville (Texas) Herald* (October 25, 1981), p. 7F.

16. Ibid. and "Reagan 'narrows' rift with Mexico," Dallas Morning News (September 18, 1981), p. H2.

17. Chavira, op. cit.

18. Ibid. and Caracas Radio Rumbos Network in Spanish (September 21, 1981) quoted in FBIS, Latin America, Daily Report, p. L1.

19. San Jose Radio Monumental (May 8, 1981) as reported in FBIS, Daily Report, Latin America (May 11, 1981).

20. "2 Bombs Give Costa Rica Taste of Latin Terrorism," New York Times (March 22, 1981) and "Terrorismo y Secuestro de Avion," La Nacion (San Jose)(December 31, 1981), p. 8D.

21. James Nelson Goodsell, "Bush finds Latin Americans concerned about sugar prices, not Castro," Christian Science Monitor (October 15, 1981), p. 3.

22. Philip Geyelin, "Two different views of Guatemala," St. Petersburg (Florida) Times (December 24, 1981), p. 6A.

7

The Struggle for Influence and Survival: The United States–Microstate Caribbean Interface

W. Marvin Will

INTRODUCTION

The recent flurry of interest in the Caribbean by the United States is both welcome and unsettling to most regional policy makers and Caribbeanists. It is welcome because there is a perceived need for a sustained U.S. focus toward the multitude of emerging nations on the U.S. doorstep rather than the "on and off" four to eight year cycles of "rediscovery" that have historically plagued regional relationships. While the Caribbean is only one of several geographic interest zones for the United States, albeit a most important one in view of socio-political-economic and security stakes linked to it, improved ties with the Northern Colossus are almost essential for the survival of many developing countries there, especially the newly independent microstates.

Once again becoming the center of U.S. attention, however, induces apprehension if not outright fear "in areas of our national subconsciousness," asserts Mexico's President Lopez Portillo, since too often in the past relationships with the U.S. have been far from satisfactory.[1] From the perspective of the Caribbean, short-term U.S. security and economic interests have had a most negative impact on governmental legitimacy, national unity, and, ultimately, systemic survival in the region. This chapter focuses on this struggle for survival in the "United States Medi-

---

Appreciation is extended to the Office of Research, the University of Tulsa, for partially funding travel expenses incurred in researching this material and to De Will for editorial and typing assistance.

terranean."[2]

The Caribbean: Many Faces

How does one define the Caribbean? There are at least three Caribbeans according to William Demas, President of the Caribbean Development Bank: 1) the Caribbean Basin; 2) the Caribbean archipelago; and 3) several cultural subsystems, including the Commonwealth or English-speaking Caribbean.[3]

In official metropolitan literature in particular, and increasingly in the region itself, one hears more and more about the concept of a Caribbean Basin in reference to the geographic macrounit which, in addition to the insular territories, includes the rim or littoral countries, primarily Hispanic, from Mexico to Venezuela and even as far east as the French Guiana-Brazilian border. The primary utility of the Basin concept lies in the political and economic potential it affords the area, but there are also cultural links between some of the littoral and insular countries by virtue of their colonial/plantation legacy, Africa-to-America and island-to-mainland migration,[4] and a rising but still embryonic sense of shared oppression/dependence.

The prevailing view of the Caribbean is that of an archipelago of islands with the Guianas and Belize usually included as mainland appendages. This Caribbean has experienced a greater sense of cultural integration than the rim countries despite its varied Spanish, French, Dutch, and English colonization patterns. "The region comprises one culture area," observes historian Franklin Knight, "in which common factors have forged a more-or-less common way of looking at life, the world, and their place in the scheme of things."[5] The independent Hispanic island states of Cuba (9.7 million) and the Dominican Republic (5.9 million) plus the (U.S.) Commonwealth of Puerto Rico (3.2 million) form the largest population segment among this group and Cuba, the size of Pennsylvania, is also the largest geographic entity among the islands. The French (or French creole) territories in the archipelago include Martinique, Guadeloupe (including half of St. Martin), and French Guiana (all departments of metropolitan France) plus impoverished Haiti, the first Caribbean state to gain independence (1804). Curacao, Aruba, Bonaire, Saba, the southern half of St. Martin/St. Maarten, and St. Eustatius make up the Netherlands Antilles group (collective population over 300,000) which is currently seeking independence, collectively or individually. One Dutch territory, mainland Suriname (formerly Dutch Guiana, population 480,000) opted for singular independence in 1975.[6]

With the exception of the U.S. Virgin Islands, the remaining areas in the archipelago, conceptually a third Caribbean, are the former and present British territories collectively known as the Commonwealth or English-speaking Caribbean, including mainland Guyana (formerly British Guiana) and Belize (formerly British Honduras). It is to this Caribbean that this chapter will direct primary emphasis due to the tremendous escalation of independent microstates emerging within the Commonwealth group during the past two decades and the questions their emergence poses for ordered change within the Basin.

The Commonwealth Caribbean: A Profile

A United Nation's study suggests that all of the Commonwealth Caribbean territories, based on geographic size, population, and overall gross national product (GNP), may be considered microstates.[7] On a per capita basis, however, this microstate group (a term used interchangeably with Commonwealth and English-speaking Caribbean in this chapter) is better developed both politically and economically than most Basin countries largely as a result of its high level of institutionalized political authority systems and its overall modernity, including literacy levels. Its natural resource base is narrow, however, and populations are small with only Jamaica having a larger or comparable total population than the smallest independent Hispanic Basin states, Panama and Costa Rica.

Jamaica became the first member of the English-speaking Caribbean to achieve political independence when in a national plebiscite in 1962 it voted to withdraw from the faltering Federation of the West Indies. The Federation, consisting of ten British colonies, had been formed in 1958 after the United Kingdom, war-torn and having lost its most valuable crown jewels in India and Africa, became anxious to rid itself of its once-prosperous islands (that were increasingly perceived as liabilities) and became an active participant with colonial leaders in an independence-through-federation effort. The Federation collapsed after four years of trial and (mostly) error failed to make the incipient organization viable and Jamaica, its largest unit (1.6 million then), opted to go it alone.[8]

When results of the Jamaican plebiscite reached Trinidad and Tobago, with the second largest population in the Federation (c850,000 then), its Premier Dr. Eric Williams asserted his post-Federation mathematical formula "ten minus one equals naught" and immediately moved for independence for his two-island state, which was also achieved in 1962. Just four years later British Guiana (soon to be renamed Guyana), then the largest of the remaining nonindependent Commonwealth countries (c600,000), also chose independence. This territory, which had not joined the 1958-1962 federation effort, is geographically the largest of the Commonwealth Caribbean states with an 83,000 square mile land mass. Barbados (c235,000 then) also opted for independence in 1966 following participation in still another abortive federation attempt, the Little Eight, which included the Leeward and Windward island groups. (See Table 1.) These four nations are today the most developed states within the Caribbean Common Market and Caribbean Community (CARICOM), which is primarily an economic intergovernmental organization (IGO) that emerged in 1973 from the Caribbean Free Trade Association (CARIFTA, founded in 1968).[9]

The Bahamas, a miniarchipelago as close as fifty miles to the Florida coast, became independent in 1973. This island grouping chose not to participate in either federation attempt nor in the CARIFTA/CARICOM movement (except as an observer) due primarily to its isolated location from its CARICOM neighbors and its socio-economic proximity to the United States.

Following the failure of the Little Eight in the mid-1960s, the diminutive Leeward and Windward island groups received semiautonomous status from the British government (1967) which permitted them to move toward independence anytime a two-thirds legislative and popular vote was secured. Thus far, urged on by rhetoric in the U.N. Committee on Decolonization, five island states in the Leeward-Windward group plus Belize (formerly British Honduras) have become independent: Grenada, 1974; Dominica, 1978; St. Lucia, 1979; St. Vincent, 1979; and near the end of 1981 the Union Jack was lowered for the final time in Belize and the two-island state of Antigua and Barbuda. None of these six newly emergent ministates has a current population level in excess of 112,000, with only

TABLE 7.1

AREA AND POPULATION OF
COMMONWEALTH CARIBBEAN COUNTRIES

TERRITORY AND DATE OF INDEPENDENCE	AREA (sq. miles)	POPULATION (000's)	LIFE EXPECTANCY
Antigua and Barbuda-1981 (L)	170	72	64
The Bahamas-1973	5,382	220	67
Barbados-1966	166	253	71
Belize-1981	8,598	149	49
British Virgin Islands	59	12	55
Cayman Islands	118	11	
Dominica-1978 (W)	305	80	59
Grenada-1974 (W)	133	110	66
Guyana-1966	83,000	884	69
Jamaica-1962	4,411	2,192	71
Montserrat (L)	39	13	55
St. Kitts-Nevis (& Anguilla?)(L)	130	66	62
St. Lucia-1979 (W)	233	112	58
St. Vincent and the Grenadines-1979 (W)	150	100	60
Trinidad and Tobago-1962	1,980	1,093	71
Turks and Caicos	166	6	

(L) = Leeward Island Group
(W) = Windward Island Group

Source: Comision Economica para America Latina (CEPAL), *Statistics Summary of Latin America, 1960-1980* (Santiago, Chile: CEPAL [1981?]); *UN Statistical Yearbook* (New York, 1978).

75,000 in Antigua and Barbuda. And much smaller territories, such as St. Kitts-Nevis and Montserrat, not to mention the Turks and Caicos Islands (6,000), are devoting varied degress of attention to an independence scenario.

A question of viability is raised[10] for, in addition to being small, the Commonwealth ministates which have achieved independence during the past decade are almost totally without a natural resource base other than their sand, sea, and energetic (albeit poor and underemployed) people. But the Commonwealth Caribbean, portrayed as a shimmering paradise by the tourist industry, consists of very real states with very real problems.

PROBLEMS IN PARADISE AND INTERNAL AND EXTERNAL CARIBBEAN POLITICS

Although national integration and communication efficiency may be expedited by the compact geographic and population dimensions of the Caribbean microstates, smallness does pose major disadvantages (acknowledged even by many "small is beautiful" advocates) such as decidedly reducing the potential for large and diversified natural resources, making the optimum development of markets of scale extremely difficult, complicating transportation routing and pricing practices, and limiting the available manpower, including retention of skilled workers and technocrats. It also contributes to the emergence of economic monocultures with their negative implications in view of highly elastic international markets. (See Table 2.)

In addition, these countries encounter major shortages of needed capital and appropriate technology and must deal with continually increasing prices for imported energy, food, and manufactured goods. Agricultural production severely lags behind domestic requirements in most islands due to a combination of territorial limitations and the negative cultural manifestations resulting from their colonial/slave heritage. This multiplicity of problems has contributed significantly to present double-digit unemployment of 20-30 percent in most islands--a rate that is more than doubled in hidden unemployment and/or underemployment.[11]

TABLE 7.2

COMMONWEALTH CARIBBEAN
EXPORTS AND TRADE DIRECTIONS

COUNTRY	MAIN EXPORTS (average % of total 1970-1976 exports)		MAIN CUSTOMERS (% of total 1976 exports)		MAIN SUPPLIERS (% of total 1976 imports)	
Barbados						
	Sugar	33	U.S.	31	U.S.	24
			Ireland	14	U.K.	19
Guyana						
	Sugar	36	U.K.	27	U.S.	29
	Bauxite	31	U.S.	20	U.K.	23
Jamaica						
	Bauxite	43	U.S.	41	U.S.	37
			U.K.	18	Venezuela	15
Trinidad & Tobago						
	Petroleum	83	U.S.	69	Saudi Arab.	26
			U.K.	5	U.S.	20

Source: IMF, International Financial Statistics (Washington, DC, 1978); UN Statistical Yearbook (New York, 1978); Virginia R. and Jorge I. Dominguez, The Caribbean (New York: Foreign Policy Association, 1981).

Potential for Relative Deprivation and Declining Political Support

Although per capita income and other development indices are relatively high in the Commonwealth Caribbean in comparison with other Third World countries, the potential for rising expectations in these states is heightened by their proximity to and resultant penetration by an opulent North American lifestyle, including its media, films, obsolescence advertising and marketing, and hoards of seemingly affluent tourists who flock to Caribbean beaches, annually outnumbering total inhabitants in some islands. The negative impact of such "modernity" is compounded by this subregion's 85-99 percent literacy in English; its well-developed communications systems, including newspapers and radio plus television in the larger islands; and the substantial pre-1970s economic progress experienced in many territories, such as Jamaica's near-world leadership in growth percentages during the early 1960s. "Champagne tastes with mauby pocketbooks" were developing, according to one Eastern Caribbean prime minister.[12]

Rapid escalation of energy costs in the post 1973-1974 period furthered a perceived decline in socio-economic conditions and provoked massive protests in Jamaica and other territories. Damage inflicted by Hurricane Allen in the Eastern Caribbean in 1980 severely affected GNP and the overall standard of living as 90-100 percent of the banana plantations were devastated in St. Lucia, St. Vincent, and Dominica. This resulted in the loss of more than one-half of export earnings and one-third of jobs in these countries and severely exacerbated the already double-digit unemployment plaguing the region.[13] Such decremental decreases, when combined with rising expectations, provide a double-barreled stimulus to perceived relative deprivation.[14]

Unemployment is always highest among youth, of course, and a near-majority of the population in the Caribbean is under sixteen years of age. During the 1960s, a substantial portion of the unemployed/underemployed Caribbean work force was able to migrate to the U.K. and other metropolitan areas, an option frequently exercised by the younger West Indians. During the 1970s, however, these legal escape valves were largely blocked by metropolitan policies and the Caribbean work force has increased by nearly 400,000, two-thirds of whom are between the ages of fifteen and thirty-four. And in some islands, as in U.S. inner cities, generations of "never employed" have been produced.[15]

These many factors combine to create a mixture fraught with explosive potential--a condition that routinely contributes to the defeat of governments via the ballot and was a probable element in the socio-political "revolutionary" upheavals that visited Trinidad in the early 1970s and overturned the Gairy regime in Grenada in 1979. By the end of 1981, continuation of such politics of violence has produced threatened coups in Jamaica and St. Vincent and a foiled mercenary plot against Dominica in conjunction with its deposed Prime Minister Patrick John.[16] But there is reason for concern. Unemployed or underemployed youths were prominent components in both the Trinidadian and Grenadian rebellions. In addition, socio-economic-political pressures in the region are currently intensifying while the ability of most of the area governments to adapt to popular demands is severely constrained by escalating budget imbalances and, in the worst cases, by International Monetary Fund (IMF)-required reductions in public services. How microstate governments cope with these demands may in fact be their most pressing crisis of the 1980s.

The IMF Crisis

Trade and exchange imbalances have become a fact of life in the microstate Caribbean, with the exception of oil-rich Trinidad, since the 1973-1974 surge in petroleum prices. Hard currency to pay the always heavy import bill is simply lacking in many countries.

The full budgetary impact of the 1973-1974 petroleum shock was temporarily delayed in the English-speaking Caribbean countries of Barbados, Guyana, and Jamaica due to high export earnings for sugar and bauxite. In Barbados, sugar prices and governmental import and tax policies combined with small-scale domestic petroleum production, which supplies one-third of national needs, to generate a substantial positive balance of payments by 1975. This surplus expanded to $50 million by mid-1979, but declining oil output helped push Barbados into the red by the end of 1981. The Guyanese and Jamaican governments, with no domestic petroleum production, embarked on heavy capital and social service expenditures and experienced major balance of payments problems as early as 1976. By September 1980, net foreign assets reflected a $101 million deficit in Guyana and $520 million in Jamaica despite heavy borrowing from Trinidad, the IMF, and, in the case of Jamaica, OPEC and even COMECON. A severe balance of payments crisis had developed in both countries, especially the latter.

A payments crisis is like a slippery slope, asserts West Indian economist Courtney Blackman. Scarcity of foreign exchange curtails purchase of needed raw materials and capital equipment which are crucial for economic recovery[17]--a problem compounded in both Jamaica and Guyana when middle entrepreneurs migrated with scarce capital and/or requested over-billing of metropolitan accounts with the overage to be deposited in Miami banks! Unless appropriate, but politically costly income and taxation policies are implemented, the beleaguered country is forced to draw down its IMF "soft fund" and even draw against its gold tranche position. "This mean[s] that any further borrowing from the Fund...would involve quite drastic and stringent conditionalities," Blackman concludes. It was Jamaica's failure to fully comply with such stringent conditions that led Michael Manley's government to its final fall from IMF grace.[18]

Prime Minister Manley and his Peoples National Party were soundly turned from office in October 1980 primarily as a result of Jamaica's continuing economic crisis, which ironically became a political crisis partly because of earlier governmental attempts to comply with IMF conditionalities! This was the eighth time that such a switch had occurred in the English-speaking Caribbean since 1976 (the thirteenth in the Basin) and established this subregion as a world leader in regime-changing elections without suspension of constitutional privileges.[19]

Microstate Foreign Policy: The Politics of Survival

In the Commonwealth Caribbean, as in perhaps no other Third World area,

> domestic constituency pressures impose on decision makers the necessity to give priority to the demands of the domestic environment. No leader who consistently turns away from such demands could seriously hope to have a long or peaceful tenure of office.[20]

Thus, foreign policy must be firmly grounded on domestic realities. In the 1960s these realities were primarily economic survival, social and economic development, and the reduction of unemployment. These aims remain paramount in the 1980s[21] and goal-seeking politics must address them as well as search out investment capital and market access. "Since all our economies are open and as such are adversely affected by world economic situation[s], and since we have limited natural resources," the Barbadian Minister of External Affairs recently lamented, "our nations are finding that they cannot provide for themselves without external assistance of some kind."[22]

There are the more traditional foreign and military policy goals, to be sure, including: 1) a measure of independence (both from the West, especially the United States, and from the more general uncertainties of the international economic environment); 2) political survivability (a regional problem with reference to border disputes, secessionist threats, and ideological challenges); and 3) a greater voice in world affairs and increased prestige among Third World states.[23] And there is also renewed Commonwealth Caribbean support for decolonization, which includes strong opposition to apartheid in South Africa, plus a resurfacing emphasis on CARICOM policy coordination. All goals, however, must yield to the primacy of national interest and economic viability--even such genuine concerns as efforts to reduce dependency or the pursuit of foreign affairs itself.

Because of the severe competition for scarce dollars, foreign/military affairs departments in the microstates must function on a very limited budget. Expenditures for the armed forces account for less than one percent of total budget allocations throughout the Commonwealth Caribbean as opposed, for example, to approximately 9 percent by Cuba. The per capita ratio of military spending to health and education expenditures in these countries (in U.S. dollars) is most positive: $4 to $228 in Barbados; $11 to $203 in Trinidad and Tobago; $9 to $113 in Jamaica; and, reflecting less political openness and more external military pressure (from Venezuela), $10 to $61 in Guyana. By comparison, the figures are $49 to $123 in Cuba; $55 to $65 in Argentina; $2 to $3 in Haiti; $262 to $565 in the United Kingdom; $394 to $271 in the USSR; and $499 to $906 in the U.S.[24]

To conserve funds, Caribbean microstates must limit their number of diplomatic missions and make site selections with great care. A typical initial representation would include an embassy in Washington, London, and perhaps Ottawa; a small permanent contingent at the UN (with a possible consulate in New York--and/or Toronto or Montreal); and anticipated missions to the Organization of American States (OAS), to Brussels and the European Economic Community (EEC), to an important African or Latin state (perhaps Nigeria or Venezuela); to a major trading partner (see Table 2); and to a major Eastern Bloc nation--plus, in the case of multiracial countries such as Trinidad and Guyana, possibly to "mother" India as well.[25] Obviously these limited diplomatic posts would, by necessity, require multiple accreditation. In some instances, countries share ambassadors, with one diplomat representing two or more countries.

By 1969-1970, seven to eight years following independence, Jamaica had established diplomatic relations with only thirteen nations and Trinidad and Tobago with twenty-three. At approximately the same time, after three to four years of independence, Guyana had embassies in seven nations and Barbados in five.[26] Barbados, as is presently the practice among several ministates in the Eastern Caribbean, initially shared an ambassador (with Guyana) and in the mid-1970s still had an extremely low budget for servicing its foreign service program:

> The initial establishment of the foreign service cadre was twenty-six persons, and since then, there has been only a minimal increase in personnel. When it is recognised that the servicing of the foreign ministry and five missions abroad is dependent upon the efforts of some twenty-nine persons, the limitations on the resources available for the conduct of foreign policy can well be understood.[27]

In Trinidad one foreign policy specialist did not find it surprising that "treaties inherited from Britain have not been fully sorted out as yet," after a decade of independence, since "there has never been more than two diplomatic officers at the same time in [the legal] division."[28]

In addition to maximizing the very limited foreign service budget allocations of these small states by multiple embassy accreditations and shared ambassadors, another most beneficial tool is their membership in the United Nations. The UN remains an important IGO for developing microstates both for the assistance it provides in the all-important sphere of economic development and the fact that these emerging countries gain access to almost every state in the world by maintaining only one small office in New York.

By gradually expanding their representation with major trading partners, fellow developing nations (such as the African, Pacific, and Caribbean group--over which Jamaica's Foreign Minister Hugh Shearer presides--that operates within the Commonwealth of Nations and the EEC), the Third World Group of 77 (to which the Commonwealth Caribbean gives both active and passive support), key countries in the Latin American/Caribbean Basin Bloc (such as Venezuela, Mexico, and Brazil), and by initiating selected contacts with Communist bloc countries (as Grenada, Guyana, and pre-Seaga Jamaica have done), the international prestige of these microstates is enhanced, sources of trade and potential development funds are kept open, and some balance is maintained against dependency on and domination by the all-powerful Northern Colossus.[29]

THE U.S.-MICROSTATE INTERFACE IN THE U.S. "MEDITERRANEAN"

A Legacy of Dependency and Domination

Cultural Dependency. The Caribbean legacy of dependency did not suddenly appear with the emergent power of North America, of course. European colonization of the region had been a long-standing reality: first, Spain; then, by the seventeenth century, colonial competition and power balancing from the French, Dutch, and the English. An ex-colonial governor described English colonization of the West Indies as follows:

> pieces in Elizabethan schemes of empire, objects of Caroline and Cromwellian enterprise, loot of eighteenth century wars, ... the West Indies have been prized with an excessive enthusiasm in one century and left to decay in squalor in the next.[30]

Native Americans in the region had been decimated. Slaves were imported in massive numbers--and were just as massively dispossessed. All, including creole

Europeans, were socialized to look first to the metropole--to learn and accept European history and values, thereby depreciating their own cultural values and structures. In short, the entire region came to suffer cultural dependence and the West Indies, to paraphrase Trinidad's V.S. Naipaul, became a "mimic society."

Political-Economic Domination in the U.S. "Mediterranean." In the post-independence Caribbean Basin, however, it is U.S. overbearance that is most directly at issue. Until the largely U.S.-imposed British Guiana-Venezuela boundary settlement in 1895-1896 and the nearly simultaneous decision by the U.K. that the Caribbean Basin was "politically and strategically expendable" in view of its African and Asian colonization schemes,[31] the United States and the United Kingdom were in competition for the role of policeman in the area. During the succeeding thirty-eight years, Washington would employ "big stick" military force and dollar diplomacy to conquer its own empire in the region and impose its political and economic will on so-called independent countries throughout the Basin, a policy officially rationalized as "the obligation of the [U.S.] Government under the spirit of the Monroe Doctrine."[32] A most candid summation and personalization of these actions is presented by Major General Smedley D. Butler, a veteran of both littoral and insular Caribbean occupations:

> I helped make Mexico and especially Tampico safe for American oil interests in 1914. I helped make Haiti and Cuba a decent place for the National City Bank boys to collect revenue in. ... I helped purify Nicaragua for the international banking house of Brown Brothers in 1909-1912. I brought light to the Dominican Republic for American sugar interests in 1916 [occupied officially until 1924, unofficially until 1934]. I helped make Honduras "right" for American fruit companies in 1903.[33]

A notable U.S. confrontation with several Basin countries regarding the 1914-1916 Bryan-Chamorro canal treaty contributed significantly to the destruction of the valuable Central American Court of Justice; "its prestige irreparably damaged,"[34] it soon disbanded. Ironically, the U.S. had aided in the establishment of the Court a decade earlier! The less interventionist

Good Neighbor initiatives of the U.S. during the 1930s and 1940s, however, produced good will in the region which contributed to a common front of cooperation during World War II, surprising even the most skeptical critics of this less belligerent policy.[35] The politics of cooperation could serve U.S. interests!

From Cold War to Detente. East-West polarization following World War II led to a renewal of interventionism in the Caribbean Basin. The prevailing philosophy of the new U.S. policy was espoused by Secretary of State John Foster Dulles: "The master plan of international communism is to gain a solid base in this hemisphere, a base that can be used to extend Communist penetration."[36] Furthermore, in the confrontation politics of this period, Third World neutrality was considered an "immoral" front for communism.

As the Soviet Union and the United States hardened their respective positions, new rules of the game were established for their respective spheres of influence. According to diplomatic historian Melvin Gurtov, these rules were first

> that access ... by U.S. diplomats, public and private enterprise, and a range of other "contacts" ... must be preserved to the broadest extent possible. A second is the obverse ... , access to the region by hostile influences should be limited or denied if they threaten (or appear to threaten) American security, political and economic paramountcy. ... A third rule [is] that the independence of ... governments is qualified to the extent they are unable to maintain political stability, promote public order against subversive forces, and protect [North] American lives and property. ... Within this sphere of influence, like the U.S.S.R. in Eastern Europe, the United States claims the powers of chief arbiter and upholder of law and order.[37]

In 1954 U.S. sponsorship of the overthrow of Guatemala's Arbenz government provided the first major Caribbean test of revised U.S. doctrine, which one Basin president termed an "international license to the United States to do ... everything [it] pleases.[39] Retarding communist intrusion became the overriding U.S. goal, especially after 1959 when Cuba and Cuban communism became the seminal issue for U.S. policy in the Basin. The militarist interventionist politics of the pre-Good Neighbor era had returned, although with new ideological wrappings, in specific U.S. policy applications that included: 1) military intervention in Cuba (1961); 2) intervention in Guyana, via the CIA, to stop Cheddi Jagan and advance the political fortunes of Forbes Burnham (1962); and 3) the forceful frustration of a potential revolution in the Dominican Republic and, in the process, significant contribution to the demise of the peacekeeping potential of the Organization of American States (1965). The Guyana intervention, which may have had worse repercussions for U.S. (and Guyanese domestic) interests than the threat posed by Cheddi Jagan, a democratic constitutionalist despite his Marxist rhetoric, was but one of several U.S. interventions in the region which contributed to very long-term change in the internal balance of power in the countries affected. The Guyana case also reveals the degree to which the British had yielded to U.S. hegemony in the Caribbean by their acquiescence to CIA involvement in one of their own colonies.[39]

Intervention continued under the Nixon and Carter administrations, but it was less overt and coercive during Carter's presidency, who was more given to ideals, especially human rights. The international economy made times infinitely more difficult during this period, but the overall political atmosphere was more tolerant of diversity in Caribbean development models and hence more conducive to experimentation and adaptation or finesse by the microstates as they attempted to maintain their precarious economic-political balance.[40]

The Reagan Corollary

Contemporary U.S. Interests and Reagan Policy. The Caribbean of the 1980s has substantial and long-term interest to the United States in addition to the crucial security and strategic concerns usually noted. As stated in recent testimony to Congress by the U.S. Agency for International Development (AID), this is due to the region's geographic proximity to the U.S., the economic interdependence that exists, the ethnic ties that bind many U.S. and Caribbean citizens, and a shared commitment to democratic political institutions as well as to human rights. Most important, however, in this era of turmoil in the Caribbean Basin, "it is in the U.S. interest that the Caribbean maintains viable and progressive economies and stable governments as the basis for cooperative U.S.-Caribbean relationships."[41] Local institutions, including the Caribbean Development Bank (CDB), were especially singled out by AID as desirable vehicles through which positive policies could be mutually developed.[42] The legitimization of such structures represents perhaps the best insurance for long-term political order in an area of crisis. The Reagan administration's response to the challenges of the region has not necessarily reflected the AID viewpoint, however.

Although the Reagan administration did not develop a comprehensive policy toward the Third World during its first year in office, it did project values with significant relevance to both the Third World and the Caribbean: that a confrontation approach toward the Soviet Union will again be pursued in an attempt to reassert U.S. power; that the Caribbean Basin is a focal point in that confrontation since nearly all unrest in the area stems from Soviet/Cuban involvement; that private investment in the economic sphere, not U.S. governmental handouts, has the greatest potential to serve U.S. needs and LDC development; and that bilateral programs are most desirable in the select cases where U.S. governmental funds are required, but that such programs should embrace only countries perceived as friends--with friends defined as those who visibly and loudly proclaim anti-communism!

Within one month of Reagan's inauguration, Department of State deliberations on a Caribbean aid program were initiated, primarily as a result of alleged Communist encroachment in the Caribbean Basin, and a pending plan "for providing major amounts of economic, political and military assistance to countries in the region"[43] was announced on May 23, 1981. Apparently as a result of influence by Assistant Secretary of State Thomas Enders, the proposed plan was structured to include a degree of coordination with other potential donor powers.

Reaganomics in the Microstate Caribbean. In a July 1981 meeting with Canada, Mexico, and Venezuela in Nassau, the Reagan administration outlined the economic portion of its Caribbean plan as a private/public Caribbean Basin Initiative (CBI). The CBI was designed to "emphasize private investment and trade [rather than] asking Congress for more aid money....[and] _the key to American participation is_ the willingness of recipient countries to 'create a good climate for private investment' with investment treaties that safeguard foreign capital."[44] Largely as a result of pressure from Mexico and Venezuela, the terms of this initiative were revised at the meeting to provide that capital assistance developed and channeled under the agreement should not be automatically denied to "enemy" countries such as Grenada, Cuba, and Nicaragua, but Washington did win agreement that each donor country could structure its own programs and choose the aid recipients.

A month later at the North-South conference in Cancun, Mexico, President Reagan amplified the private investment aspects of his assistance plan. "Poor nations should seek greater international trade, give incentives for private investment, and foster free market forces in efforts to reduce the gap separating them from developed countries," the President stated. They "must seek prosperity by pulling up their own economic socks instead of counting on handouts from the United States and other industrialized countries."[45] But many, both within the Commonwealth subsystem and the Caribbean Basin, simply have no socks to pull!

Lack of specifics relating to the Caribbean Basin Initiative has led to considerable frustration among the West Indian leadership, especially following the October 10, 1981 meeting in the Dominican Republic where the U.S. delegation appeared most reluctant to discuss aid and made very few comments about trade. "We wanted more emphasis on multilateralism," remarked a Guyanese diplomat, plus "more emphasis on trade and aid, which we are not going to get, and different mechanisms for administering the program. We won't get that either."[46] In a speech to the OAS General Assembly in Castries, St. Lucia in December 1981, Secretary of State Alexander Haig extended an offer to seek Congressional approval for select cases of one-way free trade and economic assistance. In view of budget-cutting politics and growing protectionism in Washington, however, this does not appear a very definite specific and many island leaders consider the CBI "bogged down in a mire of misplaced expectations, unsupported rhetoric, and ill-planned meetings."[47]

If all Reagan's so-called Caribbean Plan means is that we must open our countries to free access by U.S.-based multinational corporations, several Eastern Caribbean officials have commented, we are not interested since there are too many problems connected with unbridled penetration by MNCs.[48] Both former Prime Minister Williams of Trinidad and Barbados cabinet member Richard Cheltenham have expressed strong personal reservations regarding tax holiday incentives which multinational corporations routinely demand; and George Chambers, the present Prime Minister of Trinidad and Tobago, has questioned the role of MNCs in the control of crucial technology.

> The transnational enterprises are the prime sources of.... new technology...and the principal agents in the traffic in technology. They determine not only what technology is made available, not only the price at which it is available [which is astronomically high in the Caribbean], but also where the products of the technology may be sold.[49]

Real questions are also raised by West Indian leaders regarding Reagan's belief that U.S.-style development models should be emulated by emerging Caribbean nations. Such fragile economies require "truly Caribbean models rooted in our historical experience and our Caribbean purposes and values," Barbados Central Bank Governor Courtney Blackman correctly asserts. "We will, of course, continue to study alien models and modes of thought, but to obtain insight, not as molds into which our societies must be forced." West Indians, he concludes, should be "as impatient with the Free Enterprise laissez-faire ideology of Milton Friedman as ... with Marxist-Leninism."[50]

Caribbean Basin governments less solvent than Trinidad or Barbados, however, tend to be more circumspect of their placement within the U.S. sphere of interest and less critical of potential capital flows from Washington--with or without Friedman/Stockman orientations and investment guarantees for metropolitan-based MNCs. To paraphrase Dominica's Prime Minister Eugenia Charles, the CBI has moved slowly but that is because we are impatient. Weak governments must fall into line and learn to beg properly. Thus this fragile island, which has recently experienced both a mercenary invasion and an overdrawn IMF account, must court a special relationship with Washington and, possibly as an inducement, has increased rhetoric against the Bishop regime in Grenada as well as terminating a Cuban scholarship program for Dominicans.[51] Jamaica, whose Prime Minister Seaga was both the first foreign head of state to visit President Reagan and the first Commonwealth Caribbean leader to break relations with Castro, already receives $60 million in U.S. bilateral economic and military assistance and other special IMF and U.S. government treatment plus a steady flow of U.S. corporate investment and appears to be the priority country which Washington hopes to "turn around," thereby demonstrating the positive virtues of Reaganomics and the failures of socialism.[52]

The Return to Confrontation. When the Reagan administration assumed office, it inherited a most volatile Caribbean region, the "hottest corner on the globe,"[53] to use the mixed metaphor of Bogota's El Tiempo. This heat was produced by a spate of revolutionary activity that had not been equaled since the time of the Cuban Revolution in 1959. By 1979 Central America was in political flames--a flame that has also been felt in the English-speaking Caribbean in the tiny Spice Island of Grenada, not to mention a "leftist" coup in Suriname and short-term constitutional/electoral "revolutions" in Dominica and St. Lucia. To some, revolution (and socialism) appeared to be island-hopping through the area and the Reagan administration assumed a stance of dealing firmly with the situation.

The Bishop regime in Grenada provoked Washington's wrath not only by leading the first successful military overthrow of an elected (albeit corrupt) Commonwealth Caribbean government in 1979, but also by immediately exchanging ambassadors with the Cuban government; accepting economic, educational, and technical assistance from that country; and even having the audacity to cast a pro-Soviet vote in the UN on the Afghanistan invasion issue. Grenada had become an enemy! As a result the United States allegedly blocked hurricane disaster loans to that country and, without total success, pressured the EEC, IMF, CDB, and governments such as Venezuela and Mexico to abstain from granting other loans to Grenada, particularly those for construction of a new airport which was perceived to have potential for military use. There was strong negative reaction from several area governments.

Interviews with policymakers in seven Caribbean microstates during 1981 (from Jamaica to Barbados and Trinidad to Antigua) revealed multiple objections to U.S. policies in the region--from the need for Washington to revamp its import tariff and packaging restrictions to complaints about its obsession with communism, militarism, and terrorism control rather than human rights. The most unanimous and vociferous protests, however, related to the U.S. attack, as part of its confrontation with Grenada, on the legitimacy of such an important indigenous institution as the Caribbean Development Bank by threatening to withhold $4 million in contributions unless anti-Grenadian lending decisions were rendered, including funding projects for basic human needs. This action was soundly rebuffed by bank members and led the highly-respected Caribbean Contact to castigate the U.S. for "displaying some of the worst features of a superpower!"[54] Significantly, J.M.G. Adams of Barbados, one of Bishop's strongest opponents and one of Washington's most prominent supporters in the area, was among the first Commonwealth leaders to instruct CDB representatives from his island to vote against the U.S. proposition (and its money). "Why should the United States attempt to destroy our bank," another Eastern Caribbean party leader queried, "when your government is fully aware the CDB Constitution prohibits discrimination against a member state?"[55]

Recalling the 1916 sabotage of the Central American Court of Justice by the U.S., and the probable irreparable damage done to the OAS regional security system by Washington's intervention in the Dominican Republic in 1965, the most appropriate response is that this is not the first time! Unfortunately such action produces an enduring negative reaction among opinion leaders in the Basin as well as inflicting probable damage to the institutions involved. Thus, as in so many previous instances, the very legitimacy on which long-term support and security is based is often undermined by the stifling embrace of U.S. short-term security interests, however valid.

At a pragmatic level, it is also troubling to many Caribbean officials, even some who are most uncomfortable with Grenada's present reduction in civil liberties and its infatuation with Cuba, that continued U.S. confrontation with the tiny Spice Island only serves to lend heroic status to Maurice Bishop and his regime and further isolate Grenada from fellow CARICOM members--if not from the West. Such orientations are partially responsible for continued economic and political support to Grenada from area governments such as Mexico and Venezuela plus much of Western Europe. These governments are also increasingly condemning Washington's military threats against Grenada and other enemies in the region. As a consequence of this stance, the brokerage potential of Basin middle powers appears on the rise and the resultant challenge to the Northern Colossus may be contributing to a somewhat less interventionist U.S. policy such as that articulated by Secretary Haig at the December 1981 OAS meeting in St. Lucia.[56] The Colossus may yet be influenced by Ariel.

LONG-TERM U.S. INTERESTS: SOME FINAL REFLECTIONS

U.S. policy makers still have much to learn in the microstate Caribbean if long-term U.S. interests are to be realized. There remains a general lack of appreciation and/or sophistication on the part of many in the current administration regarding the nature and direction of West Indian societies in general and social movements in political democracies in particular. Although paying lip service to the importance of political democracy and institutionalized constitutionalism, Washington projects insensitivity to the complexities of this process that is transpiring on its very doorstep.

The Commonwealth Caribbean is not only one of the world's most institutionally stable areas, despite the problems noted in this chapter, but, as Trinidadian Anthony P. Maingot recently testified before the U.S. House Committee of Foreign Affairs, it is also "prone to dramatically rapid social change....In other words the most conservative of values if widely shared and if the spokesmen have access to modern institutions and mechanisms can have impacts which have revolutionary <u>dimensions</u> through something less than revolutionary goals."[57] The microstate Caribbean has such dimensions, possibly as a result of its three-century English legacy. It is institutionally conservative, yet its highly literate, Fabian-schooled society is potentially change oriented--a conservative/modern society as it were.

This theory partially explains why Michael Manley's "radical" socialist experiment could be democratically elected (and "unelected") in Jamaica and why a social, economic, and educational revolution can coexist with relatively strong private sectors as it does in Grenada.[58] The Reagan-Kirkpatrick-Allen-Fontaine resurrection of the Dulles approach, "they're either loudly with us or against us," receives little support <u>and</u> makes little sense in this area.

West Indians are most proud of their politically open democracies and culturally congruent institutional development which includes a high degree of unionization, to which most of the subregion's labor parties are or were linked. These systems are also deservedly proud that their political development has "proved the lie" that blacks cannot practice democracy with order or that former slaves only Haitianize societies. Yet, there is also widespread awareness of serious economic problems such as those noted by Foreign Minister Lester Bird of Antigua: in 1980 alone the cost of some manufactured goods rose as much as 100 percent and oil to generate electricity by 80 percent while tourism, the major generator of dollars, actually declined and resistance against Caribbean manufactured goods continued to be a fact in metropolitan markets.[59] This suggests why development models in the precariously balanced microstate economies must be precisely (and logically) tailored to local needs rather than imported from Moscow, Washington, or other metropolitan centers; why the United States should be more sensitive to local political pressures; and why, perhaps, greater appreciation should be demonstrated for the relative order which is maintained throughout the Commonwealth Caribbean. The Guyanese assistant to the Antigua-Barbuda Foreign Minster probably says it best:

> Look, we West Indians like North America, your freedoms, lifestyle, all. But we often feel as the woman jilted.... And you should understand that we didn't make our bits of coral or sand small and poor. We didn't even bring ourselves here....And we aren't in your backyard, as you like to say, but on your front doorstep. We can be [your economically] healthy friend or whatever. It is largely your choice.[60]

This is the real challenge to U.S. foreign policy that is posed by the microstate Caribbean.

NOTES

1. Peter H. Smith, Mexico: The Quest for a U.S. Policy (New York: Foreign Policy Association, [1981?], especially p. 16.

2. This term is adapted from Lester D. Langley, Struggle for the American Mediterranean (Athens, GA: The University of Georgia Press, 1976).

3. William Demas, "Foreword" in Richard Millet and W. Marvin Will (Eds.), The Restless Caribbean: Changing Patterns of International Relations (New York: Praeger Publishers, 1979), pp. vii-x. Demas focuses on the English-speaking Caribbean as one cultural subgroup. It is important to note that the several Caribbean cultural subsystems are increasingly linked by commerce and by political decisions (see 1982 program of the Centro de Estudios Economicos y Sociales del Tercer Mundo, Mexico, D.F.), yet academics from each cultural community tend to ethnocentrically exclude the other "Caribbeans" from their research.

4. See George Beckford, Persistent Poverty (New York: Oxford University Press, 1972). Migration among the islands is well known but less is known about flows from the English-speaking areas to Bluefields, Nicaragua, Limon, Costa Rica, and the Canal Zone area of Panama.

5. Franklin W. Knight, The Caribbean: The Genesis of a Fragmented Nationalism (Oxford: Oxford University Press, 1978), p. xi. "Caribbean peoples," Knight continues, "with their distinctive artificial societies, common history and common problems, seem to have more in common than the Texan and the New Yorker, or the Mayan Indian and the cosmopolite of Mexico City." (p. xi)

6. There are also active independence movements in such Caribbean French Departments as Martinique and in both Puerto Rico and the U.S. Virgin Islands.

7. This study by Charles L. Taylor identifies seventy-four "microterritories" whose upper limits are not in excess of 142,822 sq. km., population 2,928,000, and GNP US$1,583 million. At the time the study was published (1971), these limits surpassed all English-speaking Caribbean states. Study cited by Patrick Emmanuel, "Independence and Viability: Elements of Analysis" in Vaughan A. Lewis (Ed.), Size, Self-Determination, and International Relations: The Caribbean (Kingston, Jamaica: Institute of Social and Economic Research, University of the West Indies-Mona, 1976), pp. 1-2.

8. Failure of the Federation can be attributed primarily to Britain's failure to establish adequate interterritorial communication linkages during its centuries of tutelage as a colonist and to properly support sufficient central governmental authority in

the Federation's constitutional structure which could counter the stress produced by centuries of provincial thinking and decades of economic growth imbalances within the Commonwealth Caribbean. See Great Britain, Colonial Office, Cmd. 1679, Report of a Visit [by E.F.L. Wood] to Certain West Indian Colonies and to British Guiana (London: H.M.S.O., 1922); Great Britain, Cmd. 6607, West India Royal Commission Report, 1938-39 (London: H.M.S.O., 1945); and W. Marvin Will, "Political Development in the Mini-State Caribbean" (Ph.D. dissertation, University of Missouri-Columbia, 1972).

9. See Commonwealth Caribbean Regional Secretariat, From Carifta to Caribbean Community [Georgetown, Guyana: n.d.].

10. St. Kitts-Nevis, which technically claims breakaway Anguilla (population 6,500) despite the latter's secession, is making a serious bid for independence, but it has been held back in part by Nevis' threat to also leave the union. Such problems are not unique among multiisland systems in spite of their extremely small size: St. Vincent has problems with Union Island, Antigua with Barbuda, Trinidad with Togabo, and the Netherlands Antilles with Aruba. This lack of integration among the mini and microstates has led the U.S. Department of State to be greatly concerned about Caribbean viability and has contributed to the commissioning of a futurist study (1982) of the insular Caribbean, "The Caribbean Region and American Policy to the Year 2000."

11. See U.S. Agency for International Development, Congressional Presentation, Fiscal Year 1980, Annex III, Latin America and the Caribbean, pp. 10-11.

12. Interview with Errol Barrow, Prime Minister of Barbados, Christ Church, Barbados (July 14, 1970). Also see W. Marvin Will, "Mass Party Institutionalisation in Barbados," Journal of Commonwealth and Comparative Politics (July 1981).

13. Caribbean Monthly Bulletin (August 1980), pp. 16-17, in an August 15, 1980 abstract of a press release by Geest Industries Ltd., the sole buyer of Windward Island bananas, notes that bananas, which made up 43 percent of the combined Windward exports for 1978-1979 and up to 60 percent of the islands' foreign exchange, would not be available for shipment for at least eight months.

14. See Ted Robert Gurr, Why Men Rebel (Princeton, NJ: Princeton University Press, 1970), especially pp. 47-51; and W. Marvin Will and Terry Prewitt, "Pedagogies for the Dispossessed: Harbingers in the Latin American Experience" in Robert Manley (Ed.), Building Positive Peace (Washington, DC: University Press of America, 1981), pp. 218-219.

15. See Anthony P. Maingot, Prepared Statement Before the Subcommittee on Inter-American Affairs, Committee on Foreign Affairs, U.S. House of Representatives, Washington, DC (July 14, 1981).

16. [Barbados] Sunday Sun (March 8, 1981), p. 1; [Trinidad] Express (August 18, 1981), p. 13; "Grenada: Glittering Jewel," Latin American Political Report (March 16, 1979), p. 1; [Trinidad] Express (August 6, 1981), p. 13.

17. Courtney N. Blackman, "The Balance of Payments Crisis in the Caribbean: Which Way Out?", Seminar Address delivered to Guild of Undergraduates, University of the West Indies, Cave Hill, Barbados (February 5, 1979). Figures are from Caribbean Development Bank, Annual Report 1980 (Barbados: Caribbean Development Bank, 1980), p. 23; and Central Bank of Barbados, Quarterly Report (September 1981), pp. 17-21. It is highly possible that Guyana's IMF and related problems may yet surpass the Jamaica crisis, as the IMF Report on Guyana (June 29, 1981) and the Guyana Forum (October 1981), pp. 1 and 6 indicate.

18. Blackman, op. cit. Also, a "highly placed" U.S. Department of State source has verified that Prime Minister Michael Manley's final IMF package was much more demanding than the previous one and certainly less advantageous than that extended to newly elected Prime Minister Edward Seaga. According to Latin America Weekly Report (October 1981), pp. 9-11, the latter received an immediate US$610 million loan from IMF's three-year Extended Fund Facility which not only was the maximum permitted but included a special 40 percent first-year provision to address Jamaica's balance of payments crisis. The Seaga government is also the leader in the region in receipt of "soft loans" from IMF. All this and the "special relationship with Washington" has positively affected Jamaica's stand among international bankers, facilitating a climb from 76th among 85 countries in risk to a current 35th position. This, in turn, lowers the applicable interest rate.

19. Actually, there are as many as seventeen relatively open or politically democratic systems in the Caribbean Basin. See W. Marvin Will, Revolution or Order? The Politics of Change and Institutional Development in the Caribbean Basin (Boulder, CO: Westview Press, forthcoming); and Caribbean Review (Spring 1981), especially Patrick Emanuel, "Elections and Parties in the Eastern Caribbean."

20. George L. Reid, The Impact of Very Small Size on the International Behavior of Microstates, Sage Professional Papers in International Studies (Beverly Hills, CA: Sage Publication, 1974), pp. 38-39.

21. Roy Preiswerk, "The Regional Dimensions of the Foreign Policies of Commonwealth Caribbean States" in Roy Preiswerk (Ed.), Regionalism and the Commonwealth Caribbean (Port of Spain, Trinidad: Institute of International Relations, University of the West Indies, 1968), p. 23.

22. Interview with Henry Forde by Howard A. Tyner of the Chicago Tribune, printed in The [Barbados] Beacon (July 18, 1980), p. 7. Mr. Forde voluntarily left the Ministry of External Affairs following the 1981 elections to return to his more lucrative and less demanding private legal practice. This pinpoints another problem faced by the financially pressured governments of the region--retaining quality personnel in view of the work demands and submetropolitan salaries.

23. Jacqueline A. Braveboy-Wagner, "Changes in Regional Foreign Policies of the English-Speaking Caribbean" in Elizabeth G. Ferris and Jeannie K. Lincoln (Eds.), Latin American Foreign Policies: Global and Regional Dimensions, Westview Special Studies on Latin America and the Caribbean (Boulder, CO: Westview Press, 1981), pp. 223-225. This Trinidadian scholar also recognizes the primacy of national goals and of economic development. The border conflicts are, of course, Venezuela's claim to two-thirds of Guyana and Guatemala's claim to all of Belize.

24. These data are for 1978 and are abstracted from World Military and Social Expenditures (forthcoming) by "This Week in Review," The New York Times (September 22, 1981), p. 6. In the Basin, only Costa Rica ($9 to $115), Panama ($11 to $118), and Mexico ($8 to $78) have ratios comparable to the Commonwealth Caribbean states. Also see Jamaica

Gleaner (September 12, 1980); and Juan M. de Aquilla, "Cuba's Foreign Policy in the Caribbean and Central America" in Ferris and Lincoln, op. cit.; and U.S. Arms Control and Disarmament Agency, World Military Expenditures and Arms Trade, 1964-74 (Washington, DC: USACDA, 1976).

25. This scenario draws in part on the Trinidad and Tobago Draft Estimates for 1963 which are summarized by Basil Ince, "The Administration of Foreign Affairs in a Very Small Developing Country: The Case of Trinidad and Tobago" in Lewis, op. cit., pp. 321-222.

26. Braveboy-Wagner, op. cit., table on p. 234; also see George L. Reid, "The Impact of Economic Factors on the Foreign Policy of Barbados" in Basil Ince (Ed.), Contemporary International Relations in the Caribbean (St. Augustine, Trinidad: Institute of International Relations, University of the West Indies-St. Augustine, 1979), pp. 271-281.

27. Reid, "Economic Factors," op. cit., p. 279.

28. Ince, "Administration of Foreign Affairs," op. cit., p. 323.

29. See Vaughan A. Lewis, "The Commonwealth Caribbean Policy of Non-Alignment," in Ince, op. cit., pp. 1-11; also Reid, "Economic Factors," op. cit.

30. James Pope-Hennessy, quoted in Hector Bolitho (Ed.), The British Empire (London: B.T. Batsford, Ltd., 1947), p. 174.

31. Joseph Smith, Illusions of Conflict: Anglo-American Diplomacy Toward Latin America, 1865-1896 (Pittsburgh, PA: University of Pittsburgh Press, 1979); see Lester D. Langley, The United States and the Caribbean, 1900-1970 (Athens, GA: The University of Georgia Press, 1980).

32. Small Wars Manual: United States Marine Corps (Washington, DC: United States Printing Office, 1940), p. 2.

33. Quoted in Robert C. Armstrong, "From Hemispheric Police to Global Managers," NACLA Report on the Americas (July-August 1981), p. 3.

34. Langley, 1900-1970, op. cit., p. 86.

35. Irwin F. Gellman, Good Neighbor Diplomacy: United States Policies in Latin America, 1933-1945 (Baltimore: The Johns Hopkins University Press, 1979).

36. Quoted in Ydigoras Fuentes, My War With Communism (Englewood Cliffs, NJ: Prentice-Hall, Inc., 1963), pp. 50-51; also see Melvin Gurtov, The United States Against the Third World (New York: Praeger Publishers, 1974).

37. Ibid., pp. 82-83.

38. Juan Jose Arevalo, The Shark and the Sardines (New York: Lyle Stuart, 1961), p. 106.

39. Richard Millett, "Imperialism, Intervention, and Exploitation: The Historical Context of International Relations in the Caribbean" in Millett and Will, op. cit., pp. 14, 18; also see Colin V.F. Henfrey, "Foreign Influence in Guyana: The Struggle for Independence" in Emanuel de Kadt (Ed.), Patterns of Foreign Influence in the Caribbean (New York: Oxford University Press, 1972).

40. Elevating the early Carter image in the English-speaking Caribbean was special advisor and UN Ambassador Andrew Young who, because he was black, much-traveled in the islands, and sympathetic to West Indian needs, was accorded an extraordinarily warm reception during an official visit to the region in 1977. See W. Marvin Will, "Caribbean International Politics: External and Domestic Constraints" in Millett and Will, op. cit.

41. USAID, op. cit.

42. Ibid.

43. The Sunday San Juan Star (May 24, 1981), quotation on p. A1. For CBI background amplification and an assessment of the increasing amounts of military assistance to the subregion, especially for development of an Eastern Caribbean coast guard facility, see Robert C. Armstrong, "We Built It, We Paid for It, It's Ours," NACLA Report on the Americas (July-August 1981), pp. 28-31. Also see Latin American Index (September 1, 1981), p. 59.

44. The New York Times (June 14, 1981), p. A12, emphasis added. Also see concluding chapter in Charles W. Kegley, Jr. and Eugene R. Wittkopf, American Foreign Policy (New York: St. Martins Press, 1982).

45. Thomas W. Ottenad, "Reagan: Poor Nations Must Help Themselves," St. Louis Post-Dispatch (October 15, 1981), pp. A1, 18, emphasis added.

46. Washington Post (October 11, 1981), p. A22.

47. Ibid. Also see The New York Times (December 5, 1981), pp. A1, 4; The New York Times (December 3, 1981), p. A13; The Miami Herald (October 10, 1981), p. 6.

48. Interviews with John Stanley Donaldson, Minister of External Affairs, Trinidad and Tobago, Port of Spain, Trinidad (October 7, 1981) and Carl Hudson-Phillips, former Attorney General, Trinidad and Tobago, Port of Spain, Trinidad (October 8, 1981). Scholarly studies on the negative impact of MNCs include that of Trinidadian Ken I. Boodhoo, "The Multinational Corporations, External Control, and the Problem of Development: The Case of Trinidad and Tobago," in Millett and Will, op. cit. Also see speech to the UN General Assembly (October 7, 1981) by John Donaldson.

49. George Chambers, then Minister of Finance, "Statement Made to the Sixteenth Session of the Economic Commission for Latin America," Port of Spain, Trinidad (May 6-14, 1975). Dr. Cheltenham's comments were made during an interview in Bridgetown, Barbados (May 15, 1981) and at the Annual Conference, West Indian Student Association, Michigan State University (May 1978). The late Dr. Williams, frequently on record regarding MNCs, most recently addressed the topic in his "Political Leader's Address to a Special Convention of the People's National Movement" (January 25, 1981). The high cost of technology to the region is summarized by Maurice Odle, "Technology And Dependency In The Caribbean," Caribbean Studies Newsletter (Fall 1980), pp. 6 and 9.

50. Revision of a speech delivered at Chancellor Hall, University of the West Indies-Mona, Jamaica (March 14, 1980), reprinted in Caribbean Studies Newsletter (Winter 1980), pp. 3-4, emphasis added. A similar statement has also been made by the Deputy Prime Minister of Antigua, Lester Bird. Also see Howard J. Wiarda, "Toward A Non-Ethnocentric Theory Of Development: Alternative Conceptions From The Third World" (Paper presented to the Annual Convention of the American Political Science Association in New York, September 3-6, 1981).

51. Trinidad Guardian (October 7, 1981), p. 5; The New York Times (December 3, 1981), p. A13.

52. Armstrong, "We Built It," op. cit., p. 31; Tony Best, "Caribbean Basin Plan," Caribbean Contact (December 1981), p. 17. An example of the Washington-Jamaica special relationship is a special tax agreement signed in July 1981 which allows U.S. conventioneers to write off expenses incurred while participating in Jamaican conferences, a level of gratitude previously enjoyed only by Mexico and Canada. See The Jamaican Weekly Gleaner (July 27, 1981), p. 4.

53. Lilian de Levy, "Turmoil in the Caribbean: A New 'Crescent of Crisis,'" abstracted from El Tiempo in World Press Review (September 1980), pp. 37-42.

54. Caribbean Contact (June 1981). Armstrong, "We Built It," op. cit., calls the U.S. move "idiotic!"

55. Interview with Carl Hudson-Phillips, National Organization for Reconstruction, Party Chairman, Port of Spain, Trinidad (October 8, 1981).

56. The New York Times (December 5, 1981); [Trinidad] Express (September 10, 1981), p. 6. The 1980 Mexican-Venezuelan agreement to help supply the petroleum needs of several Basin countries at favorable prices has also contributed to the influence potential of these emergent powers. See chapter 4 for a detailed analysis of this arrangement.

57. Maingot, Statement, op. cit.

58. There can be no absolute assurance, of course, that the Grenadian private sector will endure. Charges against Bishop have recently amplified in connection with his reluctance to conduct elections and, most important, alleged civil rights violations.

59. "Fair Trade, Not the Beggar's Bowl," an address to Seminar on Management of Foreign Trade, CARICOM Secretariat (January 19, 1981). It must be said that a high percentage of Caribbean exports to the U.S. enters duty free, more than 80 percent in some estimations, and it is highly possible that optimum microstate manufacturing and trade potential may exist in the more developed Hispanic countries of the region.

60. Interview with Ron Sanders, Ministry of Economic Development, St. John's, Antigua (September 20, 1981) and see Note 50.

8 Conclusion

H. Michael Erisman
John D. Martz

As 1982 dawned, the Caribbean cauldron continued to bubble, particularly in Central America where El Salvador was burning more furiously than ever and the conflagration in Guatemala was spreading. Following the fiasco of their abortive "final offensive" in January 1981, the Salvadoran insurgents regrouped and by year's end had developed into a formidable adversary. Indeed at this point the consensus seemed to be that the tide of battle was shifting in their favor. For example, in late November 1981 Newsweek reported that

> The junta's 17,000-man force has been unable to rout the 4,000 to 6,000 guerrillas--and frequently cannot hold its ground against them. ...The army is helpless against increasingly effective attacks on roads, bridges and electric power stations.[1]

In Guatemala the fighting escalated slowly but steadily during 1981, with neither side being able to demonstrate any sustained superiority. An ominous sign for the government, however, was reports that the rebels were beginning to succeed in their efforts to rally the Indians, who constitute over one-half of the country's population and had previously remained aloof from the struggle.

The process of restoring civilian rule in Honduras began with a presidential election in November 1981 which was won convincingly by Liberal Party leader Dr. Roberto Suazo Cordova, who polled 54 percent of the vote. But such political progress was not matched on the economic front. The nation's 1981 GNP (Gross National Product) grew less than 2 percent while its population increased approximately 3.4 percent. High interest rates, expensive oil imports, and decreased earnings from coffee exports pushed it to the verge of bankruptcy.

> Such are the problems faced by the new government that a secret study recently prepared for the Superior Council of the Armed Forces forecast that "a general disillusionment will set in from the sixth month of the new government when the Liberals cannot fulfill the expectations awakened among the electorate."
>
> The study concluded that "if anarchy and subversion" proliferate, the armed forces may face the choice of installing either a "revolutionary military government with broad popular support" or "a civilian-military dictatorship of the extreme right."[2]

Undoubtedly Suazo Cordova is counting heavily on the United States to pull his country through its difficulties. Somoza's ouster combined with the deteriorating situations in El Salvador and Guatemala has led the Reagan administration to put increased emphasis on transforming Honduras into a bastion of pro-American stability. Consequently Tegucigalpa has been receiving large doses of U.S. economic/military aid. Concurrently it has begun cooperating militarily with El Salvador's counterinsurgency efforts. Salvadoran troops are frequently allowed to enter Honduras in "hot pursuit" of guerrillas and to search the teeming refugee camps there for rebel sympathizers. Also, there have been reports that Honduras, El Salvador, and Guatemala are planning to enter a military alliance to facilitate coordinated operations against leftists in the region. So far such cooperation, which the United States has strongly encouraged, is in its embryo stage and therefore has not drawn Honduras deeply into its neighbors' battles. But should it allow itself to become Washington's gendarme in Central America,[3] Honduras might find itself embroiled in conflicts which it cannot handle and whose subsequent contagion effect could contribute to serious polarization and violence within its own body politic.

Meanwhile the Nicaraguan Revolution abruptly shifted further to the left after more than two years of generally conciliatory domestic policies by the Sandinistas.

> Key government leaders [in Nicaragua] have dropped their formerly repeated commitment to political pluralism and a mixed economy--two tenets of the 1979 revolution. In a recent speech, Minister of Defense Humberto Ortega Saavedra declared that "our political force is Sandinista--and our doctrine is Marxist-Leninist."[4]

This radicalization along with Managua's ongoing support for the Salvadoran insurgents and its deepening Cuban ties severely strained its relations with Washington, which responded with threats of dire economic and even military sanctions.

Beyond these obvious trouble spots, other littoral states which had previously been rather quiescent were by late 1981 beginning to show some signs of increased socio-economic tensions. Costa Rica, once considered the Switzerland of Central America, was reaping the whirlwind of past financial mismanagement and was virtually broke, unable to make even interest payments on its massive foreign debt.[5] Panama, although apparently prosperous and tranquil, had yet to rectify its serious maldistribution of wealth and had lost a pillar of national unity when General Omar Torrijos was killed in a July 1981 airplane crash.[6] Finally Colombia, whose stability during the 1970s was in stark contrast to its long tradition of political violence, was once more seeing a resurgence of guerrilla activity.

Following Jamaica's turbulent election, the eastern Caribbean islands calmed down politically. However, they for the most part remained in serious economic straits. Some relief was promised by the United States, Canada, Mexico, and Venezuela, who at a July 1981 conference in the Bahamas agreed in principle to launch a joint Caribbean aid program which was soon dubbed the Mini-Marshall Plan. But by year's end no significant progress had been made in implementing it. Also, at a December 1981 OAS meeting in St. Lucia, the Reagan administration announced that it would ask Congress to approve preferential trade concessions for Basin countries (i.e., establish a one-way free trade area for most Caribbean products entering the American market). This gesture was one component of a proposed three-part package which also included special incentives to encourage U.S. entrepreneurs to invest in the region and slight increases in governmental foreign aid. While most welcomed the trade provisions, some eastern Caribbean leaders were skeptical about the idea of substantial private investment and practically all were unhappy about the low priority Washington was giving bilateral financial assistance.

> Prime Minister Vera Bird of the newly independent country of Antigua and Barbuda, said "none of us disagree" with the Reagan administration position that developing countries "must pull themselves up by their own bootstraps."
>
> "But first we must have the straps by which to pull up the boot," he said. "And we will never have the straps if the order of priority does not place the required aid at the forefront."[7]

Furthermore, the fact that Reagan's actions were clearly motivated primarily by a desire to contain communism and Castro raised serious doubts about his long-term commitment to comprehensive Caribbean development.

Within this scenario of widespread actual or potential instability, the struggle for influence outlined and analyzed in this book continued into 1982. While some competitors made tactical policy changes, the general pattern of trends noted in the preceding chapters was maintained. As such, the process of systemic transformation in the Caribbean power configuration went on.

Looking briefly at recent developments in U.S. Caribbean policy, the White House ended 1981 plagued by a vague sense of impotence.

> "The whole area is a mess," concedes one top Administration strategist. "We have not accomplished anything worth talking about. Things are a lot tougher than some people had believed."[8]

Obviously Secretary Haig's "quick fix" approach had not worked. El Salvador's guerrillas had not been defeated or even fought to a standstill; Havana expanded its presence in Nicaragua and Grenada; and the Sandinistas not only became more radical, but also proceeded, with the help of an estimated 1,000 Cuban military advisors, to build a combined militia/regular army force of 80,000 (compared with 7,000 when they assumed power) whose arsenal includes Russian-made tanks, antiaircraft guns, and surface-to-air missiles.

This mediocre (some considered it disastrous) track record sparked a year-end policy debate within the administration which concentrated on how to deal more effectively with Central America in general and El Salvador in particular. Much of the controversy revolved around Washington's military options. Regarding El Salvador, there evidently were those who felt that the situation was hopeless and that the United States should cut its losses by withdrawing gracefully. Said one senior official, "I personally think we've lost El Salvador." His sentiments were echoed by a strategist who observed that "This is a war of attrition...the kind of war that favors insurgents. It is another limited war we aren't likely to win."[9] But the prevailing sentiment was to persevere; the U.S. would continue to supply economic/military assistance, including advisors in some cases, to regimes under heavy pressure from leftists. Moreover, while professing its preference for peaceful solutions to the region's problems and offering assurances that its combat forces would not be sent into any country, the White House indicated that it might resort to other strong measures in Central America. For instance, in early December 1981 the New York Times reported that to stem the arms flow to the Sandinistas,

> ...Mr. Haig and Mr. Meese [Edwin Meese, a close Reagan advisor] refused in recent weeks to rule out such American military moves as a naval blockade of Nicaragua or the mining of Nicaraguan harbors.[10]

Yet despite hints of such unilateral intervention, which raised in some minds the specter of U.S. Marines rampaging unrestrained through the Basin, Reagan had in reality become much more committed to a collective approach to regional stability by late 1981. In contrast to his early months in office, he now frequently demonstrated an inclination to trade some freedom of action in return for multilateral participation in U.S.-initiated economic and security aid programs. The Mini-Marshall Plan was but one example of this increased emphasis on diplomatic ecumenicalism.

Although such new nuances crept into America's Caribbean policy, containment and anti-Cubanism were still its overarching themes. The administration continued to be obsessed with the notion of cutting Fidel and by inference the Russians down to size--"Haig hates Castro with a passion, and so does the President," reported one top Washington official. It was not, however, able to solve the riddle of exactly where and how to do so. Tightening the economic embargo by cracking down on U.S. firms doing business with Cuba did little harm to the island's economy, whose trade is overwhelmingly oriented toward the Soviet bloc. Attempts prior to the December 1981 OAS conference to mobilize the international community against Havana by making available to selected governments throughout the world a classified report entitled "Cuba's Covert Activities In Latin America" which sought to substantiate its contention that the Fidelistas were heavily involved in promoting subversion and terrorism in practically every hemispheric nation produced at best a lackluster response.[11] Even threats of military thrusts were undermined by the Pentagon's reluctance to give its wholehearted approval.

> The saber the White House and the State Department have been rattling in the direction of Cuba and Nicaragua has been blunted by an extremely wary Pentagon that is sending yellow caution signals against military action.
>
> There are "very, very grave doubts in the Pentagon" about risking a military solution to halt the arms flow from Cuba through Nicaragua to the El Salvador guerrillas, an administration official said.
>
> ...One reason for the lack of enthusiasm at the Pentagon is that current forces are stretched too thin around the globe.
>
> ...A second brake on military action is the American people, who appear to be deeply divided about committing U.S. forces to what could flare up to be a full-fledged war with Soviet-supported Cuba.[12]

But regardless of these frustrations, confronting Cuba remained the keystone of U.S. Caribbean policy.

Like Washington, Havana also suffered some late 1981 setbacks in the Basin power struggle.

> Cuba's diplomats have been booted out of Jamaica and Colombia; its relations with Venezuela, Ecuador, Peru, and the Bahamas are at new lows; its ties to Panama are weakening; and in the English-speaking Car-

ibbean its only friend is tiny Grenada.[13]

These diplomatic reverses slowed somewhat the momentum of Havana's long and generally successful campaign to defeat U.S. efforts to isolate it. On the other hand, it managed to keep its most important Caribbean connection--its link with Mexico--in good order. This accomplishment combined with Central America's radicalization probably in its eyes outweighed its losses. In any case, its most pressing concern was to assure that the Pentagon did not intervene in the Basin, especially in Central America. It seemed to feel that if such an eventuality could be avoided, the leftist tide would ultimately engulf much of the region, thereby giving it new allies and increased influence. Consequently it adopted a two-track deterrence strategy.

The first track relied on prudence and conciliation. Although the Cubans strongly defended and occasionally exercised their right to extend military aid to established governments (e.g., Nicaragua and Grenada), their armed forces carefully avoided any direct involvement in the Caribbean's conflicts and they vociferously repudiated repeated American accusations that they were arming and training Latin insurgents on a large scale.[14] In fact, they regularly called for compromise and negotiated settlements of regional problems, stressing their willingness to engage in the process. One reason for such moderation was, of course, to deny Washington a pretext for intervention.

The second track emphasized coercion, with Havana vowing to respond to force with force. Armando Hart, Minister of Culture and a trusted Castro advisor, exemplified this intransigence during a November 1981 visit to France when he said that Cuba would fight a U.S. military incursion in Central America.

> "We will not remain inactive. We are preparing to resist an armed American intervention. Any nation that respects itself must take concrete measures. This is what we'll do. Nothing more and nothing less."[15]

Some considered such statements empty posturing since the Fidelistas lacked the logistical capability to field and maintain an overseas army in the face of overwhelming American air/sea power. But apparently they were serious, believing that their audacity would trigger resistance from other Caribbean countries such as Nicaragua (and perhaps even Mexico) as well as from the USSR. It was the threat of this catalyst effect leading to a wider war which Cuba was counting on to deter the United States.

While the U.S. and Havana went on jabbing and feinting at one another, Caracas' Caribbean policy remained relatively stable and unspectacular. Throughout late 1981 the Venezuelans continued to support the Duarte regime in El Salvador while depending heavily on their developmental aid to exert influence elsewhere in the Basin. They also remained strongly supportive of Washington's anti-Castroism, although they criticized its suggestion that it was not ruling out the possibility of taking military action against Cuba and/or Nicaragua by reaffirming that they opposed the idea of <u>any</u> military intervention in the area.

Caracas was not, however, standing still. In a somewhat unusual move given its reputation for using petrodollars rather than arms to make its presence felt, it reached an agreement with the Reagan administration to purchase twenty-four F-16 fighter planes. This was the first time in almost a decade that any hemispheric country had managed to get the United States to supply it such sophisticated weapons and represented, according to the <u>Washington Post</u>,

> ...a significant step in Venezuelan efforts to fill what it regards as a vacuum of influence in Latin America.[16]

Pending Congressional approval, delivery is scheduled to begin in early 1984 and undoubtedly will affect the balance of regional power.

Finally, Lopez Portillo closed 1981 with several initiatives geared to give Mexico a greater visibility not only in the Caribbean, but also in the Third World at large. In late August, for example, he took the lead in trying to stimulate a negotiated settlement in El Salvador by recognizing, along with French President Francois Mitterrand, the guerrilla-led opposition as a representative political force and thereby giving it greater international legitimacy, a move which was, said a former Carter Administration official, "a not-too-gentle reminder that the United States isn't being very creative about options in El Salvador."[17] But perhaps his most ambitious project was organizing the October 1981 Cancun summit which brought together 22 leaders from developed and developing countries, including Reagan, Britain's

Margaret Thatcher, and Japan's Prime Minister Zenko Suzuki, to discuss the poorer nations' demands for a New International Economic Order. Since no U.S. President had ever before participated in such a forum, Lopez Portillo scored quite a coup in convincing a reluctant Reagan to attend. To do so, he had to persuade Castro to stay away since Reagan refused to come if Fidel was invited. Even though the conference's substantive results were negligible,[18] the very fact that it occurred at all greatly enhanced Lopez Portillo's prestige as a statesman and thrust Mexico to the forefront of world affairs as a spokesman for the globe's dispossessed (a role which, by the way, Castro has long coveted and supposedly had achieved as chairman of the Nonaligned Movement for 1979-1982).

What made Mexico's behavior intriguing was its ability to maintain generally cordial ties with both the United States and Cuba while simultaneously competing, admittedly in a rather low-key manner, with them for Caribbean (and in Havana's case also Third World) influence. Much of the credit for this belonged to Lopez Portillo, who was able to establish warm personal/political friendships with two such disparate individuals as Ronald Reagan and Fidel Castro.[19] By keeping a foot in both camps, he created the opportunity for Mexico to act as a broker not only between the U.S. and Cuba, but also between them and other Basin governments, which Alan Riding very much approved:

> Probably the only feasible broker of detente for the region is Mexico. The Organization of American States ...is not even planning to discuss the Central American crises [at its November 1981 general assembly in St. Lucia]. Venezuela has poor relations with Cuba, while the Socialist International, the worldwide Social Democratic Movement, is distrusted by Washington.[20]

In late November 1981 Mexico actually did serve as an intermediary for Washington and Managua, successfully lowering tensions at a time when the White House was threatening to take punitive measures against the Sandinistas for supposedly continuing to make large arms shipments to the Salvadoran guerrillas.[21] In short, Lopez Portillo put Mexico in a position where to a great extent the Caribbean power struggle revolved around it. That, to put it simply, is acquiring clout.

This brief survey of late 1981 developments as well as the preceding chapters cast serious doubts on the Reagan administration's perception of Caribbean instability as basically one more manifestation of a global East-West confrontation. While the Soviet Union is interested and to some extent involved in what is happening there and would like to see America's position undermined, especially if the main beneficiary would be its Cuban ally, a Cold War paradigm does not capture the gist of contemporary Caribbean reality. Actually the dynamics of recent international relations in the Basin have been and continue to be dominated by a struggle for influence involving primarily the United States, Cuba, and Mexico, with Venezuela having the potential to become a serious contender. But thus far Caracas has been overshadowed by the others; it has not yet succeeded in carving out a strong distinctive niche for itself in the Caribbean and is often seen, wrongly in many experts' opinions, as being firmly under Washington's wing due to its staunch anti-communism. Of course, should Mexico falter badly when Lopez Portillo's tenure ends in 1982 and a new president takes over, the Venezuelans could fill the breach. Also, their political stock would soar if Duarte, whom Herrera Campins has strongly supported to bolster the Latin American Christian Democratic Movement which the Venezuelan party leads, solved El Salvador's problems without becoming an American client. At present, however, his situation is to say the least precarious and his downfall would be a major setback for Caracas. In any case, since neither the Mexican nor the Salvadoran contingency is likely to materialize, Venezuela's immediate prospects for acquiring substantial regional power are problematical. Its willingness to extend generous economic aid will keep it in the race for influence, but probably as a long shot.

Within this essentially triangular scenario, Mexico is emerging as the key to a long-term restructuring of the Caribbean power configuration. There are four main possibilities regarding the direction which it might take in the foreseeable future. The first two, which are the most improbable, are:

A) It could continue to increase its influence, parlaying its present middleman status and its growing petropower to the point where it becomes the paramount nation in the Basin.

B) It could fail to maintain its momentum and effectively drop out of the picture, leaving the field to Washington, Havana, and maybe Caracas.

The more plausible alternatives are:

C) It could be drawn into the American orbit as a junior partner, thus giving it a significant but subordinate function in Caribbean affairs. In other words, it could follow what some have seen to be the Venezuelan model.

D) It could consolidate and even expand upon its current role as the regional power broker, perhaps at times leaning heavily toward the United States or Cuba in the process.

Realistically it is impossible to foretell exactly what may transpire for Mexico since much is contingent on such imponderables as its future internal development and stability, the abilities and idiosyncrasies of its presidents (who have considerable leeway in foreign policy making, but are limited to one six-year term), U.S. and Cuban actions, and events in the Basin. The last option probably represents the best prediction. Whether the Mexicans tend to swing more toward Washington or Havana will be heavily dependent on the state of their economy. If it is shaky, they will almost surely be constrained to maintain good relations with the United States, no matter how radical their rhetoric may be. But if it is good, there may very well be an upsurge of anti-Yankee nationalism and a strong willingness to cooperate closely with Havana to minimize Washington's influence in the area.

Whatever its outcome, the fact that the power struggle discussed in this book has occurred at all means that a new international political order has evolved in the Caribbean. The American Colossus has indeed been challenged.

NOTES

1. "Not Winning Is Losing," Newsweek (November 23, 1981), p. 63. For a similar assessment, see "The Death of A Thousand Cuts," Time (September 7, 1981), p. 29, which among other things notes that the casualty rate for El Salvador's security forces was a high 12 percent for the year.

2. "Honduran Victor In Overture To Foes," New York Times (December 1, 1981), p. A3.

3. For analyses charging that the United States has chosen Honduras as its new Central American gendarme, see Peter Shiras and Leyda Barbieri, "Is It Honduras Next?", Democratic Left (May 1981), pp. 8-11; and Judy Butler, "The Wider War," NACLA Report on The Americas (May-June 1981), pp. 22-24.

4. "Nine Little Castros," Newsweek (November 16, 1981), p. 59.

5. Costa Rica's economic problems are summarized in "Raiding Grandma's Cabinet," Time (September 28, 1981), p. 42.

6. For an analysis of post-Torrijos Panama, see Alan Riding, "Panama: Troubled Passage For A U.S. Ally," New York Times Magazine (November 22, 1981), pp. 78-81+.

7. "Caribbean Chiefs Cite Need for 'Straps' To Pull Their Economies Up By Boots," Washington Post (December 1, 1981), p. A13.

8. "U.S. Policy In Shambles," Newsweek (September 14, 1981), p. 44.

9. Quoted in ibid., p. 44.

10. "Latin Policy: A New Plan," New York Times (December 6, 1981), p. 20.

11. For details regarding the report's contents, see "U.S. Details 'Covert Activities' By Cubans In Latin America," Washington Post (December 2, 1981), p. 1+; and "The U.S. Vs. Castro," Newsweek (December 7, 1981), p. 54.

12. "Pentagon Wary On Central America," Erie (Pa.) Times-News (December 6, 1981), p. 5A.

13. "The U.S. Vs. Castro," op. cit., p. 54.

14. See, for example, "They React To The Exposure Of Their Lies With Even Bigger Lies" and "We Shall Resist The Overbearing, Arrogant and Fascist Policy Of The U.S. Government At Any Price," Granma Weekly Review (November 15, 1981), pp. 1 and 16 respectively for typical official denunciations of U.S. charges.

15. "Cuba Would Fight Any Intervention," Erie (Pa.) Times-News (November 8, 1981).

16. Report reprinted in "Administration Agrees To Sell F-16 Fighters To Venezuela," Today (October 16, 1981), p. 13.

17. Quoted in "U.S. Policy In Shambles," op. cit., p. 48.

18. For information regarding the conference, see "Third World: Uncle Sam's Tough New Stand," U.S. News and World Report (October 26, 1981), pp. 20-24; and "Reagan Meets The Third World," Newsweek (November 2, 1981), pp. 34-36.

19. To get some idea of Lopez Portillo's effectiveness in dealing with these two leaders, see Tad Szulc, "With Respect, We Can Do Anything," Parade (October 4, 1981), pp. 4-9; "Castro, Portillo Cite Friendship," Erie (Pa.) Times-News (August 9, 1981); and "Castro Visits Lopez Portillo For Talks," Washington Post (August 8, 1981), p. A12.

20. Alan Riding, "Mexico Has Good Cause To Offer Its Good Offices," New York Times (November 29, 1981), p. 2E.

21. Mexico's conciliatory efforts are summarized in "Haig Winds Up 'Cordial' Talks With Mexicans," New York Times (November 25, 1981), p. A7; "Mexico Will Contact Sandinistas," Washington Post (November 26, 1981), p. A4; and "Nicaraguan Envoy In Mexico For High-Level Talks," Washington Post (November 27, 1981), p. A28.

About the Contributors

H. MICHAEL ERISMAN is an Associate Professor of Political Science at Mercyhurst College in Erie, Pennsylvania. He has written numerous articles, conference papers, and book reviews dealing primarily with Caribbean/Central American affairs which have appeared in such journals as Revista/Review Interamericana, Caribbean Review, and Opiniones. He has also co-edited a Latin American monograph series. His main fields of interest are U.S. and Cuban foreign policies as well as transnationalism in the Caribbean. He is currently working on two books, one on Cuban Globalism and the other on U.S. Caribbean policy.

JOHN D. MARTZ, Head and Professor of Political Science at the Pennsylvania State University, is the author or editor of twelve books and several dozen articles and book reviews on Latin American politics. His most recent articles have analyzed the politics of Ecuador in such journals as Studies In Comparative International Development, Current History, and Journal of Inter-American Studies. His most recent book, with Lars Schoultz, is Latin America, The United States, And The Inter-American System (1980). His present research centers on parties, elections, and ideological movements in Venezuela, Colombia, and Ecuador. He served as Editor of the Latin American Research Review from 1975-1980.

W. RAYMOND DUNCAN is a Distinguished Teaching Professor of Political Science at the State University of New York-College at Brockport specializing in Soviet policy in the Third World, Soviet and Cuban policies in Latin America, Latin American politics, and Inter-American relations. He has authored or edited five books, the most recent being Soviet Policy In Developing Countries (Second Edition, 1981). He also has contributed to other books and to such journals as Problems Of Communism, Orbis, World Affairs, and Current History. During 1981-1982 he was a Visiting Scholar at the Hoover Institution on War, Revolution, and Peace, Stanford University. His current book projects focus on Soviet Policy In Latin America and Food Politics And Multinational Corporations In Latin America.

NEALE J. PEARSON is an Associate Professor of Political Science at Texas Tech University who specializes in Marxist and peasant groups, trade unions, and political parties in Brazil, Chile, Peru, Costa Rica, Guatemala, Honduras, and Nicaragua. His work has appeared in the following books: Latin American Peasant Movements; Rural Change and Public Policy in Eastern Europe, Latin America, and Australia; The Continuing Struggle For Democracy in Latin America; The Political Economy of Development; and Communism in Central America and the Caribbean. He has had articles in The Journal of International Affairs and Current History and also is a contributor to the Encyclopedia Americana's Annual Yearbook and the Yearbook on International Communist Affairs. He is currently analyzing the Honduran elections of November 29, 1981.

JIRI VALENTA is an Associate Professor and coordinator of Soviet and Eastern European Studies in the Department of National Security Affairs of the U.S. Naval Postgraduate School at Monterey, California. During his leave in 1981-1982, he received International Relations Fellowships from the Council on Foreign Relations and the Rockefeller Foundation as well as an appointment as a Senior Research Associate at Colombia University's Research Institute on International Change. His main areas of specialization are international security affairs, Soviet foreign policy, and comparative communism. He is the author of Soviet Intervention In Czechoslovakia 1968, Anatomy Of A Decision as well as numerous articles and chapters in scholarly works. He also co-edited Eurocommunism Between East And West and Soviet Decision-Making For National Security.

W. MARVIN WILL is an Associate Professor of Political Science at the University of Tulsa. His teaching and research interests focus on comparative Third World and Caribbean Basin policy. Since 1979 Dr. Will has served as the Editor of the Caribbean Studies (Association) Newsletter. In addition to numerous articles in professional journals ranging from Urban Education to the Journal of Commonwealth and Comparative Politics, he has co-edited The Restless Caribbean: Changing Patterns of International Relations (1979) and is currently authoring Revolution or Order?: The Politics of Change and Institutional Development in the Caribbean Basin for Westview Press.

EDWARD J. WILLIAMS is a Professor of Political Science at the University of Arizona. During 1981-1982 he was a Visiting Research Professor at the Strategic Studies Institute of the U.S. Army War College and previously served as a Fulbright-Hays Visiting Professor at El Colegio de Mexico. He has published widely in learned journals on Mexico and Latin American politics and foreign policy and has authored a number of books including *The Rebirth Of The Mexican Petroleum Industry* (1979) and *Maquiladores And Migration: Workers In The U.S.-Mexican Border Industrialization Program* (1982).

Index

Other Titles of Interest from Westview Press

Latin America, the United States, and the Inter-American System, edited by John D. Martz and Lars Schoultz

**Revolution in El Salvador: Origins and Evolution*, T. S. Montgomery

**The End and the Beginning: The Nicaraguan Revolution*, John A. Booth

**Mexico: A Profile*, Daniel Levy and Gabriel Szekely

**The Soviet Union in the Third World: Successes and Failures*, edited by Robert H. Donaldson

**The Continuing Struggle for Democracy in Latin America*, edited by Howard J. Wiarda

**Latin American Foreign Policies: Global and Regional Dimensions*, edited by Elizabeth G. Ferris and Jennie K. Lincoln

U.S. Policy in the Caribbean, John Bartlow Martin

**From Dependency to Development: Strategies to Overcome Underdevelopment and Inequality*, edited by Heraldo Muñoz

Unequal Alliance: The Inter-American Military System, 1938-1978, John Child

**Nicaragua: The Land of Sandino*, Thomas W. Walker

**The Dominican Republic: A Caribbean Crucible*, Howard J. Wiarda and Michael J. Kryzanek

Oil, Money, and the Mexican Economy: A Macro Econometric Analysis, Francisco Carrada-Bravo

*Available in hardcover and paperback.

About the Book and Editors

Colossus Challenged:
The Struggle for Caribbean Influence
edited by H. Michael Erisman and John D. Martz

In recent years the powerful and long-standing influence of the United States in the Caribbean and Central America has been challenged directly by Cuba, Mexico, and Venezuela and--many think--indirectly by the USSR. This struggle for dominance, which has altered and still is significantly changing the power configuration in the Caribbean Basin, is examined in detail in *Colossus Challenged*.

The book contains seven chapters by prominent area specialists. Five of the chapters focus on the Caribbean policies of the major contenders for power, analyzing the evolution of each country's policies, the main variables affecting its definition of interests and its decision making, and its prospects for exerting regional influence in the foreseeable future. The other two chapters look at the rivalry for Caribbean influence from the perspectives of eastern Caribbean and Central American governments.

H. Michael Erisman is associate professor of political science at Mercyhurst College. *John D. Martz*, professor and head of the Political Science Department at the Pennsylvania State University, is the author or editor of twelve books and many articles on Latin American politics; his most recent book (with Lars Schoultz) is *Latin America, the United States, and the Inter-American System* (1980).